# THE PSYCHIC HEALTH OF JESUS

THE MACMILLAN COMPANY
NEW YORK · BOSTON · CHICAGO · DALLAS
ATLANTA · SAN FRANCISCO

MACMILLAN & CO., LIMITED
LONDON · BOMBAY · CALCUTTA
MELBOURNE

THE MACMILLAN CO. OF CANADA, LTD.
TORONTO

# THE
# PSYCHIC HEALTH
# OF JESUS

BY

WALTER E. BUNDY, Ph.D.

Associate Professor of English Bible in DePauw University

New York

THE MACMILLAN COMPANY

1922

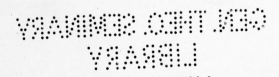

"The bible text used in this volume, is taken from the
American Standard Edition of the Revised Bible, Copyright,
1901, by Thomas Nelson & Sons, and is used by permission."

FERRIS PRINTING COMPANY
NEW YORK

TO MY FATHER AND MOTHER

# THE PSYCHIC HEALTH OF JESUS

## PREFACE

The task of coming to a newer and fresher understanding of Jesus is the bounden duty of all confessed Christians, whether orthodox or liberal, theological or lay. The present study has been made with this one thought in mind. From the more strictly scientific point of view this study aims at two things: 1) a comprehensive survey of the pathographic judgment against Jesus in both its early and its developed stages; 2) a determination of the correctness of the pathographic position as based upon a sifting of the New Testament sources.

This study makes no pretentions at psychiatry proper, for the writer is a student of New Testament literature and not a specialist in mental diseases. The field of psychopathology and psychiatry has been avoided as consistently as possible; it is entered only when and in so far as the contentions against Jesus' psychic health have forced the problem, and then only in its relation to the New Testament sources. At such times and points the writer moves with all modesty. But be that as it may, the first step is the sifting of the sources; after this has been done the psychiatrist and the pathographer may go to work.

Anyone at all acquainted with the critical works in the field of New Testament research will recognize at once the writer's indebtedness to many and various authors, which indebtedness the writer gratefully acknowledges. This is still more true in regard to the psychiatric portions of the study.

Quotations and references to the Biblical books in English are according to the Standard Edition of the American Revised Version; in Greek to the Tischendorf-Gebhardt text as employed by Huck in his *Synopse der drei ersten Evangelien.*

Quotations and references to the works of various scholars and authors are made by giving the author's name and the page of his work; the full title and particulars regarding each work cited are to be found under the author's name in the attached bibliography. In case more than one work by the same author is referred to each is designated by an abbreviation of the title.

The writer would have preferred to leave the numerous quotations from French and German authors in the original. The majority of readers, however, will welcome the English translations. These translations have doubtless lost something in the process, but the writer has tried to translate as faithfully as possible.

One reader of the original manuscript suggested the omission of the materials in Chapter III for the following reasons: *It seems a pity to give dignity to some of the very perverted views which certain men have seen fit to publish. It will shock the majority of readers. From the literary point of view, such omission would relieve the book of the impression of being repetitious.*

Many readers will doubtless agree with this opinion. The writer readily admits that such a criticism is quite to the point; in view of it he has omitted some of the more repugnant statements of Soury and Binet-Sanglé. But the writer could not omit the materials in Chapter III entirely, for one of his two chief reasons for making the present study was to give in English a precise presentation of the perverted views of each of Jesus' pathographers. This would make a certain amount of repetition in the second half of the study unavoidable. The writer, therefore, has made no effort to avoid a reproduction of identical or similar materials wherever such contributes either to the clearness of the argument or to the convenience of the reader.

The present study has its shortcomings, both critical and literary. That these are not more numerous and serious than they are the writer is indebted to Professors William J. Lowstuter and Edgar S. Brightman of Boston University School of Theology for many valuable suggestions and criticisms.

Above all, the writer is indebted to his faithful friend and teacher, Dr. Albert C. Knudson, Professor of Systematic Theology in Boston University School of Theology, not only for very substantial aid in the present study but for the constant encouragement and inspiration he has given the writer in his pursuit of New Testament studies.

The writer also takes pleasure in expressing his gratitude to Professors Paul Wernle and Eduard Riggenbach of the Theological Faculty of Basel University, Basel, Switzerland, from whose lectures and works he has learned much and whose cordial and generous hospitality he enjoyed during his Basel semesters.

*Greencastle, Indiana.*                    *August* 1, 1921.

# INTRODUCTION

*We instinctively recoil from seeing an object to which our emotions and affections are committed handled by the intellect as any other object is handled* (James, p. 9).

In the discussion of the problem of the psychic health of Jesus the argument from religious sentiment must, in as far as possible, be left out of consideration. But no one, however, would refuse to admit the strength of this argument for popular religious thought. The average Christian believer who looks to Jesus as the one and absolute religious example and leader, and the writer gladly and wholeheartedly confesses himself to this belief, will dismiss the question of Jesus' psychic health with little ceremony and less thought as positively preposterous and will immediately consign those who have passed a pathographic judgment against Jesus to the very institution for the mentally morbid whither, were he living today, they would have Jesus directed for confinement and care. But the serious student of the New Testament cannot thus so summarily dismiss the question.

Further, the problem of the psychic health of Jesus is not to be solved by an appeal to history, by citing the high, helpful and wholesome influences that have gone out from him and inspired so many fine souls and societies to sentiments and deeds of service and sacrifice.

Mental diseases in their characteristic forms, whether misunderstood or understood, worshipped or deified, tortured or treated, condemned, incarcerated or cured, have existed as far back as the earliest written records of human history. Insanity has not only always existed in human society, but it has often had a profound influence upon its history. If we confine our attention to modern times alone, we realize that great geniuses of unquestionable influence on their own and subsequent generations have manifested idiosyncrasies that have varied all the way from personal peculiarities to complete mental derangement, nevertheless they have left the world better or different because they have lived and worked. And often it has been the case that just their traits of abnormality account best for their inexhaustible energy in accomplishment. *Religious geniuses have often shown symptoms of nervous instability. Even more perhaps than any other kinds of genius, religious leaders have been subject to abnormal psychical visitations.......Often, moreover, these pathological features in their career have helped to give them their religious authority and influence* (James, p. 6f).

H. Maudsley asks, *What right have we to believe nature under obligation to do her work by means of complete minds only? She may find an incomplete mind a more suitable instrument for a particular purpose* (Quoted by James, p. 19). In discussing the unusual psychical experiences of the Apostle Paul, W. Wrede asks, *Why should these yearnings, the inspirations and struggles which took on the form of ecstasies, become less noble simply because they did assume this form? Still we shall always feel that the phenomenon itself is something morbid* (Paulus, S. 16). Regarding the social and historical significance of hallucinations Krafft-Ebing writes, *There is hardly a phenomenon of human life which, throughout the ages, has been more variously judged by the church, philosophy and natural science. The history of hallucinations contains a part of the history of the civilization of all peoples and all times, and is a mirror of religious opinions. Hallucinations have caused the most important historic events (visions of the cross by Constantine the Great), founded religions (Mohammed), and led to the most horrible errors in the form of superstition, ghosts, and persecution of witches, etc.* (p. 110f).

Psychanalysis, descriptive psychology and psychopathology do not follow the injunction and criterion of Jesus, *By their fruits ye shall know them*, nor James' supplement, *not by their roots* (p. 20). It is exactly in the roots of unusual psychical phenomena that psychopathology in particular is interested, and not in the logical and practical historical values of their productions. Its problem is not one of values, but of origins. As Dr. Moerchen writes in his little pamphlet, *Die Psychologie der Heiligkeit*, it is not the task of descriptive psychology *Werturteile ueber den Wahrheitsgehalt des religioesen Gedankeninhaltes zu faellen; weder koennen wir ueber das Wesen, den Gegenstand des religioesen Gedankeninhaltes an sich etwas aussagen, noch viel weniger Werturteile ueber den Wahrheitsgehalt dieser Inhalte* (S. 8.) Descriptive psychology is interested solely in the causes and course of psychic processes; psychopathology asks but one question, normal or abnormal? healthy or morbid?

The appeal to history may be a practical and pragmatic way of meeting a charge against the psychic health of any great man of the past, but it does not solve the problem to be solved, nor does it test the truth of the diagnosis. It may enable us to entertain a very high opinion and appreciation of the particular individual and not hinder us from deriving the greatest possible benefit from his life and work, but the judgment of the pathographer continues to stand. Rasmussen speaks of the Apostle Paul as a man whose tremendous influence and significance in the history of the world since is incontestable, yet he pronounces him an epileptic, (S. 79). In discussing the fanaticism of Jesus, Strauss remarked that the fanatic can be a noble and inspiring character, he can stimulate and elevate, and can exercise a lasting influence for good upon the course of history and the development of thought, but we today would not care to choose him as our guide and leader in life.

Of the six writers whose positions involve the psychic health of Jesus only two (Hirsch and Binet-Sanglé) fail to find something that is great, or even grand, in the person or teaching of Jesus. Rasmussen finds that it is just the pathological element in Jesus that has been preserved and has triumphed; the best in him has been neglected. De Loosten cannot praise the intellectual ability of Jesus too highly and finds his dialectic in the Jerusalem contentions without a parallel in history. Baumann praises his devotion to a great community ideal and his passion for service and sacrifice. Yet all of these concessions do not prevent these writers from diagnosing Jesus' case as epilepsy, paranoia, or excessive nervousness bordering on hysteria. O. Holtzmann presented Jesus as through and through an ecstatic character, but he is still a professor of theology.

The attitude of Jesus' pathographers (here Holtzmann is to be excluded) toward any permanent values expressed in his person or teaching and subsequent benefits to be derived therefrom is best expressed in a figure employed by two of them (Rasmussen and Hirsch): t h e   m o r b i d   m u s s e l   c a n   p r o -
d u c e   a   p r i c e l e s s   p e a r l . It is worth while to quote Rasmussen in full: *We do not go so far as to declare everything worthless that proceeds from a morbid mind. We do not deny that a morbid mussel can produce a pearl; still less do we pronounce the mussel healthy in consideration of the pearl. The lamp of the spirit will smoke if it is turned too high, and the smoke can become so dense that the flame is dimmed; but even then it can give forth light, be of benefit and valued according to its usefulness and strength. For we appraise our ideas not according to their origin, but according to their true worth* (S. 130).

For the serious student of the New Testament the problem of the psychic health of Jesus is not to be solved by religious recoil at the thought of such a suggestion, nor by an appeal to history, but it is to be faced and met on the basis of an historical and critical study of the sources of our knowledge concerning Jesus' words and deeds as found in the Gospel literature. The battle is to be fought out on the field of the New Testament, and any shift of the scene of action from this field renders the issue unscientific and indecisive.

The problem, further, cannot be considered mainly psychiatric, for the possibility of observation is hopelessly out of the question. Besides the contentions against the psychic health of Jesus have not been made by psychiatrists, but by pathographers. The problem is therefore p a t h o g r a p h i c .

As such it remains and must of necessity remain an historical critical problem. It is to be met and solved only by a critical and historical study of the literary sources. For this reason the raising of the problem is to be welcomed, and the struggle, though it be in the night time, will not pass without having imparted its blessing upon the wrestler. The problem is to be welcomed as is any problem that demands and forces a reconsideration of the character of Jesus from a new point of view.

Psychology has never been able to do much with Jesus. Such studies are usually disappointing, perhaps for the reason that we expect too much from such a promising point of view. But, as we shall see later, even the positive estimate of Jesus will find the study of his known life more interesting, instructive and inspiring from the viewpoint of abnormal than normal psychology because of the contrasting lights the former throws on his person. It is only as we begin to inquire into the healthiness of such experiences as are attributed to Jesus at the Jordan and in the wilderness, to apply to what we know of him the tests of health, that the positive psychic powers of Jesus begin fully to appear.

Christianity has been helped along in the world more by its critics than by its too sympathetic friends. We have only to cite the work of Strauss by which he threw his three great questions out into the theological world of his day and caused a commotion and confusion that has not entirely died out even down to this very hour. With his first *Leben Jesu* (1835) Strauss did more to stir the thick theological thought of his day out of its selfish sluggishness and help along the life-of-Jesus research than any other critic before or after him. Strauss compelled his contented and complacent critic contemporaries to reread and restudy the Gospels, which he knew and knew better how to use than they.

It is the high duty, and should be the pleasure, of every follower of Jesus to greet and welcome any study that will throw new light upon the person of Jesus and help to a renewed, perhaps new, appreciation and understanding of him. The raising of the problem of Jesus' psychic health, we repeat, is to be welcomed as all new problems should be, sorry to say not always have been and are, welcomed because it brings us to read our New Testament again from a different point of view and with new thoughts in mind.

# TABLE OF CONTENTS

# CONTENTS

# THE PSYCHIC HEALTH OF JESUS

# THE PSYCHIC HEALTH OF JESUS

## CHAPTER I

### The Earlier Stages of the Problem

ALBERT SCHWEITZER (GdLJF., S. 10) divides the life-of-Jesus research into two principal periods: that before and that after Strauss. This division holds good for our present study, for it is Strauss who projects the first really negative picture of Jesus in a pathological sense. The discussion during the first period was dominated for the most part by the question of miracle as treated by the rationalistic school of thought in its various stages of development. Two distinct steps were taken by this school in the explanation of miracle: 1) the reduction of the number of Jesus' miracles to the lowest possible minimum; 2) the explanation of the reduced number on a purely naturalistic basis. This did not always succeed, however, without compromising either the character and conduct of Jesus and his disciples, or the integrity of the Gospel writers. With Strauss the question of miracle was settled in a way and for a time at least. After Strauss the biographers of Jesus were busied with the new problems formulated or suggested by him.

Both periods had their *Charakterbilder Jesu.* In general, it can be said that during the first period a supernaturalistic and positive picture was taken of Jesus' person and character. During the second period, however, there arose a more naturalistic and human interpretation of the historical Jesus that was not infrequently accompanied by a tendency toward a negative view of his person and character. With the exception of Reinhard all the names that are of interest to us in the problem of the psychic health of Jesus fall within the second period.

The selection of names from the great number that have been prominent in the life-of-Jesus research for discussion in

1

the earlier stages of our present problem is, of course, determined by their relation to the problem itself.   Thus we naturally exclude some of the greatest lives of Jesus that have been
written, like those of Hase, Keim, Beyschlag, etc., all of which
projected their *Charakterbilder Jesu.*   And we give unusual
prominence to names almost unknown, like Washburn, and include names that hardly belong in the life-of-Jesus research,
like Nietzsche, except from our present point of view.

In the nineteenth century, the century great in its lives
of Jesus, only some half dozen men are of interest to us.   The
problem proper of the psychic health of Jesus belongs to the
twentieth century, but, as we shall see, it had its roots well
planted in the nineteenth.   (For Binet-Sanglé's history of the
discovery of the insanity of Jesus see his work, IV 297-326.
He represents it as beginning with Mc 3,21 and coming to its
conclusion in his own research).

### 1)   David Friedrich Strauss

Strauss is the first critic of significance to project a negative picture of Jesus in the psychopathic sense, but he did not
do this in his first *Leben Jesu* which appeared in two volumes
in 1835.   In spite of his almost entire elimination of miracle
from the ministry of Jesus and his complete rejection of the
Fourth Gospel as a trustworthy source of historical knowledge concerning what Jesus said and did, nevertheless Strauss'
view of Jesus' person and character in his 1835 *Leben Jesu* is
purely positive, for he defends Jesus against any serious suspicion of fanaticism (*Schwaermerei*).

It is worth while noting just here that the pathological
problem in the case of Jesus arose in connection with the first
attempts to construe and give some sort of an historical account
of Jesus' self-consciousness and its contents.   In the entire history of the question of Jesus' psychic health the *Schwerpunkt*
of the discussion has always remained just here and is the predominant factor in the 1905- form of the question.

Strauss attempted no systematic psychological survey of
Jesus' self-consciousness as was later done by Baldensperger,
H. J. Holtzmann, and others.   But the question of Jesus' psy-

chic soundness, though it did not thus form itself so definitely for his thought, is touched upon by Strauss in his discussion of Jesus' claim for his consciousness. In his first *Leben Jesu* he comes upon the problem in two short passages: the first, regarding the Johannine claims of Jesus for himself; and the second, regarding his Synoptic claims.

The first passage (I 542ff) has to do with the Johannine representation of Jesus claiming for himself the prerogative of preëxistence. Such passages as Jn 3,13 and 16,28 are not real claims for preëxistence but are rather to be regarded as a *symbolic designation of a higher, divine origin* (I 542). However, such passages as 6,62; 8,58 and 17,5 cannot be explained in any such figurative fashion. Strauss inclines strongly to reject these as real words of Jesus because they are purely Johannine and without parallels in the Synoptic discourse materials, and further, to assign all these claims for preëxistence in the words of Jesus to the composition of the author of the Fourth Gospel. He goes on to say, *Thus it will always remain doubtful whether it (the claim for preëxistence) belongs to Jesus' own view of himself or only to the reflection of the fourth evangelist* (I 546). But if it is allowed that Jesus really spoke these words out of his supposed recollection of a prehuman and pre-worldly state, it simply means *the destruction of healthy human consciousness and exposes him to a fanaticism from which he otherwise shows himself free* (I 543f).

The second passage (I 553f) has to do with Jesus' outlook in the Synoptics (Mc 13,26; Mt 24,30; Lc 21,27) for his return in the role of the Son of man in the sense of Daniel 7,13. Strauss took no offense at this word of Jesus, which, he says, taken apart from the apocalyptic atmosphere of the times in which it was spoken would be, in and of itself, a very audacious and adventurous notion. There is no reason for rejecting this idea of Jesus because it would seem to make a fanatic of him, as DeWette seems to have thought and against whom the following statement seems to be directed: *Whoever shuns this view of the background of the Messianic plan of Jesus simply because he fears that thereby he would make a fanatic of Jesus, let him consider how exactly these hopes corresponded to the*

*long cherished hopes of the Jews, and how easily upon the su-*
*pernaturalistic soil of that time and in the secluded circle of the*
*Jewish nation a conception in and of itself adventurous, if it*
*were only nationalistic in character and besides had its true and*
*splendid elements, could win for itself even a prudent person*
(I 553f).

Thus we see in his first *Leben Jesu* that Strauss comes upon the question of Jesus' fanaticism, but decides it in a very
positive way designating Jesus as *einen besonnenen Mann*. But
this is not true of his second life of Jesus which appeared in
two volumes in 1864 under the title *Das Leben Jesu fuer das*
*deutsche Volk bearbeitet*. This second work of Strauss was
translated into English and published under the title *A New*
*Life of Jesus*. The quotations below from this English translation are according to the second edition, 1879; the references
to the original correspond to the twenty-first German edition.

The transition of Strauss' turn to a negative view of Jesus
is seen in a letter addressed by him to Kaeferli dated June 15,
1862, just a year and a half before he finished his second *Leben*
*Jesu* (Jan. 24, 1864), in which he writes: *If one surrenders*
*the orthodox view of Jesus, then one has before him a fanatic,*
*and such a fearful fanatic, that it is difficult to conceive of*
*such a combination of so much fanaticism and so much reason*
(Quoted by Wellhausen, Einl. S. 150, Anm. 1). Strauss' turn
toward a pathological view of Jesus is to be best explained by
the personal embitterment that he cherished in consequence of
the unhappy fate that his first *Leben Jesu* brought down upon
him.

From the scientific point of view Strauss' 1864 *Leben Jesu*
marks a distinct degeneration in the critical character of his
work. It contains too much that is the product of resentment
and too little of his earlier careful, clear and consequent criticism. In this work he comes again to speak on the same two
questions of Jesus' claim of preëxistence and his apocalyptic
aspirations in the same connections as in his first work, but here
we find an unsympathetic and negative tone that is totally lacking in his 1835 work. Concerning the Johannine claim of
preëxistence he writes: *It is indeed inconceivable to us that any*

*person in the flesh should remember an ante-natal existence, even independent of the fact that in the present case it is supposed to have been a divine existence reaching back to a period before the creation of the world. It is inconceivable to us, because in accredited history no instance of it has occurred. And if any one should speak of having such a recollection, we should consider him a fool or, if not, an impostor* (Eng., I 271f; Ger., I 101f). *But a man, whoever he may have been, could never, if his heart and head were sound, have uttered such speeches about himself as are put into the mouth of Jesus in the Fourth Gospel. . . . . . The speeches of Jesus about himself in this Gospel are an uninterrupted Doxology, only translated out of the second person into the first* (Eng., I 272; Ger., I 102). They run along too characteristically in the tone of the fourth evangelist's thought in his prologue, and too foreign to the thought of Jesus as represented in the Synoptics, to be ascribed to the historical Jesus. *But when he* (the enthusiastic Christian) *goes so far as the Fourth Evangelist, and puts the utterances of his own pious enthusiasm into the mouth of Jesus in the form of his own utterances about himself, he does him a very perilous service* (Eng., I 273; Ger., I 102).

In his 1864 *Leben Jesu* Strauss devotes fuller consideration, a whole separate paragraph (39), to the Messianic return. He says: *To a human being no such thing as he here prophesied of himself, could happen. If he did prophesy it of himself, and expect it himself, he is for us nothing but a fanatic; if, without any conviction on his part, he said it of himself, he was a braggart and impostor. . . . . . He who expects to come again after his death, as no human being has ever done, is in our opinion not exactly a madman, because in reference to the future imagination is more possible, but still an arrant enthusiast* (Eng., I 322f; Ger., I 120). But Strauss regards these words of Jesus concerning his return as historical; they are not to be denied or neutralized by some unnatural explanation. Then he asks: *Or, lastly shall we make him bear the burden of them in the full meaning of the words, and therefore be compelled to admit that he was a fanatic, and not a common one either?* An affirmative answer to this question, he says, is not *something altogether in-*

*conceivable* (Eng., I 323; Ger., I 121). *The expectation of such a thing* (Mc 13,26), *on one's own behalf is something quite different from a general expectation of it, and he who expects it of himself and for himself will not only appear to us in the light of a fanatic, but we see also an unallowable self-exaltation in a man's* (*and it is only of a human being that we are everywhere speaking*) *so putting himself above everyone else as to contrast himself with them as their future Judge* (Eng., I 331; Ger., I 124). *It might be ever so disagreeable to us with our Christian habits of thought, but if such should prove itself to be the case* (that Jesus was a fanatic) *as the result of historical research, then our Christian habits of thought must give way. Further, one has no right to say that a fanatic could not have had the historical influence that has gone forth from him nor have been capable of the high and wholesome insights we have been discussing. This may be true of an impostor whom we leave out of consideration entirely. But the discovery of high gifts of mind and superiorities of soul combined with a prominent element of fanaticism* (mit einer Dosis Schwaermerei) *is not such an unusual occurrence, and it can be asserted of the great men of history that not one of them has been wholly free from fanaticism* (Ger., I 121).

But this idea of Jesus' expectation of a personal return became still more intolerable to Strauss, and he wrote to Lang on October 16 of the same year that he finished his second *Leben Jesu*: *For me this idea borders close on insanity* (Ziegler, II 609).

Strauss finished his *Der Alte und der Neue Glaube* in October 1872. Paragraphs 4-32 deal with the first of the four questions which Strauss seeks to answer in this book: *Are we still Christians?* This question he answers in the negative: *It is my conviction that, if we refuse to resort to subterfuge, if we will not turn and twist words, in short if we want to speak as serious and honest persons, we must confess: We are no longer Christians* (S. 61).

To paragraph 30 Strauss gives the title: *Das Schwaermerische in seinem Wesen.* Here Strauss, in substance at least, repeats his position in his 1864 life of Jesus regarding Jesus' expectation of his own personal return: *If he was not this* (a higher, superhuman being) *but only a mere man and yet cherished this expectation, then we can help neither ourselves nor him; according to our conceptions he was a fanatic. This word has ceased long ago to be an affront and insult such as it was in the last century. We know that there have been noble and intelligent fanatics. A fanatic can rouse and elevate, and his work may be historically lasting, but we shall not want to choose him as a guide in life. He will lead us into devious paths unless we place his influence under the control of our reason* (S. 52f).

Thus Strauss ends by definitely designating Jesus as a fanatic, conceding that even a fanatic can be of considerable historical significance, but entirely omitting the reference to the apocalyptic atmosphere of Jesus' time by which he defended Jesus against the charge of fanaticism in 1835. The last sentence above quoted makes clear Strauss' turn toward the hated rationalism which he made so ridiculous in his first *Leben Jesu*.

## 2)   Ernest Renan

Renan was the first to attempt to come psychologically close to Jesus. His success, however, is very questionable. O. Holtzmann praises Renan as the first who saw in Jesus' enthusiastic faith the real source of Jesus' power (WJE., S. 9, Anm. 1). Renan confines this enthusiastic element to the last weeks of Jesus' public career.

The degeneration which Renan found in the character and career of Jesus was not psychological, but moral. In the last period of his career Jesus degenerated from the genial aphoristic philosopher of optimistic morality to a sinister preacher of pessimism appealing to the popular thought of his day by undertaking the role of a political revolutionist and professional thaumaturge (p. 170). Jesus' resort to miracle constituted a collapse in his morale. This was brought about by his increasing unpopularity with the masses, the growing opposition of the religious leaders, and the earlier unwholesome influence of the Baptist whom Providence kindly removed from the scene before Jesus' moral break became complete, as it threatened at the beginning. If it had come when it threatened to do so earlier in Jesus' public career, the break would have left Jesus only *an unknown Jewish sectarian* (p. 78).

Upon his last return to Galilee, Jesus begins to ascribe to his own person entirely new functions in the realization of the kingdom of God. The kingdom can now come only by violence, and Jesus regards himself as the indispensable victim. But this is not all: *After his death the Son of man is to come with glory, accompanied by legions of angels, and those who repel him are to be confounded* (p. 170).

Here Renan does not take offense, as did Strauss in his later life, and as have the recent formulators of the question of Jesus' psychic health. The audacity of this conception is not at all surprising, says Renan, for Jesus had long before set himself in a relation to God as a son to his father. On the contrary, this claim of Jesus stands in closest correspondence with his character and is not at all out of place for him: *That which in the case of others would be intolerable pride should not in his case, however, be characterized as an outrage* (p. 171). It, therefore, does not raise a pathological problem for Renan as it has for others.

All great movements in history have been inspired or accompanied by a certain amount of illusion. *The admixture of illusions heretofore to be found in all great movements, whether political or religious, is not a sufficient reason for refusing to accord to these movements our sympathy and admiration.... .. One can love Jeanne d'Arc without admitting the reality of her visions* (p. 12). Jesus' illusion regarding the immediate proximity of the end Renan designates as *an illusion common to all great reformers* (p. 186). He further excuses Jesus on the basis of this idea not being peculiar to himself but common among his contemporaries: *Let us pardon him his expectation of coming in triumph on the clouds of heaven. Perhaps this was the error of others rather than his own* (p. 186). Jesus' errors of judgment, according to Renan, were merely those innocent errors common to childish credulity and beautiful piety, and were due to his childish idea of the familiar relationship existing between God and man and his exaggerated faith in the ability of man. These were *the happy errors which constituted the principle of his force* (p. 31), and gave to him the power of making an impression on his time which no one, before or since, has been able to exercise in a comparable degree.

Renan unconsciously hints at the pathological problem, but it does not seriously occur to him; otherwise he would have given it some sort of definite consideration. He solves the errors of judgment in the great men of history by the appeal to history: *Till now the alienated mind has never been able to influence seriously the course of human history* (German translation, Reclam, S. 85). Renan's chief regret in the case of Jesus is his surrender of his early Galilean idealism which he yielded under the pressure of events. He thus finds only a moral degeneration in the character of Jesus.

## 3)  Eduard von Hartmann

Eduard von Hartmann's book, *Das Christentum des Neuen Testaments* (1905), is the second and revised edition of his *Briefe ueber die christliche Religion* which appeared shortly before the outbreak of the Franco-Prussian war in 1870 under the pseudonym F. A. Mueller. In this work von Hartmann will show, among other things, that both the personality and teaching of Jesus are *a much too narrow foundation for the erection of a religious structure* (S. 15).

Von Hartmann rejects the teaching of Jesus on ethical grounds. Jesus, as the Baptist, was a decided pessimist; his was not the metaphysical pessimism of Buddhism, but an *Entruestungspessimismus* (S. 86). Jesus is the world's most determined pessimist, not only in an ethical, but in a physical sense. His optimism is transcendental (S. 130). Moreover, Jesus' ethics are purely plebeian; they not only exclude the aristocrats of social standing, property and fortune, but even the aristocratic select spirits. There is an anti-Semitic tone running throughout von Hartmann's book; Jesus was a Jew from head to foot and was not free from the characteristic *semitischen Rohheit* (*Semitic coarseness*).

The personal and private ethics of Jesus are primitive and have long since been outgrown by cultured civilization. He taught the control of conduct with the outlook for recompense in terms of rewards and punishments.  This von Hartmann describes as *a moral doctrine devoid of ethical character and the immorality of pseudo-morals* (S. 123f).  The two great commandments (Mc 12,28ff) are in no wise original with Jesus but were adopted by him from Deut. 6, 4ff.  The Golden Rule (Mt 7,12) Jesus borrowed from Hillel; as an ethical principle of conduct it is injurious:  *Understood as motive the instruction concerning the reciprocity of services rendered is an uncouth Philistine morality which may be very useful in practical life but which goes straight to the door of the most prudently calculating egotism and injures true ethical sentiment* (S. 134).  Jesus' idea of God is too thoroughly Old Testament and cannot be accepted today because it belongs to a period when the moral conscience was coarse and undeveloped, and it naturally bears the features of the primitive stage of culture from which it comes.  Jesus, further, requires the individual to renounce all insistance upon, or claim of, personal rights (Mt 5,39f).  In Mt 18,16-18 Jesus sets *in the place of state justice the lynch justice of the democratic community.*

Von Hartmann finds that Jesus' social ethics are just as inadequate as his personal and private ethics.  He demands the renunciation of earthly goods and expropriation; property and economy are foolishness and crime, nevertheless he does not hesitate to accept from ministering women gifts over which they had no rightful legal disposition, and to destroy a herd of swine that belonged to a third person which today would have brought a suit in court for indemnity.  He shared the primitive Jewish view of labor as a curse upon mankind and had no appreciation of the dignity of labor such as the modern world has, *which not only punishes shiftless vagabondage and begging, but in so far as possible the giving of alms to the unemployed capable of work, and which would convert all aid into insurance* (S. 50).  Jesus broke with his own family and not only permitted but encouraged others to do the same; nowhere do we read that he told the women in his following to go back to their homes and husbands.  Then von Hartmann concludes: *He who regards the world simply as a waiting-room and sees the true home of man exclusively in the other world, his teaching, frankly spok-*

*en, can be nothing other than destructive for all those institu-tions founded upon the contrary supposition that man should strive to make himself at home in the world and be comfortable here* (S. 158).

Von Hartmann's rejection of the personality of Jesus as a sufficiently firm foundation for the construction of the relig-ious life of the modern world is the principal point of inter-est with him in our present problem of the psychic health of Jesus.

In the first place, Jesus' personality cannot constitute a religious standard for modern life because the sources furnish a too inadequate picture of Jesus: *The historical Jesus remains for us ever a problematic figure about whom we can make only more or less doubtful conjectures; what we can say of him with any degree of probability amounts to an extremely meagre sub-ject-matter with which, from the religious point of view, noth-ing is to be done* (S. 20). In his determination of the most re-liable materials, von Hartmann sets the principle which P. W. Schmiedel followed in the selection of his "Grundsaeule" in the historicity debate: *Positive features of the historical Jesus we shall recognize preferably in those elements which have sur-vived independently or even in contradiction to the doctrinal conceptions of the original documents by the unperceived law of continuity and the naïve faithfulness of epic tradition* (S. 20). This principle of selection naturally brings von Hartmann up-on those more distinctly human features of Jesus, more espe-cially characteristic of Mc, which lend themselves most readily to the pathographic point of view.

Intellectually Jesus was a mediocre mind. His teaching, for the most part, is made up of a selection of materials already taught or preached by the old prophets, John the Baptist, the order of the Essenes, the Talmud, or the Old Testament Apo-crypha. Further, Jesus' selection is not always the most for-tunate for he does not select the best. Jesus' own independent productions are not better than mediocre. The much admired moral aphorisms are only citations or revisions of Old Testa-ment and Talmudic matter.

Jesus' parables show no originality either in form or content, and are often very inferior to those of the great Jewish rabbis. The sources from which Jesus drew most of his parables are unknown, but this does not let us conclude that they are his own original productions. Some of them are really *very finely felt and crystal-clear*, as for example Lc 10,29-37; 15,11-32 and 18,10-13 (S. 44). But Mt 13,3-8; 13,12-23 and 18,22-34 manifest *neither specially ingenious nor poetic originality, but for the most part only a fortunate choice and skillful combination of pictures* (S. 45). Then comes a longer series of short parables which in no respect transcend *the niveau of mediocrity, in which one finds as little to praise as to blame* (S. 45). Many (Mt 9,16-17; 12,33; Lc 15,8-9; 12,37) are trivial. Von Hartmann has so little understanding of the parable as a form of address as to call Jn 10,1-16 a parable which no genius would have stooped to speak and so illogically thought out as to have one character alternately play the part of shepherd, the door of the sheep, and then the shepherd again. Jesus often violates the very principle of the parable by representing a scene that is unnatural or contrary to historical fact, viz., the parable of the wise and foolish virgins. In the parable of the pounds (?), Mt 25,14-30, *the point in the illustration itself is miscarried*, in that the servant who brings back the original sum intact is condemned and the two immoral profiteers are praised. *A sure mark of the intellectual ability of a man is this: whether he improves or impairs materials which he finds in a certain form and adopts* (S. 46). Jesus did not improve upon the borrowed materials which he employed; for example, the Talmudic parallel to the parable of the wise and foolish virgins is much clearer and less offensive to our taste than the Christian form in Mt 25,1-12. The two parables in Lc 11,5-8 and 18,1-7 not only show bad taste, but a high degree of impropriety (S. 47).

In the matter of dialectic Jesus could have learned much from the Jewish schools of his day, *if this had not been so strongly repugnant to his intuitively fanatical disposition* (S. 48). Jesus was by nature too unargumentative and unreflective to engage in longer discussion and discourse; he, therefore, confines himself to gnomes and parables without once attempting to give a rational reason for his position. When he is forced to debate, he comes out either by side-stepping the issue or by uttering some sophism. Jesus' defense in Mt 12,27 is unsound; of this Jesus himself is aware, for he turns to a personal attack on his opponents to save himself. His argumentation in Mt 22, 31f is weak and unconvincing. To the precise questions of Nicodemus in Jn 3,4ff Jesus gives no precise reply, but indulges in a monologue not at all pertinent to the issue presented.

Jesus' intellectual abilities could not have given him the success he had. His unusual oratorical power could not have done it. He could not have won his followers *without the charm of an imposing and winning personality* (S. 49) ; *he must have possessed personally something uncommonly binding. That with which he won hearts, roused admiration and confidence, was above all else the comforting gospel of the Baptist that the end of the people's suffering was at hand, the fanatical glow of his enthusiasm and the stirring warmth of sentient expression with which he knew how to accredit his message, and a suggestive power of personal appearance and demeanor by which he accomplished his miracles of healing* (S. 71).

The constituency of the personnel of his following accounts for a great deal of Jesus' success; *the greater part of it was made up of eccentric persons, epileptic and insane, in part too perhaps of such as believed themselves healed by him* (S. 49). Then von Hartmann states the advice that Jesus would receive were he living today: *According to our present-day conclusions in psychology and psychiatry a healthy religion cannot grow on such a morbid soil, and today we would give a religious reformer or prophet the advice to eliminate in so far as possible such elements from his following, since they can compromise only too easily both himself and his cause* (S. 49f).

Another element that contributed to the success of Jesus is to be found in the general religious restlessness and the feverish Messianic expectations of the time. The social and national depression under which the Jewish people groaned had aroused the popular fancy to a high pitch. It is not at all surprising that it would occur to some insane person that he was the Messiah (S. 55). *To believe one's self the Messiah was in*

*the very atmosphere of the time like a kind of epidemic idea*
(S. 67). Messianic claimants were numerous, and it is against
these possible rivals that Jesus warns his disciples in Mt
24,23ff (Mc 13,21ff; Lc 17,22ff).

It is von Hartmann's delineation of the consciousness and
character of Jesus that forms his chief point of interest for us
in the earlier stages of the problem of Jesus' psychic health.

During the first part of his public career Jesus seems *almost an impersonal being* (S. 63). His message is so thoroughly objective that his own person plays no part in it and
he seems to regard himself as only *an indifferent instrument.*
During this period Jesus is only the prophet of the imminent
world-catastrophe and the approaching kingdom of God. Even
in the second period he does not yet possess his Messianic consciousness. Nevertheless, at the end of the first period the idea
begins to strike root; he hints at it and seeks confirmation by
public and private opinion in the second period. The fanatical
female element in his following was doubtless the first factor to
encourage Jesus in the thought of his Messiahship: *There is
nothing more probable than that it was these woman who, if
they did not awaken in Jesus the idea of his Messiahship, at
least nourished it and by their idolizing hopes caused it to strike
root* (S. 49). In the last period of his public career he begins
to lay aside his former reserve; Mt 12 is full of his exaggerated
self-exaltation. With the entry into Jerusalem *his personal
estimate of himself is aggravated according to the measure of
the demonstrations in his honor* (S. 65). The anointing in
Bethany augments this feeling. During his Jerusalem days *he
falls into a condition of abnormal aggravation of self-consciousness* (S. 66). The nearer he comes to the end of his life,
according to the Synoptics, the stronger his Messianic ambition
appears as the decisive motive of his action. *Then, as he saw
death approaching, he summed up the results of his life, saw
his work wrecked, his person and cause deserted of God, and
died with the unanswered question on his lips, why God had
forsaken him* (S. 74). His belief in his Messiahship was only
a fanatical fiction to which he had committed himself.

In his estimate of Jesus' character we come to von Hartmann's pathological judgment against Jesus which, as we shall see at once, is much more severe than that of Strauss.

Jesus taught humility and meekness and he was *in general certainly a gentle and quiet nature;* for the same reason he was also, in the main, *eine unpraktische Natur* (S. 68). His meekness was by no means a merit, for it was natural to his personality; *but it swung immediately into fierce energy and implacable exasperation whenever he encountered serious opposition to the realization of his fundamental idea* (S. 68f). This is seen in Lc 12,49ff, Mt 23,19 33, and in the cursing of the fig tree where, if historical (it might be a miracle variation of the parable in Lc 13,6-9), his anger shows itself capable of flaring up on a very harmless occasion and venting itself in a most uncritical way on an innocent object (S. 69).

In his summary sketch of Jesus' personality von Hartmann writes: *Not a genius, but a talented individual, who with complete lack of genuine culture produced on an average only moderate materials and who was not able to guard himself against numerous weaknesses and grave aberrations; a quiet fanatic and a transcendental enthusiast, who in spite of a natural geniality hated and despised the world and its concerns and looked upon every interest for it as injurious to the one true transcendental interest; an amiable youth, who through a curious chain of circumstances arrived at the then epidemic idea that he was the Messiah and perished in consequence of it* (S. 72).

Von Hartmann does not completely reject every feature in Jesus' personality: *Certainly one can exhibit many features of the personality of Jesus which even today can serve as models* (S. 70), viz., his piety and his resignation to the divine will. But in order to be an ethical example, all, and not just some, of the features of a personality must be faultless. Evolution itself eliminates Jesus as a religious ideal for the modern world; each age must seek its moral ideal in itself and not in another, and Jesus belongs to another age long, long in the past and completely outgrown.

Strauss pronounced Jesus a fanatic (*Schwaermer*); von Hartmann is more specific in his definition and more severe in his judgment. He designates Jesus as a *stiller Fanatiker und transzendenter Schwaermer*, to whom the fortunate fate was allotted of appearing in history in an uncultured time and among an uncultured people that prepared for him as a religious fanatic only a tragic end.   Modern society would have been more merciful, and yet more merciless, and consigned him to that confinement and care which would have precluded all possibility of subsequent influence.

Von Hartmann thus closes his chapter on the personality of Jesus : *Man kann es als ein glueckliches Vorrecht jener ungebildeten Zeiten und Voelker preisen, dass sie solchem religioesen Schwaermer wenigstens ein tragisches Ende ermoeglichten; die moderne Kultur wuerde ihm bloss ein trauriges Los bereiten, das jede Nachwirkung ausschloesse* (S. 74).

#### 4)    Friedrich Nietzsche

Nietzsche's *Also Sprach Zarathustra* (Thus Spake Zarathustra) is, in reality, a contrary counterpart to the Gospels themselves, or better perhaps to the Sermon on the Mount.   The book is composed chiefly of addresses by *Zarathustra*, but these are interspersed with bits of transition narratives that often read as though they were modelled after the narrative matter of the Gospels.   These narrative bits, however, are introduced only as they furnish a setting for, or make some sort of contribution to the discourse materials.

In fact, Nietzsche fashioned his presentation of the career of *Zarathustra* after the course of the public career of Jesus. The very first line of the book tells us that *Zarathustra*, as Jesus, entered upon his public career when he was thirty years of age (Lc 3,23).   He leaves his home and the sea of his childhood and goes into the mountains where he spends ten years instead of forty days as Jesus did ; Jesus came out of the wilderness too soon.   At the end of this period he enters upon his public career during which he, as Jesus, makes his frequent retreats to solitude, not for prayer but for meditation.   He early draws and retains unto himself disciples, who, in so far as possible, are his constant companions and whom he instructs concerning the superman, who forms as constant a theme in *Zarathustra's* message as does the kingdom of God in the preaching of Jesus.

In the course of his career *Zarathustra* goes through a very highly symbolic and imaginary itinerary; he visits the city called *"Die bunte Kuh"* and the isles of the blessed. He pronounces his woe over *Die grosse Stadt* as Jesus does over the Galilean cities (Mt 11,20ff; Lc 10,13ff). His favorite retreat is a mount of olives and toward the close he democratically, yet very exclusively, celebrates a last meal with his disciples and a few other trusted and sympathetic friends. But Nietzsche's *Zarathustra* does not die; his hour comes but in the form of a moment of transfiguration in which he grasps the greatest of all truths, *suffering with the superman.* Darkness does not cover the earth at midday (Mc 15,33) and his last cry is not *My God, My God, Why hast thou forsaken me?*, but he goes forth from his den to his work in the world with the strength and glory of the rising sun and issuing his challenge, *This is my morning; my day approaches; come, come, thou great noonday* (S. 476). It is *Zarathustra* who really lives; it is God who is dead.

Nietzsche's book is, in reality, a condensation and crystalization of a spiritual struggle that waged in his day and lands in the souls of many of his contemporaries, and which he felt with special keenness: the struggle of the individual against the whole. Nietzsche hated Christianity, as he conceived it, because it tended to institutionalize the individual. He regarded Christianity, therefore, as the sickness of humanity. Jesus preached an ideal community, the kingdom of God; but *Zarathustra* preaches the ideal individual, the superman.

As Weinel writes, *Nietzsche's philosophy is the history of his own life* (IBN, S. 143); we might add that his *Zarathustra* is his psychological autobiography. For many years Nietzsche suffered fearfully with stomach trouble, excessive nervousness and weak eyes. And before he had finished the last part of his *Zarathustra* (1884) his brain and mind had become seriously affected. His thought came thus to center about the two opposite poles of health and sickness, except as it flashed brilliantly back and forth between them. It would seem only natural, then, that the question of Jesus' health would suggest itself to Nietzsche; and it did, but not in the 1905— form of the question. It was the ethical and moral teaching of Jesus that Nietzsche found to be morbid.

More than all else Nietzsche wanted what nature had denied him: to be healthy, strong, able to work in the world, and to do in a splendid superhuman way. Above all else he wanted to really live and enjoy life. And he was impatient with what he found in the Gospels to be Jesus' low estimate of this life and his hatred for this world. Jesus was constantly pointing his followers to the life of another world and order of things, the kingdom of God. Therefore, Nietzsche has *Zarathustra* say:

> *I implore you, my brethren, remain true to the earth, and believe them not who speak to you of supermundane hopes! They are mixers of poison whether they know it or not.*

> *They are despisers of life, paralyzed and themselves poisoned, of whom the earth is tired; may they pass away* (S. 13).

Jesus and Christianity had stripped all the joy out of life. In his address at the last supper *Zarathustra* asks, *What has been hitherto the greatest sin here on earth? Was it not the word of him who said 'Woe unto them who laugh'* (Lc 6,25. S. 427). Nietzsche's chief objection to Jesus was that he never learned to laugh. If Jesus found no occasion to laugh he sought badly; even a child finds reason to laugh. Jesus did not love enough, for he did not love those who laugh. Instead he pronounced woes on them. This for Nietzsche is a lapse of taste on the part of Jesus, but only to be expected for Jesus came from the proletariat. *Zarathustra* admonishes his hearers to avoid all such teachers:

> *Avoid all such uncompromising persons! They are a miserable morbid kind, a rabble class; they look upon this life as bad, they have an evil eye for this earth* (S. 427).

Nietzsche thus finds something morbid, not in the mind and person of Jesus, but in his view of the world and his spirit of living life. He is offended at Jesus' teaching concerning life's ideals; and this, as Weinel says, made Nietzsche the strongest enemy of Christianity.

Nietzsche does not regard Jesus' teaching as the product of his morbid state of mind, but of his youthful immaturity. Jesus died too soon; his mind was not yet ripe for public instruction on life's ideals. Jesus had not been alone with himself enough; he was in the wilderness only forty days. *Zarathustra* remained ten years in his first retreat to the mountains without becoming tired. *Many die too late, and some die too soon; therefore Zarathustra teaches, "Die at the right time"* (S. 105). Jesus was one of those few who die too soon, for his death prevented him from retracting his teaching.

*Of a truth, too soon died that Hebrew, whom the preachers of slow death honor; and since it has been fateful for many that he died too soon.*

*Then he knew only the tears and melancholy of the Hebrew, together with the hatred against the good and the righteous,—the Hebrew Jesus; then the yearning for death overtook him.*

*If he had only remained in the wilderness, and far from the good and the righteous! Perhaps he would have learned to live and to love the earth—and to laugh besides!*

*Believe me, my brethren! He died too soon; he himself would have retracted his teaching if he had lived to my age!* (It is interesting to note that Nietzsche was only thirty-eight years old when he wrote this). *He was noble enough to retract!*

*But he was still immature. Prematurely the youth loves, and prematurely he hates both man and earth. His soul and the wings of his spirit were still tied and heavy.*

*In the man there is more child than in the youth, and less melancholy; he understands himself better with regard to death and life* (S. 107f).

Nietzsche was not without admiration for Jesus; he could call him *noble enough to retract*. In fact, he felt great sympathy with much in Jesus' character and expressed the regret that the proper person had not known and been with him who would have understood and helped him. *It is to be regretted that a Dostojewsky did not live near this interesting decadent; I mean some one who would have known how to appreciate the captivating charm of such a mixture of the sublime, morbid, and childish* (Quoted by Weinel, IBN, S. 149).

### 5)   Jules Soury

Soury (1), one time secretary to Renan, is the first to make a definite diagnosis of the psychic malady of Jesus. Jesus was a case of progressive paralysis of the brain. He opens his preface thus: *Après le dieu et l'homme, le malade* (p. 5). Since the work of Strauss and Renan there remains of Jesus but the sinister shadow of a sufferer. *Jesus appears here for the first time as a morbid mind of which one attempts to trace the development of the disease* (p. 6). The nervous trouble with which Jesus was afflicted was very serious, in fact incurable. This disease has never been idle; it has produced millionaires, kings, popes, prophets, and even gods of poor devils (*diables*) with disordered brains. It has produced more than one Messiah. The study of morbid psychology demonstrates that the founder of the Christian religion died in a more or less advanced stage of this disease; the cross saved him from complete insanity.

Soury proposes to conduct his investigation on the basis of three orders of fact as attested by the oldest and most reliable witnesses of the life of Jesus. 1) The exalted religious sentiment, then general in Galilee, drove Jesus into the wilderness of Judea where he for a time lived the ascetic life of a prophet. Dominated by *l'idée fixe* that he was called to announce the Messiah, he left his family and native village, where he was little more respected than in his own home, and, followed by a few fishermen, he went about through the cities and villages of Galilee announcing the imminent approach of the kingdom of God. 2) Little by little Jesus came to the belief that he himself was the very Messiah he had been announcing. The

---

(1) . *Jésus et les Evangiles,* (1878, 190 p.)   The writer is indebted to the Public Library of the City of Boston for access to this now rare edition of Soury's work.

progressive swooning away of his natural self-consciousness can
be detected from the time of the incident at the foot of Mt.
Hermon until the day when he boldly declared himself to be the
Messiah before Caiaphas and Annas.  3) His cursing of the
fig tree, when it was not the season of figs, and his violent
cleansing of the temple are manifestly absurd acts.  During
this period Jesus' self-consciousness rose to the point where he
believed that he was permitted to do anything and that nothing
was impossible for him.  For a long time Jesus had manifested
a clear perversion of natural sentiment and affection, especially
in regard to his own family.  His fits of frenzy against the
Jerusalem authorities, his exaggerated words and deeds, his delirium of his Messiahship were followed by a marked decline in
his mental and physical faculties, *un affaiblissement intellectuel
et musculaire* (p. 10).

In each of these periods of his life pathological conditions
of Jesus' constitution can be discovered.  The first effect was
a precipitation of the course of the blood, an abnormal dilation
of the blood vessels, and a congestion of the brain.  Every
chronic congestion of this organ is attended, from the point of
view of the subject, at first by an intensely moral life and an
extraordinary activity of the imagination rising even to the
point of hallucinations; later, ideas of power and absurd delirious delusions of grandeur appear.  *The violence and irritability of aliens is then very great* (p. 11).  The progress of the
disease is rather slow.  There are at times remissions during
which the reason seems to return, but if the affliction continues
for some months or several years the result is a complete intellectual and physical debility.  *That is how Jesus would have
ended if, evily inspired, the Jews had preferred to see Barabbas
on the cross* (p. 14).  This *méningo-encéphalite* has been called
the sickness of our century, but, since it has a moral origin, it
is the disease of all centuries.  Religious and political passions
were no less active in Judea then than in our own lands.  Mes-
sianism spread over Palestine in Jesus' day like an epidemic;
Jesus caught this mental malady and died of it, *Voilà tout*.  It
is probable that Jesus was predisposed to infection because he,
in all probability, came from a tainted family.  What we know

of his brother James does not permit us to doubt this much.
One third of the cases of general paralysis are due to heredity.
One would suppose that there were *maniacs, epileptics, suicides
or drunkards* in Jesus' family. *He was wise to remain as chaste
as an ascetic* (p. 18f).

But one does well to proceed cautiously in consideration of
the eminence of Jesus' moral faculties and religious genius
which morbid heredity seems able to admit. Moreau de Tours
writes: *The dispositions of mind which enable a man to distinguish himself above other men by the originality of his thought
and ideas, by his eccentricity and the energy of his affective
faculties, by the superiority of his intellectual faculties, have
their origin in the same organic conditions as the various moral
disorders of which insanity and idiocy are the most complete
manifestation* (quoted by Soury, p. 19f). It is often the case
that men liable to states of ecstasy and hallucinations have most
profoundly modified the world's thought and influenced the
course of the world's history. The historian cannot afford to
neglect hallucinations, for a confirmed paranoiac has often
proven himself capable of some of the most brilliant feats of
the human mind.

Soury attempts to trace the evolution and maturity of the
morbid germs that lie secreted in every organism, and to prove
that the superior manifestations of heart and mind have a neuropathic origin. In this study he does not desire to grieve or
hurt the simple soul that delights to devote itself to the ideal
that it loves. He will advance no hypothesis, but simply point
out certain features in the character and personality of Jesus
based on one or more passages of the Gospels. *Our portrait of
Jesus is identical with that of the Gospel itself* (p. 26).

The Gospel writers picture Jesus as a morbid mind. His
modern biographers have not perceived this for the simple
reason that they have not looked for it. Today when Jesus is
no longer considered divine, but merely a man, he, like the majority of other great men, is for the historian only a problem in
morbid psychology. Excellent equilibrium of physiological
functions can bestow only long life upon us. *In order that the
genius may appear it is necessary that this equilibrium be brok-
en* (p. 34).

The Galilean prophet was not always of a sweet and even disposition; he allowed himself to be seized by choleric fits against the world of men and things. He was often rude toward the sick and the infirm who came to him for relief; nothing equals the harshness with which he dismissed those whom he had cured. *Jesus was a thaumaturge or he was nothing.* (p. 128). He was not the amiable person that Renan pictured, but a fanatical and visionary Jewish thaumaturge subject to fits of frightful frenzy and violence. In our day he would be accounted insane. But it is in the malady of Jesus that the finest features of his personality are to be found.

Jesus' contemporaries, even his own family, regarded him as insane. So must we. If Mary and the brethren of Jesus, when they came from Nazareth to Capernaum to fetch him, had brought him again to his home in Nazareth, the Galilean prophet perhaps would have passed an obscure existence in some dark corner of the paternal house held by a chain as was the demoniac of Gadara.

The exasperated state of Jesus' mind is clear in his woes on the Galilean cities, in the subtilty of his reasonings, the ambiguity of his responses when he was put with questions, and the ruses he employed in escaping the hands of his enemies. *This blending of intense violence and instinctive prudence, of consummate cleverness, although unconscious, is thoroughly characteristic* (p. 68).

Jesus' words at Caesarea Philippi have all the indications of the state of those who are already in the way of general paralysis; this delirium of his Messiahship was born of his intense faith in his prophetic call and mission. It was only gradually that it came to obscure his natural personal consciousness and identity.

His Jerusalem words and acts are pathological in character, not because of their vehemence and violence, but because of their absurdity. Being in the advanced stages of general paralysis, Jesus doubtless took the mockings of the Roman soldiers in all seriousness. Only some of the half-demented women who had followed him up from Galilee witnessed his execution.

The pathographic part of Soury's book is confined to the preface and the introduction; in the subsequent chapters he hardly touches upon the question, and does not prove what he promised. However, it is interesting to note that Soury anticipated de Loosten and Binet-Sanglé in the idea that Jesus suffered affliction under the burden of morbid hereditary influences.

In the third edition of his book which appeared in 1898 under the title of *Jésus et la Religion d'Israel* Soury entirely omits the pathographic sections of the first edition (1878) and in his preface expresses his regret for the offense caused by the first appearance of his book (see A. Schweitzer, GdLJF, S. 363).

For an appreciation of Soury and a refutation of his diagnosis—see Binet-Sanglé, IV 311-320; against Soury in particular and the pathographic position in general—see Ninck, S. 230f, 245ff.

### 6)  L. K. Washburn

Washburn's pamphlet, *Was Jesus Insane?*, hardly deserves mention in the discussion of our present problem, for it is too clear in its purpose and too uncritical in character to be taken seriously and is wholly undeserving of criticism. Though he quotes from the Gospels a number of times, Washburn cites only four references; three by chapter (Mt 23, Mc 3, and Jn 8), and one by chapter and verse (Lc 19,27). (All other references are supplied by the writer). His only answer to the question as he states it in the title of his pamphlet is cheap rhetoric of which the following is a characteristic specimen:  *To believe this* (that Jesus was divine), *we must write Imbecile on the brow, tell truth to wear the mask of hypocrisy, bid honesty put out its sight, lead to the grave the shining virtues of our race and drape manhood in black. Why, the very majesty of nature must crawl in the dust and the lips of truth kiss the feet of falsehood* (p. 16). This pamphlet appeared in 1889 and contains only 18 small pages (1).

---

(1)  It is out of print and the writer is indebted to the kindness of The Truth Seeker Company in New York for lending him a copy from its publication files, which kindness enables him here to survey briefly its contents.

Washburn's complete lack of orientation in the study of the New Testament literature is seen in his estimate of the sources. The accounts of Jesus in the New Testament are not to be depended upon. Thirty years intervened between the death of Jesus and the time when the earliest Gospel is said to have been written; *but it is by no means certain that any account of Jesus was written for one hundred years after the time of his death, and if an account was written it is impossible at the present time to know what it was* (p. 4). *To assert that the gospel account of what Jesus said is reliable, is to declare that we have the exact words which he spoke and a faithful description of what he did...... Common report, hearsay, gossip, imagination, furnished the writers of the gospels with their materials* (p. 5). We see how mechanically Washburn conceives of tradition when he says, *We must have a phonographic record of his speeches when delivered and an accurate account of his acts by an eye-witness...... Will anyone presume to say that the gospel story was written by an eye-witness, or that the Sermon on the Mount, the parables, and the exclamations of Jesus were phonographically reported?* (p. 4f). Take for example the Sermon on the Mount, *Among those who heard Jesus do you think there was one who would be able to repeat every one of the 2,473 words of his sermon thirty years afterwards exactly as it was delivered* (p. 5).

It is not Washburn's purpose to point out the inconsistent and contradictory character of the Gospels, *but rather to hold up the picture of this person in the light of those extravagant expressions which have been accepted as proof of his divinity, but which seem rather to indicate his insanity* (p. 6).

Since the Gospels are completely silent on physiological details, we can judge the character of Jesus only by his speech and behavior. *Let us see what Jesus said and did, and find, if we can, whether a God once lived upon the earth, or whether a man, under a mental delusion, tried to play the part of a god* (p. 7).

*How do we prove a person insane? Is it not by his words and acts, by what he says and what he does? If a person uses foolish and extravagant language, if he performs deeds for*

*which can be offered no good or rational excuse, he is adjudged
insane.  Did any person ever make use of a more irrational
speech; ever put forth claims to more preposterous power;
ever utter more intemperate, insane language, than the person
called Jesus* (p. 7).  The world seems possessed with a fear of
the name of Jesus; this is *moral cowardice.  The name of Jesus
is the name of a man, and it was a name that was quite common
in the time of Josephus.  It is a name that we need speak with
no particular reverence* (p. 8).

*The language of Jesus is not sensible, not rational; cer-
tainly not the language of a sane mind* (p. 8).  If a man today
*about whom there was nothing particularly remarkable* should
speak the words that Jesus speaks in Jn 10,30, *we would say
that he was crazy, and every medical expert in the United
States would sign a certificate of his insanity* (p. 9).  Such
words merely *mirror the moods of a shattered brain; but it was
easier to be a god then than now.*

Jesus was only *an ordinary individual so far as his earthly surroundings were concerned,* and we might think that we
are reading von Hartmann again when Washburn says that
Jesus had the *habits of the lower classes* (p. 10).  *It is difficult, if not impossible, to account for the extraordinary career
of Jesus upon the ground of sanity.  There is only one way to
explain the gospels—either Jesus was insane or the person that
wrote his life was* (p. 10).

It is generally admitted that mentally sane persons are
not easily moved to anger or led into an excited condition
which expresses itself in violent speech or action whenever they
encounter opposition or contradiction.  (Here we have an anticipation of one of Rasmussen's points).  But Jesus denounces
people with apparently little cause; this cannot be reconciled
with his own teachings.  His teaching in Lc 6,28 is contradicted by Mt 10,33 and Lc 12,51f (Mt 10,34).  In Mt 10,
35f (compare Micah 7,6) *a more fiendish mission could not
have been undertaken; it is the scheme of a madman* (p. 11).
He pronounced woes on the cities that were irresponsive to his
teaching (Mt 11,20ff; Lc 10,13ff).  He raved violently
against the Pharisees (Mt 23,1-36; Lc 11,39-51).  *Jesus*

*could not brook opposition and he was moved to anger at the slightest pretext* (p. 11).

Mc 3,21 is the *verdict of every sensible person who reads the gospels today, and had this verdict of the friends of Jesus been respected, the world would not have been shrouded in the terrible darkness of Christian superstitions for over a thousand years* (p. 12). Further, a great many meaningless details and expressions in the Gospels go to prove that Jesus was not in his right mind, Mc 3,31-35; Jn 2,4. A man making such a foolish statement in our day as Jesus made in Jn 8,56-58 *could be sent to the insane asylum; wills have been broken with less evidence of the testator's lunacy. This foolish speech of Jesus ought to cost the Christian world all respect for the speaker's intelligence* (p. 11f). It is no wonder that Jesus hid himself (Jn 8,59) after making such a statement.

All of Jesus' references to his return on the clouds in the role of the Son of man are merely *the utterances of an unbalanced mind* (p. 14). But there was a method in his madness; his mind was filled with the idea that he was to rule the world, and *any means, no matter how cruel, that would hasten the fulfilment of his designs, were sacred* (p. 15). His delusion concerning his Messiahship is the *faith of a diseased more than of a rational mind* (p. 17). We can explain his Messianic claim only *by believing that he was insane.*

Then Washburn triumphantly closes his eighteen-page discussion of the insanity of Jesus with the remark: *After a fair and impartial reading of the gospels, the world must be convinced that Jesus was not divine, but insane* (p. 20).

One feels bound to apologize for including Washburn in the same chapter with men like Strauss, von Hartmann and Nietzsche, for these men struggled with real problems and attempted serious solutions. Washburn deserves mention only because we aim at a comprehensive survey of the literature on the subject in hand.

However, it is to be noted that Washburn, in spite of the tasteless tone that dominates his pamphlet, did touch very directly upon some of the Gospel passages that figure prominently in the 1905— pathographic judgment against Jesus.

(H. J. Holtzman, MBJ, S. 81, Anm. 1, cites Albert Dulk, *Der Irrgang des Lebens Jesu; I. Teil* 395S. 1884, *II. Teil* 1885 302S., as figuring in the pathographic contention. This work was not accessible to the writer.)

## CHAPTER II

### Factors Contributing to the Rise of the Problem
#### 1) Philosophical

It is our general world-view that, for the most part, justifies our judgments and determines our decisions in the great majority of the matters of life. It is this *Weltauffassung* or *Weltanschauung* that, usually unconsciously, rises as a kind of subliminal self to affect the formulations of our thoughts and the guidance of our conduct in any particular instance. Our world-view may grow and develop or even undergo a radical revolutionary change with age and education. But we never escape it entirely; in one aspect or another, it sets itself before our eyes as a kind of invisible colored screen through which we regard the world and life. Nowhere is this truer than in the field of religion. The world-view of the free-thinker makes his religious ideas and attitudes perfectly natural and comfortable to himself, which to his traditionally orthodox neighbor seem shockingly irreligious.

World-view has played an important role in the pathographic judgment against Jesus. Naumann regards the works of Rasmussen and de Loosten as the inevitable confirmation of the indications of the modern spiritual barometer. The spiritual atmosphere responsible for the charge against the psychic soundness of Jesus has been variously analyzed. Kneib complains against the modern *Willensrichtung* and the general inclination toward a departure from the long accepted Christian traditions. He says that religion has dwindled down to religious psychology, and the latter to psychopathology which would explain religion and piety as a degeneration. Werner sees in the modern rejection of the supernatural element in religion and the substitution of a naturalistic interpretation the underlying cause which is responsible for recent judgments

29

passed upon the emotions and experiences of the religious life as abnormal and morbid phenomena. Naumann finds that the answer to the question of the psychic health of Jesus is dependent upon the answer to a much more general question, namely: Is an actual contact and relation between the finite and the infinite possible? If the answer is negative, as it frequently has been in recent times, then Jesus was a paranoiac. Hollmann writes, *Fuer die Beurteilung wird hier schliesslich entscheidend sein, ob man an ein Wirken goettlichen Geistes im Menschengeist glauben kann;* S. 275.

It is quite essential to understand the world-view of those who have contested the sound state of Jesus' mind. With the coolest conceivable composure de Loosten, Binet-Sanglé and Hirsch pronounce judgments against Jesus, which for the conservative Christian conscience are the blackest blasphemy. The ease with which these men do this is at once clear when one understands their materialistic, atheistic and free-thinking viewpoints. Rothenburg and Rasmussen add to this their hatred for Christianity and all of its traditions. The latter sees in all founders, prophets and champions of religions only analogies to typical cases of epilepsy; their sincerity and seriousness is not to be doubted, for both are only symptoms of their sickness. Holtzmann's liberal viewpoint accounts for his book; he enjoys the ecstatic element in Jesus, for liberal theology has always been fond of the study of Jesus in the light of psychology.

The best designation of the world-view which has formed the background for the denial of Jesus' psychic health has been fortunately framed by Professor James as *medical materialism*. By *medical materialism* we mean that view of mind which regards all psychic phenomena as purely products or phases of the physical, chemical, or electro-chemical functionings of the brain. Exceptional psychic appearances are at once explained by the assumption of nervous disorders or disease. It is very interesting to note that Professor James (p. 13, note 1) cites Dr. Binet-Sanglé as a typical representative of this *medical materialism* (Against *medical materialism* see James, p. 11ff).

The above representations serve to show that, for Jesus' pathographers, the question of his psychic health was decided by their world-views even before they had entered upon their work. On the other hand, the Christian world-view, particularly the Christian estimate of the person of Christ, has kept Christian believers from taking their work at all seriously.

## 2) Scientific

The conflict between religion and science is as old as the latter. The history of modern science has determined to a marked degree the history of religious thought; the former has relentlessly forced compromises and concessions from the latter. Astronomy has compelled Christian believers to surrender their geocentric ideas of the earth on which they live. Geology finds the earth infinitely older than a calculation of Biblical genealogies back to the first man and creation would show. Even theistic philosophy finds that creation was not completed on the sixth day and that God rested on the seventh, but that creation is a process that is still going on and that God never rests. The work of Darwin and its subsequent more scientific revisions have not been able to find man originally in a garden of Eden, or any other paradise; at best he has emerged from a state of savagery and barbarism by a hard climb to civilization and culture. Psychology has a very different story to tell of the ego than that found in Genesis where Elohim breathed a soul into Adam and he lived. The unlocking of the scriptures of the Orient and the comparative study of religions have not only compromised and reduced the originality of many Biblical narratives, but of many of the Biblical teachings. Historical criticism would make very radical rearrangements if it were to catalogue chronologically the canonical books as they now stand in both Testaments; to Biblical personages that have long enjoyed highest repute it assigns a minor role, and some of the long neglected and almost forgotten minor prophets are raised to the seats of honor.

Thus one might go on through all the experimental and theoretical sciences in their modern forms and conclusions. Practically every one of these sciences that have appeared since the Renaissance has made, either directly or indirectly, in one form or in another, its reflections, often direct attacks, upon the Biblical narratives, teachings, or personages. Beginning with Semler and extending down to this very hour Christian theologians have been busy trying to bridge over the gap that has been repeatedly reopened or widened between Biblical religion and science. During this struggle for survival the Christian religion has proved its *Lebensfaehigkeit* by its acknowledgment, adjustment, and assimilation of newly discovered truth. This has often been such a slow and delayed process that Christianity has not always claimed the modern mind.

It is only natural that some of the sciences should raise questions concerning the central figure of the Bible and the Christian religion. Beginning with Reimarus and continuing on down through the life-of-Jesus research the person, work, and teaching of Jesus have been persistently pressed to a problematic point from many and sundry angles. Natural science has asked: Did Jesus really rise from the dead? Was Jesus born of a virgin? Did he actually perform miracles? Historical and textual criticism has asked: What of the sources of our knowledge concerning Jesus, are we to accept the Synoptic or the Johannine representations? What of the literary relation of the first three Gospels, in how far are they historically reliable, how much of their reports is the product of myth and legend? How much is to be assigned to the reflections, colorings, reworkings and revisions of earliest Christian piety and thought? Linguistic studies have pried into the meanings of Jesus' self-designations in the third person. Psychology has tried to force its way into the mystery of his self-consciousness, and has asked: Who was Jesus? What did he think of himself? Biographers of Jesus have asked: How long was Jesus' public career? What was its course, compass and chronology? What was Jesus' plan and purpose? Others have investigated and sought to interpret the teachings of Jesus, and have asked: To what extent is his teaching original, or borrowed? Is Jesus the first and main master of the parable? How are we to estimate and evaluate his teaching in the light of modern morals and ethics? In how far is his moral and ethical teaching defendable and retainable from the modern point of view? Does Jesus have anything pertinent or practical to say on modern social questions? Or are his teachings so historically conditioned by the thought of his day and people and the stage of culture and civilization in which he lived that he has nothing to say to the individual or group life of today? Others have asked: Where did Jesus' own thought center, on eschatology and the imminent cosmic catastrophe and the advent of a new supernatural order of things, or did he foresee a long future and history for his following and church? Historians have asked: What is Jesus' relation to the beginnings and rise of Christianity? Is the founding of Christianity really not the work of Paul rather than that of Jesus? In how far has historical Christianity preserved in its purity the religion and thought of Jesus? Has it not seriously swerved from the course upon which Jesus started his first disciples as it has struck out into the currents of civilization and culture? Does not traditional Christianity bear the marks of Pauline theology and Hellenistic philosophy rather than the simple yet profound thought of Jesus' Sermon on the Mount and his incomparable parables? Students of the religions of the Near East, and particularly of the mystery religions and secret devotional cults of the Roman empire, have asked: Did Jesus ever live or exist as an actual person of history? Is it necessary to presuppose and postulate a personal founder for Christianity, or any religion? Did not Christianity rise rather from a pre-Christian Jesus cult? Or did it not spring up by spontaneous combustion as the result of the friction of hidden social and religious forces fermenting in the Roman empire? Or is the story of Jesus only a variation of a Babylonian myth, or simply that of an historicized mythical divinity?

From the above it is clear that the person of Jesus has become increasingly problematic with the rise and development of the experimental and theoretical sciences, and that the problem of Jesus' person cannot be solved by a mere reading of the accounts of him in the New Testament. And it is just this fact that Jesus remains forever problematic that gives him charm, and fascinates and stimulates to renewed study and investigation.

In recent years medical science has been pushing energetically into the field of psychic research, which it had not heretofore entirely neglected yet had left undeveloped. This particular task has fallen to psychiatry, the youngest branch of medical science. Psychiatry has had a hard fight with superstition, but this it shares in common with all the sciences; they have all had a long struggle before they were able to convince the popular mind of the seriousness of their intentions and their ability to render service. But the psychiatrist has proven not only that he can render service, but that his services are indispensable. He cures, or cares for those unfortunates of society who are not sick in body but diseased in mind. He is summoned to prisons to observe and before courts to testify to the mental health of those who have broken society's laws or committed crime. In the recent war he had his hospital behind the front where he ministered to those who had suffered temporary psychic derangement in battle.

The psychiatrist is interested chiefly in abnormal psychology, or psychopathology. He proceeds to study abnormal and morbid psychic phenomena independent of the field and the connections in which they appear. This sort of scientific procedure necessarily brings him into the realm of religious experiences where unusual psychic phenomena seem to be especially frequent and abundant. Here he cannot proceed differently than in the other realms of experience, nor employ special methods because he is treading on hallowed territory. As Dr. Dorner writes, *There is no s p e c i a l psychology of religion; there are only those laws which are universally valid in the field of psychology and which condition the religious life in so far as it is a psychological process* (S. 188). The growing closeness of the relation between theology and medicine in certain circles of investigators is clear from the sub-title of the periodical from which this quotation is made, *Die Zeitschrift fuer Religionspsychologie.—Grenzfragen der Theologie und Medizin.* Krafft-Ebing writes: *In its relation to theology, psychiatry is interesting since it shows the psychopathic origin of numer-*

*ous religious errors and sects; and in history it shows how many of the mysterious acts of historic personages find their true explanation in psychopathic conditions* (p. 24).

The raising of the problem of Jesus' psychic health cannot be laid at the door of the psychiatrist, but it is in connection with this new science that the problem has appeared. Psychopathology conducted under scientific observation has suggested comparative psychopathology in cases where observation is no longer possible. Rasmussen's *Jesus* is evidence enough of this. He designates his book as a study in comparative psychopathology, applying to Jesus the tests of psychic health. His general principle of investigation he states thus: *If we find no parallels to their experiences* (the religious pioneers and leaders) *in the healthy world, and we do find very similar appearances among the diseased, then no serious investigator can escape the surmise that there exists between these quite homogeneous phenomena some real connection* (S. 55).

The latest appearance in the field of comparative psychopathology is pathography. The pathographer pursues a purely pathological programme in that he peruses the biographies, autobiographies and confessions of the great personages of history in quest of those psychic phenomena which are more usual in cases of mental disease than health. Kneib writes: *It has become almost a mania to test great men as to their psychic health. Instead of biographies "pathographies" are the order of the day* (S. 21) (1). The tendency is not only to test the genius mind by the standards of psychic health, but to explain genius itself by the assumption of mental morbidity and thereby to depreciate all that hitherto has been admired and loved as great, or grand, or good in the particular personage under investigation. Besides, the genius mind has often manifested psychic anomalies which have appeared in earlier or later life, and have varied all the way from personal peculiarities, eccentricities, excessive irritability and nervousness to

---

(1)   *Das Bestreben die Traeger ungewoehnlicher Geistesgaben unter die psychologische und speziell die psychiatrische Lupe zu nehmen, ist in neuerer Zeit sehr hervorgetreten,* Moerchen, MKP, S. 422.

a complete psychic degeneration which has robbed the genius of his former creative powers.

In certain circles of investigators genius has been defined as degeneration. The psychology of genius as a problem in pathology is as old as Aristotle who said, *Nullum magnum ingenium sine mixtura dementiae fuit.* In more recent times the judgment passed upon the genius mind by those who have attempted to write its health history has been still harsher. *The extreme mind is cousin to extreme insanity* (Pascal). Lamartine speaks of *that mental malady which one calls genius* (See de Loosten, S. 7). Dr. Moreau writes, *Genius is but one of the many branches of the neuropathic tree;* Dr. Lombroso, *Genius is a symptom of hereditary degeneration of the epileptoid variety, and is allied to moral insanity;* Nisbet, *Whenever a man's life is at once sufficiently illustrious and recorded with sufficient fullness to be a subject of profitable study, he inevitably falls into the morbid category...... And it is worthy of remark that, as a rule the greater the genius, the greater the unsoundness* (Quoted by James, p. 16f).

The pathographer regards the pathological element in the genius as the seat and secret of his power to influence his own and subsequent generations and win for himself a niche in history's hall of fame. Even psychologists find psychopathic personalities, under certain circumstances, at a distinct advantage in the race for renown and in the possibility of influencing their contemporaries. James writes: *Borderland insanity, crankiness, insane temperament, loss of mental balance, psychopathic degeneration, has certain peculiarities and liabilities which, when combined with a superior quality of intellect in an individual, make it more probable that he will make his mark and affect his age, than if his temperament were less neurotic* (p. 22f).

The three outstanding pathographers of recent times are Moebius, Loewenfeld and Lombroso. Dr. Moebius made a study of great men like Rousseau, Goethe, Kant, Schopenhauer, etc. L. Loewenfeld made a similar study of great artists like Michel Angelo, Raphael, Dürer, Millet, Boecklin and Feuerbach (*Ueber die geniale Geistestaetigkeit mit besonderer Berueck-*

*sichtigung der Genies fuer bildende Kunst. Grenzfragen des Nerven—und Seelenlebens. XXI. Wiesbaden).* These works were not accessible to the writer except in *résumé.*

In its German translation Dr. Lombroso's work bears the title, *Genie und Irrsinn.* His book is a rather helter-skelter collection of anecdotes and biographical details from the lives of outstanding men of modern times. He casts no direct reflections on any Biblical character; in fact, he scarcely mentions any of the great men of antiquity. He is far from identifying genius and insanity, though he does hold that the great majority of the geniuses of history manifested at times symptoms of more or less serious types of mental alienation. As instances of insane genius he points out Harrington, Boylan, Codazzi, Ampère, Schumann, Tasso, Cardano, Swift, Newton, Rousseau, Lenau, Széckenyi, and Schopenhauer.

It is worth while to quote at length some of Lombroso's main conclusions concerning the relationship between insanity and genius: *Is one justified without further ado in drawing the conclusion......that genius is always neurosis or insanity? It is here that error begins. It is true that there are moments which are common in the stormy and passionate life of the insane person and the genius; common to them are the periodic rises and falls of the affective life and the subsequent exhaustion, the originality of their aesthetic productions and discoveries, the unconscious and involuntary creation and employment of peculiar expressions, the frequent distractions, the inclination toward suicide and not infrequently toward alcoholism, and common to both a pronounced vanity. There are geniuses that are insane, or become so; there are insane that manifest a flash of genius in consequence of their affliction. But to conclude from this fact that all persons of genius must be insane is an altogether overhasty formulation of judgment, and is only the repetition of the error of those primitive peoples that worshipped the insane as divinely inspired beings...... If genius were always insanity how is it to be explained that Galileo, Kepler, Columbus, Voltaire, Napoleon, Michel Angelo, Cavour, men who besides their genius had only too great misfortune to bear, never manifested the least sign of mental alien-*

*ation* (S. 338f).  The interesting differences between genius and insanity as pointed out by Lombroso are too extensive to be quoted here; they are to be found on pages 339-341 of his work.

A. Hausrath, *Luthers Leben,* 2 *Baende* 1904, accounts for the phenomenal psychic elements in Luther's personality by the assumption of a type of neurasthenia with which he was afflicted.

It is therefore not at all surprising that such pathographic studies of the genius mind, sooner or later, would come upon Jesus, whom the Christian world has always looked upon as the greatest of all and greater than all geniuses, discover alongside his greatness, grandness and goodness a prominent pathological element, and declare as pathological just that in him which the Christian believer has always regarded as his exceptional uniqueness and believed to be the divine dignity of his person.

It is the works of the first three that suggested to de Loosten his pathographic study of *a genius like Jesus Christ* (S. 8f).

Against the insanity of genius and piety, Naumann writes: *As genius is not insanity, so the highest religious life is not insanity but a powerful concentration of inner forces and activities which has only the most superficial resemblances to insanity* (Sp. 271).  Against genius as a degeneration Weidel writes:  *Perhaps the truth is to be reached by the reversal of popular medical opinion: the genius is the true man who fully exhausts the capabilities of human nature, while "normal" persons often remain imbedded in the merely animal side of life* (S. 83).  To explain all extraordinary, unusual and creative genius as a mark of mental morbidity *means the conversion of history into a madhouse, for everything really worth while in science, art and life would be the work of aliens.  A man like Jesus is not to be wedged within the forms which psychological observation has taken from the average man.  Of necessity he shatters them because they are too cramped for him* (S. 28).

### 3)   Historico-critical

During the first two decades of the present century liberal

German theology has had no easy sailing. W. B. Smith has told the liberal theologians that their Jesus never existed as an actual man of history. A. Schweitzer writes that the real Jesus of history is all-too-historical, and that the liberal theologians are guilty of a false psychology; their modernized Jesus never existed. F. Loofs holds the liberal German theology responsible for the rise of the problem of the psychic health of Jesus. Hermann Werner pronounces the Jesus of liberal theology insane (*ein Geisteskranker*). It is the last two named that interest us here in the historico-critical factors contributing to the rise of our present problem.

Friedrich Loofs' book *Wer War Jesus Christus?* (*Fuer Theologen und den weiteren Kreis gebildeter Christen eroertert*) is the German revision of his Haskell Lectures delivered at Oberlin College, September 26 to October 4, 1911, which appeared in book form in 1913 under the title, *What is the Truth about Jesus Christ?* The occasion of this German revision, as Loofs says in his *Vorwort* (*Es war Wernle's "Jesus", der mich dazu bestimmte, S. V*), was Wernle's *Jesus* which Wernle finished at Christmas time in 1915 and which was published about six months before Loofs completed his revision on July 25, 1916. Though Loofs devotes his book to the refutation of two current views of Jesus, namely: the one that Jesus was a purely divine figure who never existed as a man of the world's history as represented by W. B. Smith, Arthur Drews, etc., the other that Jesus was merely a man as held by the liberal German theologians, of whom he singles out Wernle as a typical representative, it is to the second view that he devotes by far the greater amount of attention.

Loofs' book is of special interest to us here because he holds the modern liberal theology of Germany chiefly responsible for the rise of the pointed problem of Jesus' psychic health. He begins with Reimarus and goes down through the life-of-Jesus research showing that the liberal interpretation of Jesus as merely a man has set a false goal for itself (S. 2), has suffered ship-wreck as attested by its own history (S. 3f), and shows itself utterly bankrupt of resources to cope with the recent form which the question has taken.

Loofs quotes and agrees with H. Windisch to the effect that *the life-of-Jesus research presses toward a psychiatric problem* (*Theologische Rundschau, XVI. Jahrgang,* 1913, 12. *Heft,* S. 441; Loofs, S. 54). (H. J. Holtzmann writes, *Fast scheint es, als wolle sich die auf dem grossen Weltmarkt gefuehrte christologische Debatte zuletzt in dieser Richtung zuspitzen;* MBJ, S. 81, Anm. 1). According to Loofs, the raising of the question of Jesus' mental health is only the consequent culmination of the attempt to understand and interpret Jesus in a purely historical fashion as any other great man of history is to be understood and interpreted. The liberal theologians of Germany have been the chief champions of this view. (For a concise statement of the "liberal" view of Jesus, see Case, *The Historicity of Jesus,* Chapter I, pp. 1-31). Though Loofs would not load the responsibility for such works as those of Rasmussen and de Loosten on to the shoulders of liberal German theology (S. 53f), yet he does regard the general question, *Was this Jesus a psychically normal man?* and Oskar Holtzmann's book, *Was Jesus an Ecstatic?* as directly the product of the attempt to explain Jesus by the historical methods as employed by the liberal German theologians.

Loofs finds that the liberals are making concessions in the psychiatric direction, and he cites Heitmueller and Hollmann as concrete instances. Heitmueller writes in his *Jesus* (S. 89): *As reliable data of tradition we have Jesus' consciousness of commission which transcends the compass of the prophetic and the fact that Jesus laid claim, at least in some sense, to the Messianic dignity. It is not necessary to point out that both facts constitute difficult psychological puzzles. And when, as has recently been the case, the psychic health of Jesus is called in question and he is presented as pathological, the attempt has here at least a possible point of departure. But it has not succeeded and it never will. The creator of the parables, the framer of the sayings was as healthy as any man. Much can be cited to render this puzzle less difficult, but we are not in a position to solve it* (Loofs, S. 54f, Anm. 5). In discussing the books of Rasmussen and de Loosten in the *Theologische Rundschau, IX. Jahrgang,* 1906, 7. *Heft,* S. 275,

Georg Hollmann writes: *Thus a very considerable reduction of the materials used by both authors will certainly come. But even then there will still remain elements about which one can contend,—all that which comprises the ecstasy of Jesus......* *But even if we were to find in Jesus traces of psychic abnormality, they would as little hinder us in laying hold of the eternally worth while elements in him as they do in the case of Paul who was an epileptic. Even then the consideration is available which de Loosten himself brings out when he looks upon the psychic abnormalities of the specially gifted as the high ransom which they must pay for their prominence. For the present we must await the results of further unbiased research* (Loofs, S. 55, Anm. 1).

Holtzmann, Heitmueller and Hollmann make it clear to Loofs that the liberal theologians are threatened with the retention of their purely historical interpretation of Jesus at the expense of his psychic soundness, and this shows him clearly the pitiable plight of the research that reckons with Jesus as with any other individual of history. *If the liberal life-of-Jesus research were pressed to the point where it could retain its purely human Jesus only by surrendering his psychic health, then everyone who is convinced that faith has an historical right would be able to hold such a judgment inadmissible and to see therein only an avowal of the bankruptcy of a life-of-Jesus research that reckons with a purely human Jesus* (S. 55). The purely historical interpretation of Jesus must concede, either that we know next to nothing about Jesus due to the inadequacy of the sources, or that he was one of those religious fanatics who mean well but who are the victims of irrational and impossible hopes which bring them into a megalomaniacal state of consciousness.

That the liberal life-of-Jesus research has pressed toward the psychiatric problem is clear from its earlier stages in the preceding chapter. The writers of the two greatest lives of Jesus in the nineteenth century witness to this. In his 1864 *Leben Jesu* Strauss insists that Jesus was a fanatic, for *it is only of a human being that we are everywhere speaking* (See above p. 6). In his *der Alte und der Neue Glaube* he again repeats, if Jesus were a mere man (*ein blosser Mensch;* see above p. 7) and expected to return personally to the earth, he was for us a fanatic. Thus Strauss was insistent on the point of Jesus' fanaticism, if he is to be interpreted in a purely human way. Keim also saw the direction the whole question was taking when he defined certain characteristics which he discovered in the temperament of Jesus: *I myself in "Der Geschichtliche Christus"* (Zuerich, 1865) *assumed a strong threefold temperamental endowment of Jesus, sanguine, melancholic and choleric. To these three, each strongly developed, one will always come back . . . . . . (only the phlegmatic is lacking)* (I 442, Anm. 1).

We are further reminded in this connection of the opening sentence of Soury's book: *Après le dieu et l'homme, le malade* (see above p. 20). Kneib, from the Catholic viewpoint, laments the widespread inclination on the part of certain groups and schools of theologians to surrender the divinity and deity of Jesus as opening the way for the questioning of Jesus' psychic health: *If once the d i v i n e in Jesus Christ is surrendered, then the u n i q u e n e s s of this historical personality must be explained as p u r e l y h u m a n* (S. 6). Hermann Jordan also takes this view of the issue of the attempt to explain Jesus on a purely human basis (JMJB, S. 54).

The harshest of all judgments against the liberal theologians in this connection is that passed by Hermann Werner in his 45-page article in the *Neue kirchliche Zeitschrift* (*XXII. Jahrgang, 5. Heft*, 1911, S. 347-390), *Der historische Jesus der liberalen Theologie—ein Geisteskranker.* Werner says point blank that the historical Jesus of liberal theology is insane. *The end of a course is the best criterion of its truth* (S. 347), and the path struck out by the liberal theologians has brought them face to face with the question of Jesus' psychic health; it thus comes to pronounce the fatal verdict upon itself. The liberal attempt to strip Jesus of all the elements that extend beyond the confines of a purely human consciousness has been a delusion. Fresh disappointments are at hand, for the morbid Jesus of liberal theology has nothing left that recommends him either to the present or the future; he is religiously inadequate. The course of the liberal life-of-Jesus research is fatal; it brings us to a Christianity about to collapse. As typical liberals Werner mentions Harnack, Hausrath, Weinel, Rudolf Otto and A. Schweitzer. The picture of Jesus delineated by these men, according to Werner, proves Jesus a paranoiac because of his exalted self-consciousness and deliriant delusions of grandeur; they went out to discover the historical Jesus and came back with a paranoiac. *The historical Jesus of liberal theology is and remains a morbid man with a morbid mind* (S. 383).

Historically the problem of the psychic health of Jesus is perhaps directly connected with the liberal attempt to interpret Jesus in a purely historical way. But the liberal theologians are not as bankrupt of resources and as helpless as Loofs and Werner would have us believe in the meeting of the present issue.

### 4) Popular Psychological Presentations

The popular psychological presentations of Jesus by liberal theologians have not only been very strong in their psychological emphasis, but have pointed out those unusual experiences of Jesus and the exceptional psychic elements of his character in a way that makes them border closely on the abnormal, if not the pathological.

In his *Jesus* Bousset asks, *Did he not live a good share of his life in those spheres beyond the confines of clear consciousness?* (S. 11.)

Weinel writes in his *Jesus im 19. Jahrhundert*: *Whether Jesus knew those devotional moments of ecstasy, as did Buddha and Paul, can be stated with less certainty. Narratives such as those of the baptism and the temptation, in spite of all the objections that are urged against them, afford us a glimpse into such special hours in which he "heard" the voice of God and wrestled with "Satan"...... What for us duller souls remains only inner experience transformed itself in the great soul of the prophet into such sensuous hearing and seeing* (S. 92).

Rudolf Otto in his *Leben und Wirken Jesu* says of the dove and the voice at the baptism, *All this is simply an objectifi-*

*cation of an unspeakable inner experience in which all of those indicated conceptions played their part even to the extent of "hallucinations"* (S. 31f). It was against these very men that Werner proceeded in his above mentioned article; see above p. 42.

Still more pronounced in its psychological emphasis in the direction of psychic abnormality is Karl Weidel's character study, *Jesu Persoenlichkeit.* (Weidel, head-teacher in Magdeburg, is a student of Wrede's; see A. Schweitzer's enthusiastic appreciation of Weidel's book in his GdLJF, S. 580ff). Weidel finds in the Jesus of the Gospels what Nietzsche sought in vain, *the man of will (den Willensmensch); in a very unusual strength of moral will directed upon itself lies the secret of this personality* (S. 26). Jesus' influence on subsequent history is not to be found in any contribution of new knowledge on his part, but in his personality, more particularly in his moral will. (A. Schweitzer also finds Jesus an authority only in matters of the will; see his GdLJF, concluding chapter).

The character of all great men is full of contradictions, for they carry within their breasts all the contrasts of human experience. For Weidel, the chief charm about Jesus is the variety of contrasts in his character. *With the highest reverance for paternal tradition and law he was at the same time the greatest revolutionist and revaluer that history knows. Capable of the most passionate fury and anger, an austere judge, a fiery fighter, and again a man full of gentleness and kind-ness, meek and forbearing, and a friend of sinners . . . . . . clear, calm, determined and sure in his action, and then again passionately stirred, rashly aggressive, as though "beside himself" and driven by higher compulsion . . . . . . king and beggar, hero and child, prophet and reformer, fighter and prince of peace, ruler and servant, revolutionist and sage, man of action and poet: he was all of these in one person* (S. 23f).

*An ordinary man would have collapsed under the tension of such inner contradictions. But Jesus leaves nowhere the slightest impression of a man inwardly broken . . . . . . Only a very powerful self-control was able to support, without harm to itself, such a variety of contrary capacities and propelling forces and to assemble them for compact common action. A weaker will than his would have perished because of the very richness of its gifts and powers...... The flaring fire of his soul would have consumed any other; but he was its master and he cast firebrands into the world that even today are not extinguished* (S. 26f).

His claim for his person and words *does not testify of a morbidly roused, eccentric or fanatical mind, but is rather proof that all of these utterances are the natural expression of his being* (S. 30). His life was one continuous conflict. He turned on his opponents with a scathing sharpness and passion that was almost unjust. *By his very nature he was of unquestionably passionate temperament; readily roused, impetuously irascible, capable of burning anger, and ruthless whenever the cause of God was at stake...... It was not without reason that his family feared that he was "beside himself" and desired to bring him home again by force. What a foolhardy attempt to try to extinguish the fire of a volcano* (S. 33f).

There is not the slightest trace that he ever advised with his disciples. *He knows what he will, and what he will he carries out. Here he knows neither obstacles nor deliberation. He offers no good advice; he does not discuss various possibilities; he permits no objections, no ifs and buts, no indecision and uncertainty; he knows only to command* (S. 35). His word concerning mountain-moving faith is more than mere parable; it is the expression of his volition. Reason played no role in his religion, emotion was not the source of his piety; he was too much a man of will for rational reflection or mystic meditation. His religion was purely moral will. *He did not allow himself to make the least concession concerning the unconditional right of morality to sole recognition, neither because of the so-called considerations of utility, the question of feasibility, the rules of prudence, nor because of regard for social, legal, state or other regulations* (S. 46). Jesus knew nothing of our modern considerations of kin, surroundings, public opinion, professional duties, custom, tradition and reputation.

Jesus' extraordinary creative endowment laid a heavy task upon his soul. He could not be called happy, for in solitude he must battle for the balance of his soul.

Although Weidel makes only three references by chapter or verse to the Fourth Gospel, his character study of Jesus is taken in the main from that Gospel.   When he writes,  *concerning any kind of vacillation in his  calling, of a gradual growth and becoming certain of his convictions, or any uncertainty regarding their correctness and an arrangement of matters with the popular expectations......we read nowhere a word...... From the very beginning his whole action is carried along by an unswerving certainty and confidence; from the first moment of his public appearance he has left all vacillation and doubt behind him* (S. 21), when he says that Jesus directly identifies *h i s* thoughts, desires and ends with those of God, that he goes to Jerusalem to die a voluntary death and that the scene in Gethsemane is legendary because Jesus' emotions on this occasion do not correspond to his character, as Weidel conceives it, we clearly see that Weidel's picture of Jesus comes chiefly from the Fourth Gospel and not from the Synoptics.

Weidel, with the others who have written popular presentations, protests strongly against the psychiatric judgment against Jesus, but from such pronounced psychological emphasis as dominates his character study of Jesus it is only a step, and not a long one either, only an approach from a bit different angle, to the pathographic studies presented in the following chapter.   If normal psychology with such strong inclinations toward the exceptional and abnormal psychic phenomena can profitably study Jesus, why cannot abnormal, even morbid, psychology study Jesus with its own interests and thoughts in mind?

## CHAPTER III

### The Problem Proper

Geographically the problem of Jesus' psychic health has been fought, but not fought out, on German soil. Rasmussen's book comes from Denmark, but is best known in its German translation. Binet-Sanglé's work, the longest but not the best of all, appeared in France and (to the writer's knowledge) has not been translated into any other language; A. Schweitzer says that his work has remained unknown in Germany (GdLJF, S. 365), and we might add in the rest of the world. One work comes from the United States, the large volume of Hirsch which appeared first in German (1910) and is better known in Germany than it is in English (1912) in the United States. England, to the writer's knowledge, has made no attempts at the problem. Sanday's *tentative modern christology* which locates the seat of Jesus' divinity in the *subliminal* self by drawing a horizontal instead of a vertical line (*Christologies: Ancient and Modern*, Chapter VII., pp. 161-185), and which some regard as pathological because it shifts the seat of the divine in Jesus from the center of his consciousness, cannot come into consideration here, for Sanday is discussing a christological problem; ours is historico-critical. All negative pictures of Jesus in the psychiatric sense, other than the two above exceptions, have come from Germany.

Further, the question can be said to be almost exclusively German, for all the replies have appeared in the German language and by Germans. The Anglo-Saxon mind seems never to have taken the question seriously; at least it has never busied itself with it. One reason for this perhaps is the fact that the liberal German theology with its purely human understanding and interpretation of Jesus has never gained any very extensive foothold on Anglo-Saxon territory. But this geographical

confinement of the question to German soil is not due to any
special apologetic interest on the part of the German theologians to defend the central figure of the Christian faith, for
academic interests have played a prominent, if not predominant
part in the discussion which has furnished the conservative,
liberal and eschatological schools an opportunity to lay very
compromising charges at each other's doors.   The liberals have
attacked the eschatologists, the eschatologists have launched
a counter-attack, and the conservatives have started an offensive along the whole front against both.

The professional distribution is also very interesting and
will become clear as we take up the study of each of the six
men in question.   Three of the six works are written from the
medical point of view; Hirsch, Binet-Sanglé, and de Loosten.
Rasmussen is a philologist and writer, once a student of theology; Holtzmann is a professor of theology; Baumann is a
professor of philosophy.

### 1)   Jesus—an Ecstatic

#### Oskar Holtzmann

Oskar Holtzmann's (Professor of Theology at the University of Giessen) book, *War Jesus Ekstatiker?   Eine Unter-
suchung zum Leben Jesu*, is a supplement to his *Leben Jesu*
which appeared in 1901.   (Holtzmann finished his second book
in January, 1903; it was published in the same year in Giessen
by C. A. Wagner and contains 143 pages).   In his introduction (S. 1) Holtzmann agrees with J. Weiss against Wellhausen, who represents Jesus' soul as moving along in a constant harmony and uniform quiet and sees in Jesus the complete culmination of the process of the elimination of the ecstatic element from piety which began with Jeremiah.   Holtzmann sees in Jesus' person *heights and depths of spirit;* he is
*often passionately impetuous, again calmly composed* (S. 2).
There is no necessary contradiction between ecstasy and piety,
for *ecstasy is a constantly recurring form of vigorous piety*
(S. 3).   Jesus had a strong inclination toward ecstatic piety,
but no one would claim that Jesus was o n l y an ecstatic.

Holtzmann defines ἐξίστασθαι as *ausser sich kommen;*

ἔκστασις *bezeichnet einen hoechsten Grad geistiger Erregung, da ueber e i n e m Eindruck das sonst gueltige Mass der Dinge vergessen ist* (S. 3, Anm. 1).

Holtzmann begins his process of proof by showing that Jesus was an ecstatic both in his own judgment and that of his contemporaries. That his contemporaries so regarded him is clear even in the Fourth Gospel: 7,20; 8,48-52; 10,20-21; the last reference being the Johannine parallel' to Mc 3,22-30.

Πνεῦμα ἀκάθαρτον ἔχει in Mc 3,30 is the usual designation for possession (Mc 7,25; 9,18 25; Lc 4,33; Acts 8,7). Jesus did not deny being possessed; his enemies had distorted the kind of possession; it is *by the spirit* (Lc 11,20 *finger*) *of God* (Mt 12,28) that he casts out demons. *Just here it is quite important to note that Jesus was convinced that he was possessed and driven by a superhuman spirit. As strange as this may seem to us we must hold fast to the fact that Jesus conceived of this spirit as a personal being that dwelt within him* (S. 13). Jesus seems to have left the impression on his contemporaries that he acted under the influence of an overpowering spirit that was not identical with his own ego: *The impression of the activity of Jesus was of the sort that he seemed less to be acting than being acted upon* (S. 14). *He acts under the pressure of intense moods and thoughts; even his speech is not the expression of composed reflection but is given him by the superhuman spirit* (S. 14).

That he was possessed Jesus knew as well as did his enemies. His family knew it too, for they came to fetch him by force (κρατῆσαι) ; they could account for Jesus' conduct only upon the assumption that he was beside himself (Mc 3,21) ; here the very word ecstasy (ἐξέστη) is used.

Thus we find in Jesus all the distinctive marks of the ecstatic: he is active as the agent of a being foreign to himself; he acts only when impelled by the spirit which manifests itself in unexpected or violent action; he speaks what this spirit gives him to speak which becomes clear when his speech suddenly springs out beyond the usual compass of the ideas natural to common consciousness, or bears a tone and passion which does not correspond to his usual manner (S. 14, Anm. 1).

After discussing the trustworthiness of the sources (S. 16-34) Holtzmann proceeds to list the traces of ecstatic character in Jesus (S. 35-113). His catalogue is composed of six groups including biographical incidents, Jesus' ministry of healing, and his teaching.

1)  The baptism of Jesus must be conceived, as Mc 1,10-11 represents it, as a private and personal experience of Jesus; to think of it as public as Mt 3,16-17 and Lc 3,21-22 present it makes the later course of Jesus' career impossible. The baptism is not a later legend that sprang up in the early Christian community in connection with the rite of baptism, but is a real historical incident that marks the beginning of Jesus' public career. Jesus actually presented himself for baptism and was baptized by John; this fact is not only evinced by the account itself, but by the strong impression which Jesus' retains of the Baptist and the high estimate that the Baptist enjoys in Jesus' opinion. The chief point of interest in the incident of the baptism is what it meant to Jesus personally. It is here that he gains his full Messianic consciousness for the first time. This consciousness he attains in a state of ecstasy, for *the Messianic claim is for Jewish thought so strikingly daring that the conviction of one's right to make such a claim for one's self can in reality be gained only in ecstasy* (S. 39). And this is the only incident in the earlier career of Jesus that would furnish sufficient occasion for such ecstasy. Thus Jesus' public ministry had an ecstatic beginning. *Jesus knew that he at that time came under the control of a being formerly foreign to himself and which now had taken possession of him; this was the spirit of God* (S. 40f). This ecstatic experience took on the form of a vision and was purely subjective. He thought he saw the spirit descend in the form of a dove and heard a voice from heaven. This spirit, which took possession of Jesus, was *der ruhende Geist* and did not as in ordinary possession stir to restlessness. *The assurance of the love of God may be won in a state of ecstasy, but it gives a quiet that is usually foreign to the ecstatic nature. Thus in one state of ecstatic inspiration Jesus came again to composure* (S. 42). At the baptism Jesus wins a highly fantastic, enthusiastic and

ecstatic faith which constitutes the essence of his being and which expresses itself in both his words and deeds. *To this faith Jesus owed the imperturbable steadiness and virile confidence of his demeanor* (S. 43). Jesus could bear at the same time the features of an ecstatic and of a quiet determined person; the ecstatic element in him appeared only when he must defend his faith against obstacles and opponents.

2) By psychological necessity the temptation has its place just after the baptism. It shows us why the ecstatic element within Jesus did not impel him to fantastic enterprises. Here Jesus' moral will shows itself stronger than the fanatic fire that burned within him. It is this very ecstatic element that drove him into temptation (Mc 1,12), but Jesus forced this spirit back within its proper confines; it must not be the sole source of the Messianic moment in his consciousness as it threatened to become. The temptation was an inner experience vitally connected with Jesus' self-consciousness, and it marks his suppression and control of the ecstatic element by his O. T. piety. But the temptation itself is a product of ecstasy and it is just here that we learn to know Jesus as an ecstatic. *The temptation begins in a state of ecstasy and ends with a word of Scripture. The being carried away to a mountain, being set on the pinnacle of the temple, the dream of forty days fasting in the wilderness are ecstatic* (S. 49).

3) We further recognize the ecstatic element in Jesus' preaching of the imminent nearness of the kingdom of God. This Jesus inherited from the Baptist, who, in the tone of his preaching and eccentric habits of life and dress, was a still more pronounced ecstatic than Jesus. This idea of an immediate collapse of the old order and the advent of a new one is not the product of composed reflection, but is a conception that is foreign and strange to the commonality of men. It, therefore, must be designated as ecstatic. This ecstatic expectation Jesus sometimes expresses in a strongly stimulated spirit (Mc 13,26f; 14,22ff; Mt 12,28; 19,28; Lc 11,20; 17,22-37; 22,30), and at other times in a more quiet reflective manner (Mc 4,1-9; 4,26-29; Mt 13,18-21; 13,44f; Lc 13,18-21; 17,20f). Jesus' conception of the kingdom of God was escha-

tological and apocalyptic as is evinced by his own words and
the fervent eschatological hopes of Paul and the early Christian community; both are ecstatic.  Holtzmann concludes thus:
*The belief in the nearness of the judgment and the kingdom
of God, the belief that he was the Messiah, that by his work
he was preparing the way for the kingdom of God, and the
assurance of the kingdom of God to individuals*: all this might
and must be regarded as ecstatic (S. 71).

4)  Jesus' preaching of repentance in view of the approaching kingdom *had its ground in an ecstatic faith* (S. 71).
This faith was from the beginning determinative in Jesus'
whole ministry.  His Messianic consciousness gave him a triumphant confidence which enabled him to stand independently over
against the world.  This enthusiastic confidence expresses itself in Mc 4,39f; 9,23; 11,14; 11,22-24, and Jesus seeks to
impart it to his disciples in Mc 2,19; 8,34-9,1; 14,24; Lc 10,17-
20; 11,5-13; 12,22-32; 18,2-8.  *The ability to withstand
storm and stress, which Jesus would give his disciples, was also
ecstatic* (S. 74).  The ecstatic element in Jesus gives rise to
a new moral conscience as is seen in Mc 7,6-15; Mt 23,13-16
23 25 27 29 (Lc 17,39-52), and in Lc's Sermon on the Plain,
6,20-49.  *Only an ecstatic can promise and warn in the name
of God without reference to some previous revelation; only he
can declare so frankly the will of God* (S. 77).  Jesus' protest
against the assertion of individual rights, his demand for strict
self-discipline, his prohibition of the oath, and his attitude toward the institutions of marriage and property show that he
was *not a calculating nature but a divinely inspired personality
who acted less in response to outer occasion and more according to inner impulse.  The ecstatic background of his faith and
being never disappears entirely* (S. 92).

5)  Jesus' ecstatic character further manifests itself in
his miracles, in so far as they can be considered historical.  The
chief group of cures, the healing of demoniacs, Jesus affects
by restoring permanent composure to the disordered minds
of the victims.  This constitutes the marked peculiarity of
Jesus' ecstatic temperament over against the usual type of
ecstatic, who communicates his contagion to others; Jesus re-

stores composure to the deranged and disturbed. Nevertheless, we find that Jesus is not unaware of the contagiousness of the ecstatic within him as Lc 12,51f (Mt 10,34ff) well witnesses. Other cures of sickness and affliction, the precise nature of which we do not know, are to be explained by suggestion and autosuggestion. In all of his cures it was Jesus' sense of duty that drove him to give relief and help to the needy and sick; it was his ecstatic faith that gave him the power to actually effect them (S. 98).

6) Jesus' prophecies of his passion and death are not to be regarded as the result of rational reflection, but as an ecstatic intuition of the impending future. *It is not an idea based on the grounds of reason when Jesus, after the Messianic confession, greets Peter with the words: "Upon this rock I will build my church; and the gates of Hades shall not prevail against it"* (S. 103). Jesus' determination upon his suffering and death was an ecstatic decision; it is this ecstatic experience that sends him on his way to Jerusalem to die. His law of gaining life by losing it, Mc 8,35, is a paradox in which the means for reaching an end consists in the renunciation of the end itself. *To submit one's self to such an unusual order of things means that one is an ecstatic* (S. 104). In his word to the sons of Zebedee (Mc 10,39ff) the thought of his death seems almost to curb his ecstasy, but the very thought of the Messiah giving his life as a ransom (Mc 10,45) for many is *not a conclusion reached by rational reflection upon his death* (S. 105). His address at the last supper is *a highly ecstatic address; it transcends the whole compass of human consciousness when a son of man declares that, because of his death, God will forgive the sins of many and will arm them against future sin through his grace* (S. 113).

Thus the ecstatic element in Jesus gives to him certain constant convictions: that the kingdom is near; that he is the Messiah; that he knows the essence of the will of God; that he can guarantee to certain individuals entrance into the kingdom of God. These Holtzman sums up as Jesus' *Gewinn aus der Ekstase* (S. 114).

But Jesus was not an ecstatic only. Sometimes he appears as the bitter enemy of the very essence of ecstasy. He banishes the disturbing demons; he does not permit his disciples to fast; he does not allow himself to be led to fanatical views and practices; he declines disposition over the places of honor in the kingdom of God, and knows not the day or hour of its coming. These are *marks of soberest discretion* (S. 116).

To the non-ecstatic ministry and teaching of Jesus Holtzmann reckons his recognition of the state (Mc 10,42; 12,13-17), temple tax (Mt 17,24-27), his high estimate of the necessity and value of labor (Lc 6,47-49; 13,6-9; 14,25-30), his emphasis upon loyalty to personal profession and the world's work, his maxim of service (Mc 10,42-45), his conception of his own and his disciples' preaching as labor, his opposition to the social seclusion of the Pharisees, his exalted estimate of the single soul (Lc 15,4-10), his task as he conceived it as caring for souls, and his own personal loyalty to his own calling and commission. From this point of view Jesus does not wear the least trace of the ecstatic character, and these very features are so thoroughly characteristic of Jesus' person and character, *that in view of them one could easily overlook everything ecstatic* (S. 123).

Holtzmann closes his book in the conviction that we have gained a clearer and more vivid picture of Jesus, for we see in him a constant transition from ecstasy to composure (*Wechsel von Ekstase und Ruhe*). It is just in this change from one contradiction to the other that the charm of Jesus' personality is to be found. *It is often just the presence of contradictory and conflicting elements that makes a personality attractive. The contrast between clearness and ecstasy in Jesus may have been that which from the beginning bound hearts to him, and in this combination of two apparently opposing features is to be found much that accounts for the secret of his first great successes* (S. 139).

Holtzmann's presentation of Jesus as an ecstatic is not altogether convincing for he allows so much in Jesus that is non-ecstatic, he must so search, shift and strain materials, he is forced to note so many exceptions where he does constitute a greater or less degree of ecstasy, and so often finds that

Jesus' ecstatic conduct and character so radically and peculiarly varies from what we would naturally expect of an ecstatic, that we cannot help but feel that after all Jesus does not fall within the ecstatic group. If Jesus was to any degree an ecstatic, it was merely accidental and played no such significant role either in the career or in the consciousness of Jesus as Holtzmann represents.

Holtzmann further leaves us in uncertainty in so far as Jesus' psychic soundness is concerned. He does not tell us whether he considers ecstasy in general, or the degree to which Jesus possessed it in particular, as psychopathic. He seems to represent Jesus as bridling any ecstatic impulse or experience that would threaten his psychic balance, for he considers the ecstatic element in Jesus as making a distinct contribution to his character and conduct.

Perhaps Holtzmann's *Leben Jesu* of two years before will help us out on this point. In discussing Jesus' vision at the baptism he gives to the third paragraph of page 106 the marginal title, *Nothing Morbid*, in which he says: *But one wants to hear nothing of such visions because they are marks of a morbidly excited imagination. Against this view two facts are to be urged: first, Jesus in his subsequent public life proves so abundantly the clearness and reliability of his judgment and the strength of his will directed toward definite noble ends that the deduction of his visions from a psychic malady is quite impossible; secondly, a religion has never yet been founded by a personality that by its imagination could not raise itself above the ABC's of the ordinary run of things.* Then in note 2 on the same page: *It would be well in general to do away with the conception of visionary experience as a mark of morbid excitement, unless one will pronounce all inspiration morbid.*

Holtzmann's definition of ecstasy as *ein hoechster Grad geistiger Erregung, da ueber e i n e m Eindruck das sonst gueltige Mass der Dinge vergessen ist*, is so inadequate and indefinite as to constitute no definition at all from the psychological point of view. As O. Schmiedel writes in commenting upon Holtzmann's book, *At least a definition of ecstasy on a broader basis of the history of religions is to be desired* (HPdLJF, S. 73). But Holtzmann neglects this. However, we cannot agree with the cutting and unjust criticism which Schmiedel offers against Holtzmann's delineation of Jesus as an ecstatic character: *W h a t   k i n d   o f   a   p i c t u r e   o f   t h e   S a v i o r   d o   w e   g e t !   Jesus for the most part "in a highest degree of psychic stimulation," like a v o l c a n o  which with thunderous rumblings after brief pauses discharges stones, lava, mud and fire* (S. 75).

But when Holtzmann declares the stilling of the storm and the cursing of the fig tree to be historical because *Jesus must not perish in the storm, and the withered fig tree must furnish an occasion for the word about mountain-moving faith*, when he leaves Mt 16,17-19 in the mouth of Jesus instead of ascribing it to the early Christian community, and sees in Lc 12,51-53 (Mt 10,34-36) Jesus' own confession of the ecstatic contagion that went out from him, we feel that Holtzmann is more interested in making out a case of ecstasy for Jesus than in exercising careful critical judgment.

### 2)   Jesus—an Epileptic

### Emil Rasmussen

Rasmussen's (1) book, *Jesus: Eine vergleichende psychopathologische Studie* (Leipzig 1905, 167 S.), was translated from Danish into German by Arthur Rothenburg (The book appeared in Danish in 1904). Rothenburg's enthusiastic 21-page prolegomena to Rasmussen's *Jesus* is almost as interesting as the book itself. Rothenburg hails Rasmussen as the modern champion of the consequent criticism of Strauss in the shattering of the traditional picture of Jesus. By his emphasis on the psychiatric moment the Danish scholar has swept away all the artifices, affectations, and pitiable make-shifts of the theologians and has enriched the life-of-Jesus research. For the first time Jesus' emotions are subjected to energetic investigation with

---

(1) Danish philologist, author, and one time student of theology, of Copenhagen; other works of Rasmussen are *Ein Christus aus unseren Tagen, David Lazzaretti*, Deutsch 1906 Leipzig, 233S; *Der Zweite Heiland! Ein Passionsspiel in vier Aufzuegen*, Danish 1906, German 1911.

the result that Jesus belongs to the mentally morbid (S. XXII). Jesus falls into the category of the prophets who are all aberrations from the normal type of the race.

Jesus was a great reformer. His ethics mark a distinct advance beyond that of his contemporary Jewish countrymen. But his hatred for the family as an institution and his recommendation to live by alms and faith have not been accepted by the modern world. If by a genius we mean a man who is original and productive, we cannot call Jesus a genius. Jesus was a man worthy of our deep pity whose tragic, yet splendid, fate deserves our heartiest sympathy. Rothenburg's remarks have a distinct von Hartmann tone. Jesus' morbid nature forever forbids that he should become a law for the healthy soul. As a prophet he is simply one of the many; as a man he is by no means an absolute ideal. History must, and in fact does, reckon with the complete collapse of Christianity, for it has no assurance that to Christianity is reserved the great guarantee of being the fullest, or even fuller, revelation of God. Christianity is not the one and only religion, but is simply a religion among many others.

Rasmussen's book falls into three parts: 1) the Son of Man (S. 1-49); 2) the Men of God (S. 50-134); 3) the Prophet Jesus (S. 135-167). He opens his book with the statement that the old alternative, Jesus was either the one whom he gave himself out to be or he was the greatest impostor that ever lived (Rasmussen says that this alternative was forced upon him during his days as a student of theology), is false. There is a third possibility: a man may not be the one he represents himself to be, and yet not be an impostor; he may be beside himself, insane. It is therefore our duty to look into the Gospels and determine two things; what Jesus thought of himself, and what the apostles thought of him. *Rather one investigation too many than one too few* (S. 3).

In answering these two questions Rasmussen excludes the Fourth Gospel, *where all the words of Jesus have an absolutely strange and improbable tone which in truth is the author's own* (S. 4). The Synoptics are to be used with caution, for they often contradict each other on important points and are openly propaganda in their purpose. The evangelists have concealed and painted over the most original features of Jesus, but we have the means in our hands for restoring the damaged parts. The Gospel writers were too naïve in their art to be successful in their attempt to conceal certain things that might be unpleasant to their readers.

### 1)   The Son of Man

Rasmussen devotes the first part of his book to the position that Jesus was not the Son of God, that is, not divine. The idea of a man becoming divine was possible on Roman and Greek soil, but impossible on Jewish soil. Strict Jewish monotheism excluded this possibility; even the expected Messiah was a purely human figure. The term *Son of God* in the strict sense of deity was linguistically foreign to the old Hebrew and the Galilean Aramaic. When Jesus spoke of his relation to God as that of son to father, he did not ascribe to himself a relationship that was unique and peculiar to himself but a relationship shared by the apostles and others (Mt 23,9; Lc 20, 36). Nowhere in the first three Gospels does Jesus claim the prerogative of deity for himself, but he clearly expresses a relation of decided dependence and knows nothing of a state of preëxistence (Mt 23,39; 12,32; Mc 10,18). *If Jesus did not regard himself as God, then there is naturally no reason for endeavoring to be wiser than he* (S. 10). The narratives of the nativity, the miracles, the resurrection and the ascension constitute no proof of Jesus' divinity. Jesus regarded himself as simply a man well-pleasing in God's sight and over whom the spirit of God had come as in the past upon kings and prophets.

Jesus not only regarded himself as a prophet and a man, but the early Christian community saw in him only a man and a prophet (Acts 10,38). Paul shares this same view, otherwise his proof of the resurrection would lose all point. Paul's conception of Jesus' relation to God as a son in the sense that all men are sons of God is identical with Jesus' own conception of himself; Paul and Jesus are sons of God in the same sense.

Jesus spoke of himself as the Son of man, but the disciples drowned out the voice of their master with the cry, Messiah, Messiah! *Who was right, the disciples or the Master? I think, the master* (S. 26). Jesus never gave himself out to be the Messiah, and the claim of the evangelists to the effect that he did *is a blow in the face of the Master and their own reports* (S. 39). The idea of Jesus being the Messiah is the conception of Jesus' environment which triumphed over and suppressed Jesus' own conception of himself as the Son of man in the sense of Dan. 7,13; but he is here undertaking a role which no single soul, human or divine, could fulfil, for the close of the chapter in Daniel represents the Son of man not as a single individual, but as the chosen people (S. 49).

## 2)   The Men of God

It is in this second part of the book that Rasmussen develops his position by a study in comparative psychopathology as the title of his work promises. Jesus was a prophet as the multitudes proclaimed him in Mt 21,11; this is all he aspired to be and, in order to understand him, we must try to understand these *Men of God* as they have appeared in history.

The fundamental characteristics of the great religious pioneers are as follows: They possess a singular power which springs from their contagious and unshakable faith that defies every hindrance to a degree that corresponds closely to the fixed idea of the paranoiac. With set rudder they steer ruthlessly toward their goal. Yet they have moments in which they would seem to falter (Jeremiah; Jesus in Gethsemane), but their faith bolsters them up to every test. Their minds are occupied with but few thoughts and their intellectual and spiritual horizon usually narrows down more and more as time passes and passion grows. They have their times of visitation when their faith is reinforced by voices and visions. These are moments of highest exaltation when the very heavens open before their eyes. These unusual experiences, which the dervish produces by dancing and some of the old prophets by striking upon stringed instruments, come naturally of themselves and without artificial assistance to the born prophet (S. 51ff).

But these moments of exaltation are purchased at the

price of hours of high-tensioned fear; this is the chief characteristic of the *Men of God*. This fear is, for the most part, unmotived and groundless and approaches borderland insanity. It can express itself in morbid melancholy, or in the idea of being pursued and pressed by foes (Jeremiah and Kierkegaard), or in plans for suicide (Mohammed). It often gives rise to horrible hallucinations (Luther). It is usually an indefinite and general fear which interprets itself in terms of personal, family, or national guilt and vents itself in passionate prayer or in prophetic threats. There is further an impulse toward renunciation of the world and a desire for suffering as something not just to be faced, but forced.

The principal feature of the religious pioneer is the fact that the content of his conviction or faith has been experienced by him. *He makes his life, his inner experiences a law, a religion for others* (S. 53). Religious pioneers are not to be designated at once as mentally morbid. It may be a painful process to discover diseased defects in some of the greatest personalities of history, but we must satisfy ourselves as to the precise nature of these defects and study them feature by feature.

The two psychic maladies to which great religious leaders are specially liable are hysteria and epilepsy; the two may combine in a given case, which is to be diagnosed as hysterico-epilepsy, for they are often due to the same causes and manifest themselves in very similar symptoms. Rasmussen is interested only in epilepsy.

The sure stigma of epilepsy is the well-known and classic epileptic attack, (see page 254ff) (1). The victim has the inclination to conceal the attacks. The attack is usually preceded, or even sometimes displaced, by a fit of unmotived and insane fear. This fear is usually accompanied by visual

---

(1) The writer did not feel justified in omitting a review of Rasmussen's delineation of religious epilepsy, even though epilepsy from the more general psychiatric viewpoint is reviewed in the last chapter. A presentation of Rasmussen's description of the religious epileptic is specially to the point because he singles out those particular features which he intends to demonstrate as present in the case of Jesus.

and auditory hallucinations which drive the subject to flight, or prayer, for relief. As suddenly as the attack comes it can go again leaving the subject clearly conscious and fearless. In more serious cases the victim falls into spasms of madness and even commits acts of violence without afterwards recalling what he has done during the attack; this serious form of attack is known as *grand mal.*

This disease can express itself in fits of convulsive merriment which works contagiously upon its surroundings. In cases of *absence* the subject loses consciousness for a moment, halts in the midst of a conversation, stares expressionlessly in front of him, becomes himself again and seeks to conceal what has happened by taking up the conversation again just where it was broken off. If this condition is more persevering and serious, the patient lies or kneels down and is insensible to all impressions from the outside world; this is epileptic *stupor.* There are further instances in which the patient is for even days in a twilight state of consciousness; during this period sub-consciousness controls either the minor or major actions, yet all the time the subject may carry on the regular routine duties of his daily life.

The religious epileptic suffers deliriums which are religious both in character and content. During these states of delirium the subject can be in terrible torture or believe himself indescribably blessed; or he can suddenly be reversed from one to the other and back again. Often these deliriums are attended by such a degree of clear consciousness that the ordinary person detects nothing wrong and thinks he is witnessing a marked instance of divine inspiration. Between times the patient can be as clearly conscious as any healthy person and he has no difficulty in convincing his surroundings of his soundness and health. It is a further peculiarity of this affliction that it affects the emotional life for a considerable period before the intellectual faculties are attacked. During these intervals of clear consciousness the subject, nevertheless, develops a series of pronounced peculiarities, such as ungrounded fear, melancholy and sudden swings of mood and temper; these can also swing about into their very opposites. The epileptic character is full of contradictions.  The sense of his own guilt, usually imagined, or that of others presses him to an excessive piety.  He possesses a sense of the closeness of the divine to himself in particular and he carries the commission to suffer for others, or to reform the world.  He is impressed with his own greatness and suffers under the delirium of megalomania. He is an egoist, an egoarch.  There often appears the idea that he is pressed or compelled to do this or that, and this idea, whatever it may be, controls the whole of his subsequent life. He imagines that he has behind him a glorious line of ancestors.  His case becomes most serious when all of these ideas begin to systematize themselves.  He becomes restless, inconstant and vagabond.  He is often physically and intellectually capable of almost superhuman accomplishments.  His sex life is often abnormal, either to the extreme of excess or entire continence.  He often suffers severe headaches, dizziness, exhaustion and violent attacks of perspiration.

As the disease progresses the victim continues to degenerate.  His thought and speech become less coherent, and he is constantly returning to the one theme or set of fixed ideas. He loses the ability to take up, rework and assimilate new ideas. Trivial incidents he comes to regard as events of world-wide importance; his world becomes exclusively egocentric.  He loses his ethical and aesthetic sense and judgment.  He is irritable and falls into fits of frenzy without proper provocation; he is distrustful and regards the whole world as his enemy.  The attacks of fear, of being pursued and hard pressed, and the hallucinations become more frequent.  Finally he succumbs to the malady or dies at his own hand.

This short survey of epilepsy and the epileptic character will serve to show that the great religious pioneers and seers possess many stigmata in common with epileptics and are to be regarded as in a greater or less degree epileptic (S. 67ff). In his catalogue of the religious pioneers whom he describes as milder or more serious cases of epilepsy Rasmussen lists Elijah, Elisha, Amos, Hosea, Isaiah, Jeremiah (4,19; 16,1 5; 15,10; 17,18; 18,21; 20,10 13; 39,26), Ezekiel (3-4; 33), Buddha, Paul (I. Cor. 14,2 16 18 19 23; II. Cor. 10; 12; Gal 4; Acts 9;

21,13; 27,10) who would found a new religion upon the basis of a few epileptic hallucinations, Mohammed, Sabbataei Lewi, Mohammed Ahmed, Oreste de Amicis, David Lazzeretti, Anna Lee, Swedenborg, Soeren Kierkegaard, Johannes Holbek; even Caesar, Luther and Napoleon.

The names in this catalogue prove that epileptic persons can be capable of remarkable and worthy accomplishments and productions. The diagnosis of their maladies, however, should serve as a guide in the appreciation or depreciation of what they have said or done and in our acceptance and use of both. Here Rasmussen expresses himself in the figure of the morbid mussel and the pearl cited above, p. XIV.

### 3) The Prophet Jesus

In the third part of his book Rasmussen comes to the theme for which he has prepared the way in the first two parts (S. 135-167). His book can be regarded as taking on the form of a syllogism in which the minor premise precedes the major: Jesus was a prophet (premise and part I) all prophets are to a greater or less degree epileptic (premise and part II); therefore Jesus was an epileptic (conclusion and part III).

Rasmussen regards Jesus as no exception to the psychiatric principle; he by nature belongs to the prophetic type of temperament which is to be observed daily in our psychiatric clinics. Jeremiah, Paul and Kierkegaard are Jesus' psychic kin. The Gospel materials are very meagre in those particular details which would interest us most from the psychopathic viewpoint. In fact, the evangelists intentionally concealed those very features that would betray Jesus' demented state. Yet they were not entirely successful.

Jesus was swayed back and forth with a pendulum-like regularity between fear and violent boldness as were the old prophets before him. He sometimes breaks forth into uncontrolled frenzy and employs the coarsest insults against his opponents. Lc 12,50 and 22,36 contain Jesus' own confession of his fear; so also Mc 10,32, as well as Jesus repeated retreats to solitude. Mc tells us that fear of entering the cities keeps him apart in the desert places. Gethsemane is without doubt

an attack of epileptic *petit mal.* *No healthy person has experienced anything similar, not even when in danger of death* (S.
139). It is not an ordinary attack of fear, for healthy fear
continues until the danger is past. The apostles were fully
cognizant of Jesus' condition. The cleansing of the temple is
an attack of *grand mal;* in spite of its religious character this
act of Jesus cannot be described as that of a healthy and kindly nature. The whole scene is simply the expression of Jesus'
disordered and afflicted soul.

Jesus tells us nothing of his inner experiences; we see only
his executed acts. That he suffered with hallucinations is clear
from the incident at the baptism and Lc 10,18.

The portrayal of Jesus' character in the Gospels is just
as decisive and tragic. He rejects home and country. His
character is full of the most extreme contradictions which are
tense to the point of rupture: noble beauty, quiet dignity, ve-
hement hate, brutal violence, and infinite goodness and gentleness. Jesus' character cannot be determined. He is neither
a meek and melancholy, nor a brutal choleric temperament; he
is neither courageous nor cowardly, neither affable nor unsociable. He is all of them alternately: melancholy, courageous and affable; choleric, cowardly and unsociable. *The malady
is the restlessness which compels him to swing like the pendulum
from one extreme to the other* (S. 143).

Jesus' self-exaltation (*Selbstgefuehl*) expresses itself not
only in his claim for superhuman dignity but in his ridiculous
attitude toward the Pharisees and in the lack of agreement between his instructions and his own conduct. He is not the meek
person that he recommends others to be, but accepts *every possible deference from any sort of person.* He regards himself
as a reformer and would make his own abnormal conduct and
character a law and religion for all humanity. He cannot be
bound by either law or custom, and one could extend to him the
sincerest sympathy and support on this point if he had been
consequent instead of creating new regulations peculiar to his
own person and trying to force them upon others, such as his
command to hate the family, his prohibition against saving and
economy, divorce, assertion of self-rights, and his recommend-

ation for continence. No normal and healthy person could carry out these precepts.

Jesus' idea of his suffering atoning for the sins of others is the product of his epileptic megalomania. Early Christianity looked upon Jesus as a model of gentleness and love, but the evangelists give us quite a different picture. Jesus hated his own family, and his family in turn hated him. It is true that he was kind to the sick and the poor, but that belonged to his supposed calling; besides, they offered no opposition to him. But not one of the first three Gospels tells us that real friendly sympathy attached him to any person. His disciples were his servants, not his friends; they were also the objects of his distrust. Jesus is represented as a friend of children, but we are not once told that he sought them out because of real love for them; they rather furnished useful illustrations for his teaching. Jesus never knew what it was to be thankful; a word of gratitude never crosses his lips. He accepts everything as a mere matter of course. The author of the Fourth Gospel feels this coldness in the Synoptic picture of Jesus and attempts to tone it up a bit by introducing the beloved disciple, Jesus designation of his disciples as his friends, his strange love for Lazarus, and his dying word in behalf of his mother. It is to be regretted that we cannot place confidence in this Johannine representation.

Jesus was seized by a vagabond restlessness that does not correspond to the Old Testament prophecy concerning the Messiah. He, further, placed a too low estimate upon the relation of the sexes. He was unmarried and recommended the same state to others. He looked upon the sex life as something low and declared that such relations would not obtain in the kingdom of God. Only a sick person could entertain such a view. Jesus' mental and spiritual horizon narrowed down until he saw nothing but himself, his mission, and whatever might contribute to both. His parables with their monotonous theme of the kingdom of God evince the unvaried and confined compass of his ideas. His contemporaries and his own family pronounced him insane.

Jesus' teaching sprang from three sources: 1) his own

peculiar and pathological nature; 2) his set convictions concerning the imminent kingdom of God; 3) his circle of followers. The first forbids that his teaching should become normative for religious conduct. The second gave him an opportunity to pronounce his dogmatic precepts and vent his wrath against his opponents. The third satisfied his selfish ambition to be the center of a circle of admiring followers. His followers must catch his restlessness in order that his teaching might be propagated; it was therefore necessary to remove every point of attachment by demanding the full surrender of home and property. Jesus further recommended living by alms, an untenable solution of the social question. In both the form and content of his teaching Jesus was only an imitator of the prophets and rabbis.

In his emphasis upon the disciple's fate as dependent upon his relation to his own person the affliction of Jesus again comes to light. His emphasis upon the value of faith is simply a revival of Habakkuk and has never convinced the world of men. *The whole of humanity assumes in fact and in practice that the worth of a man does not depend on what he believes, but on what he does* (S. 156).

Against this diagnosis of epilepsy in the case of Jesus one cannot raise the objection of Jesus' extraordinary influence. His influence and impression upon his contemporaries was very meagre and in no wise to be compared with that of Mohammed or David Lazzaretti; Jesus had not more than a few score of disciples at the time of his death, but theirs numbered millions and both were demented. The objection that Jesus' moral and spiritual qualities forbid that he was a diseased mind is without forcefulness, for even a genius may be an epileptic. *There cannot be the least doubt that Jesus could have been morbid and genial at the same time* (S. 160).

We recognize von Hartmann again in the closing paragraphs of Rasmussen's book when he writes: *Not even the clericals want to follow the ideal* (Jesus). *The ideal of our day is the human, sociable and patriotic person, the faithful worker, the good father of a family who in tolerable fortune strives to surround himself and his family with beauty and happiness*

...... *Jesus is the polar opposite of all this*...... *Why then not be honest and say that Jesus is no longer the ideal of our time?* (S. 162f). Life's ideals are not given by God or man, but rise from within one's own breast. It was the morbid element in Jesus' message that won for him his triumph; all that was best in him has been neglected.

In conclusion Rasmussen defines his attitude toward Jesus: *If we should sum up our fundamental attitude toward Jesus it would be a genuine sympathy for an exceedingly unfortunate nature with a tragic yet splendid fate* (S. 164). *Soeren Kierkegaard was right again when he said to Lewin: You are fortunate; you are free from Jesus* (closing sentence, S. 166).

The more one reads Rasmussen's *Jesus* the less is one impressed with it. There is a tone of ingenuineness that pervades it from beginning to end. It contains frequent lapses of taste in certain course materials cited (see pages 92f, 100f, 105) which do not have the remotest parallel in the life of Jesus. Rasmussen's syllogism (see page 63) is neither convincing nor sound, for he draws his conclusion from a false premise; that all the religious pioneers and prophets were epileptic is a wholesale sweeping statement devoid of historical basis. The historian cannot thus toss all prophets and champions of religion into the same pathological pot. Of the total of 167 pages of his book Rasmussen devotes less than thirty pages to the point to be proven, namely, that Jesus was· an epileptic. Within these thirty pages he deals in dogmatic generalizations; he cites only thirteen references to the Gospels by chapter and verse. Rasmussen is hardly to be classed among the pathographers of Jesus, for he undertakes no systematic sifting of the sources as the three next writers do. However, he is more careful and critical in his use of the sources than those who diagnose paranoia in the case of Jesus, for he excludes the Fourth Gospel and even notes the weak textual basis for such a passage as Lc 22,43-44.

### 3)   Jesus—a Paranoiac
#### Dr. de Loosten (Dr. Georg Lomer)

Dr. de Loosten is a pseudonym for Dr. Georg Lomer, head-physician at the Holstein Provincial Institute for the Insane in Neustadt. His pathographic study of Jesus bears the title, *Jesus Christus vom Standpunkte des Psychiaters. Eine kritische Studie fuer Fachleute und gebildete Laien* (Bamberg 1905, 104S). (Other similar studies by de Loosten are: *Ignatius von Loyola. Vom Erotiker zum Heiligen. Eine pathographische Geschichtsstudie*, 1913; *Krankes Christentum. Gedanken eines Arztes ueber Religion und Kirchenerneuerung*, 1911; *Das Christusbild in Gerhart Hauptmanns "Emanuel Quint." Eine Studie*, 1911).

In his preface de Loosten states that he has undertaken his pathographic study of Jesus in the effort to throw new light upon certain points in the life of Jesus that are in need of illumination, and that he was encouraged to carry it out in the hope that a physician would feel free to recognize and express certain things in the character of Jesus which the theologian, for very good reasons, must pass over in silence. He intends to offer a critique of the career of Jesus from the unprejudiced viewpoint of a modern specialist in mental disease as based on the literature that has come down to us concerning Jesus.

In the first part of his book de Loosten makes a brief survey of the psychology of genius as it has been studied from the psychiatric angle. The appearance of any man in history is as natural an event as any other phenomenon of nature and is bound up in the same chain of causation as any other natural fact. The influence of a genius on his time is possible only when his ideas already lie unformulated and unexpressed in the minds of his contemporaries; it is just this ability to formulate the unformulated and express the unexpressed that makes him a genius.

The great geniuses of history have been studied from the psychopathic point of view; then de Loosten asks, *Does such a critical investigation dare approach a genius like Jesus Christ in the expectation of finding sufficient materials for such a precarious discussion and in the hope of not being misunderstood?* (S. 8f). He believes that this question can be answered in the affirmative; however, such a study is reserved for those, as the supplement to the title of his book indicates, who are capable of distinguishing between the person and the words of Jesus and of retaining the pure kernel of an immortal teaching. Present-day science does not look upon the eccentricities of the genius as the stigmata of a mental malady, but, if such are present, *as the high price, as the great ransom*, which these gifted souls must pay for the preference which they enjoy over against the tens and hundreds of thousands of less gifted mortals. History teaches, *that a psychopathic constitution, if it is otherwise highly and strongly gifted, can influence in a formative way the succeeding centuries and bring millions under its spell* (*Mohammed*) (S. 10).

The problem at hand is not to be solved by orthodox theologians whose authority is *dogma* and whose slogan is *believe;* even the liberal theologians have avoided the real alternative, *morbid or healthy* (S. 16). Medical experts alone are qualified to pass a judgment of sickness or health. *Seeing and knowing is better than believing; and the removal of the bandages* (faith), *which have become unnecessary, from eyes that they may see and know is the purpose and goal of all science* (S. 17).

In the second part of his book (S. 18-91) de Loosten goes to the problem proper of Jesus' psychic health. The physical and mental health of an historical individual is to be determined along four lines of investigation: 1) his anthropological and social extraction; 2) the environment in which he lived and grew; 3) his words and acts; 4) the impression he made upon others and their judgment of his physical and mental health. These four principles must also guide in the study of the psychic health of Jesus.

1) We know nothing of value concerning Jesus' ancestry or descent. The birth stories of Mt and Lc are religious fictions; they really go to show that Jesus was of illegitimate birth, for they know nothing of Jesus' father. The legend of the supernatural birth in Mt 1,18 and Lc 1,35 is an invention to cover up the disgrace. Further support of the fact of Jesus' illegitimate birth is found in Origen's *Contra Celsum* (See Keim's *Celsus' Wahres Wort*, S. 11f) and the Talmud report where Jesus is represented as the son of a Graeco-Rom-

an soldier.  Besides Jesus manifested psychically so many non-Semitic features that he could well have been *a half-caste of pure Jewish and of perhaps Greek or Greek-Lesser Asiatic blood* (S. 21).  We know more of Jesus' mother and kin.  She was related to Elizabeth whose son, John the Baptist, was declared to be insane by his contemporaries (Mt 11,18; Lc 7,33).  The possibility that Jesus suffered by hereditary transmission through this relationship of the mothers cannot be gainsaid.  Perhaps Jesus' brother James was similarly affected.  (Soury also made this point; see above p. 21).

2)    Jesus was born in a time of the most turbulent national fomentation.  *A directly paranoiac type of thought* (S. 25), which was born of a feverish hope for political deliverance, swayed great masses of the people in Jesus' land and day.  The Jews believed that they suffered because of their own sinfulness: *What psychiatrist is not involuntarily reminded by this type of thought of typical clinical cases of melancholia! A part of Israel had in fact become morbid* (S. 25) from the nervous shock of Roman oppression.  This popular consciousness of guilt found a crystalization point in the person of the Baptist.  That John was demented is evinced not only by the judgment of his contemporaries but by his eccentric habits of life and dress; he was an excellent example of *kultureller Verwilderung* (S. 28).

3)    Jesus was born in a province of mixed bloods and dialects.  His training at home was doubtless that of every orthodox Jewish boy of the time.  Of his youth and childhood we possess only apocryphal legends, yet some of these may contain a grain of truth now and then.  Incidents in the Gospels of Thomas and the Hebrews picture Jesus as a not altogether lovable boy.  His reply to his mother in Lc 2,49 is impious and his whole attitude is to be described as unnatural to a child of his age.  If his parents expected a word of childish love or request for forgiveness, to which they were entitled after three days of anxious searching, they were disappointed.  Jesus' previous discussion with the doctors in the temple shows an exaggerated self-consciousness and premature intellectual ripeness.  De Loosten describes Jesus' characteristics as a child as fol-

lows: *A prematurely keen mind, a strongly developed self-consciousness, and possibly an ethical defect in matters of natural human affections* (S. 32).

Of Jesus' life from twelve to thirty years we know nothing. But the Jewish scriptures played an important role during these years. Jesus' exaggerated self-consciousness does not seem to have left him; it was because of this doubtless that the break was brought about between Jesus and his family, for he considered himself superior to them and entertained a condescending attitude toward them. Perhaps their knowledge of his dishonorable birth augmented their dislike for him. The foreign blood in his veins doubtless accounts for the differences with his family, and it is to be regarded as an instance of hatred due to race prejudice. Jesus was gifted much more richly than his brethren and this would bring about a natural estrangement as the years passed. His own family seemed to show not the least understanding for him.

Jesus, *captivated by his own peculiar thoughts that stormed high heaven,* was not only separated from his family, but a great gulf came to separate him from his fellow-countrymen. His self-consciousness, unhindered by its own self-contradictions, grew gradually toward an infinite exaggeration. His idea that he was better than his contemporaries came to constitute an essential element of his ego. Step by step he came to interpret the prophetic promises as pointing directly to his own person. This was a purely pathological process which the psychiatrist describes as *Wahnbildung* and without which the character of Jesus' subsequent conduct is inconceivable. The world of ordinary thought, as rich as it was, satisfied him no longer. The turbulent complex of ideas that surged in his brain sought for an avenue by which they could discharge their energy and relieve their subject by bringing him into action. John the Baptist furnished this occasion.

It was this subjective tumult that brought Jesus to the Baptist, and this step marks the culmination point of a long process of inner incubation that had been working within Jesus' soul. At his baptism Jesus experiences a vision which strongly influenced his later decisions. Psychologically the vision was an hallucination with apperceptive connections and was attended by an abnormal emotional upheaval.    The increased psychic pressure drove Jesus into the wilderness where he could be alone for the necessary inner adjustments. During the period of the temptation Jesus doubtless had other hallucinations or visions which centered about his exalted self-consciousness. Jesus' physical condition was pathologically altered as the result of long fasting and furnished fertile soil for such hallucinations as Mt and Lc record in their three temptations.    The temptation period, then, marks a physiological and psychic crisis in which Jesus determines upon a role never yet attempted in the world of his day.

Jesus' first step in public was to win a respectable following; in doing this he did not even shun an occasional *captatio benevolentiae* as in the case of the winning of Nathanael. His feeling of superiority again expresses itself in his attitude as a junior rival of the Baptist, to whose disciples Mt 11,11 and Lc 7,28 are an open challenge to desert their teacher in favor of himself.    In this Jesus was not altogether successful, for the Baptist's reputation was too well established for an innovator to uproot; Jesus' real success begins only when the Baptist has been removed from the scene.    The unfortunate sermon in Nazareth (Lc 4,18-27) shows that Jesus' idea of his own excellence over against his countrymen could lead him to violate the simplest dictates of prudence.    He was forced to transfer the scene of his ministry to Capernaum.    Jesus laid important stress upon his miracles as is shown by the fact that he is angered when he fails to find faith; his teaching he subordinated entirely to his ministry of miracle as is seen by his reply to the Baptist's deputation (Mt 11,5ff; Lc 7,22ff). Jesus' teaching contained nothing essentially new.    His parables, for all their poetic perfection, center selfishly upon his own person.    Jesus did not make his points by careful logic, but by ready reference to Old Testament prophecy.    Jesus never knew how much he hurt his cause by not allowing his disciples to choose between his person and his teaching.    *In order that they might assimilate those elements in his person-*

*ality that held promise for the future, they had to take the pathological elements in the bargain* (S. 47).

Jesus laid greatest stress upon the pathological element in his person and regarded himself as nothing short of divine. He commanded silence on the point of his identity after the confession at Caesarea Philippi because he had not yet sufficient following to carry out his plan. Mc 8,30 *was an act of the healthy prudence which he still possessed sufficiently at that time in order to avoid too irrational actions* (S. 49). Peter's confession met with Jesus' full approval and satisfaction, for it must have been a matter of no little worry to him that the first to confess his Messiahship were deranged demoniacs who hardly belonged to the intellectual élite of the land; now one of his own healthy-minded disciples makes the longed-for confession. This incident combined with his increasing following and successes brings Jesus' *Selbstgefuehl* to still higher heights. He now makes the conditions of discipleship still more exorbitant (the rich young ruler) and they constitute an anarchy against regulated civil order. Mt 8,19-22 (Lc 9,57-62) and Lc 14, 26 33 show that Jesus had lost all natural human feeling.

It is interesting to note de Loosten's comment on Jesus' regard for children, for he finds this the most human and lovable feature in Jesus' character. *The same man who otherwise had lost the domestic sense almost entirely affectionately devotes himself to children* (S. 53).

Jesus never lost his natural intellectual ability; he possessed a striking dialectic that never missed the mark and stood always at his disposition. This native gift combined with his extraordinary command of the Jewish scriptures enabled him to defeat his opponents on their own ground. *The manner and method with which he despatches the Pharisees and Sadducees in numerous disputes still await their parallel* (S. 53).

4) We now come to Jesus' impression upon his contemporaries and their judgment of him. In order for one individual to influence another the two must have a great deal in common in both character and thought; few points of common contact bring about certain conflict. A genius can always work best among men of his own race and land; his ideas must be

organically born out of his own people's thought in order to make a real and lasting impression.  A study from this point of view throws an interesting light on Jesus.  Christianity made its progress in the Occident and lost the Orient where was the cradle of its infancy.  This fact dates back as early as Jesus' choice of his first disciples who came from Galilee and of the peasant class from which Jesus himself came.  In Galilee Jesus was successful; he was put to death in Jerusalem where he was not understood.  Jesus' lowly origin explains his injustice and prejudice against the rich (Lc 16,19-31).  Jesus was not careful enough in his associations to appeal to the better classes of people.  He had no appreciation of the state, and he was not interested in the artistic architecture of the temple which one of the disciples called to his attention (Mc 13,1f).  All these things show that Jesus was a son of the lower social scale that knows nothing but the struggle for bread which engages all its energy.

De Loosten joins von Hartmann (see above p. 13f) in his complaint against the personnel of Jesus' following, particularly the female element.  The disciples were won by Jesus' superior moral teaching, but it was the pathological element in his person that attracted the women who were themselves mentally afflicted and believed themselves healed by him.  Further, Jesus was a *sexuell refraktaer* (S. 58).  He pictured the future as supersexual.  Mt 19,12 is *an immortality directly dangerous to the state* (S. 59).  This lack of sex sensitiveness combined with the absence of any appreciation of the family as an institution is a mark of psychic degeneration *par excellence*.

How frequently Jesus was subject to hallucinations during the course of his career we do not know and we cannot say in how far he was influenced by them.  However, it seems very probable that he was quite dependent upon them for his decisions.  Experiences similar to that at his baptism must have repeated themselves frequently (Lc 10,18) ; our general knowledge of this abnormal psychic phenomenon would lead us to suppose this.  His disciples were occasionally witnesses of this type of ecstatic experience which he enjoyed, as at the trans-

figuration where Jesus' command for silence indicates his own
consciousness of the pathological moment in the incident. Lc
9,36 represents the disciples as holding their peace of their
own accord. Here we strike a Rasmussen tone: *If the incident as a whole had been uplifting and truly religious, one that
could have served the cause of Jesus, they* (the disciples) *would
have been the first to have spread the report of it far and wide,
and that jubilantly* (S. 61). Here the disciples seem to have
detected the pathological background of Jesus' experience and
voluntarily held their peace. That Jesus' hallucinations were
religious in character and content is to be explained by his
predominant religious interests.

A mentally abnormal person can long pass for healthy and
sound with those who know him best; if they do discover something wrong, they usually seek to understand sympathetically
or excuse his condition. But when he comes out of his local
surroundings where he is less known, then criticism is keener
and more merciless. That Jesus was charged with mental de-
mentation is clear from Lc 4,23; his own family said he was
beside himself (Mc 3,21). That this opinion was rather wide-
spread is evinced by Jn 8,48f and 10,19ff. On Jn 7,19f de
Loosten comments, *This surprising and anxious outcry of
Jesus has quite the marks of a suddenly appearing delusion
of persecution and is very characteristic of the tense state of
soul in which he found himself at this time* (S. 62). Mc 3,22
is a Synoptic confirmation of the general opinion concerning
Jesus' state of mental health. The above references suffice to
show *that Jesus was regarded by many of his contemporaries
as actually insane and that from this fact certain conclusions
can be drawn regarding the personal impression made by him*
(S. 64).

Jesus' temper was by no means uniformly composed, but
seemed to rise and fall according to the successes he was able
to register against his opponents. He was often exposed to
peculiar and apparently ungrounded depressions of spirit as
Jn 12,27 shows. His word in connection with the cure of the
woman with an issue of blood in Lc 8,46 (this notice is not
found in Mt's parallel, and is not a word of Jesus but a remark

of the evangelist in Mc 5,30) testifies to an abnormal process
of perception. *He had some sort of abnormal peripheral sensation, perhaps in the cutaneous field, and sought for this an
explanation. That he found this at once in the person of the
afflicted woman is a mere accident which he—shrewd as he was
—guarded himself against declaring as such* (S. 66).

Jesus was ruthless in his disregard for the religious rites
and customs of his people. He could brook no opposition and
answered objections with insult and sarcasm. He was even dis-
courteous in his remarks to his more distinguished hosts. He
was never cautious in his words with friend or foe. It is not
surprising that he did not win more friends. He would have
had a greater outward success if he had unfurled the flag of
political revolution, but Jesus seems to have lacked all talent
for organization. Rather than augmenting the number of his
following, he was more interested in binding those already won
more closely to himself by awakening within them exorbitant
expectations in terms of Dan. 7,13f. But he would consider
no special requests; his followers must take what came. To
share in the future glory required unconditional subordination
and absolute surrender to his own desires.

Jesus' lack of success with the Jews turned him to the
Gentiles; by a dim race instinct he felt himself drawn more
strongly to the Gentile than the Jew. As he grew increasingly unpopular *the rash thought gradually matured in
his brain of carrying out by himself his long nourished claims,
which he had expressed in a thousand ways, by a kind of kingdom of violence* (S. 72). Had Jesus been capable of sound reflection he would never have undertaken the fatal journey to
Jerusalem. He saw clearly that his star was about to set, but
the impulse within him drove him ahead like possessed. However, he did not neglect to prepare his disciples for a possible
defeat in Jerusalem which they already had feared as is clear
in the anxious undertone of Peter's word in Mc 10,28. In his
prophecies of the passion Jesus trampled the Messianic ideal
of his people under his feet; for this they could not forgive
him, and they were too sound-minded to take any pleasure in
the Messiah's passive passion.

During his Jerusalem days Jesus found himself in a high-tensioned and excessively nervous state of mind.  It is only out of this state of soul that his senseless cursing of the fig tree is to be understood.  He had lost the calm composure of his Galilean days.  The cleansing of the temple was an act of striking violence and branded Jesus as dangerous to the civil peace in the eyes of his Jerusalem enemies.  The Pharisees knew that the plan of a mentally morbid dreamer for a social-religious revolution was inadequate to the situation.  Among the disciples Judas alone had retained a clear head, and his betrayal and subsequent suicide is only the expression of his regret for having wasted his time and energy in the discipleship of Jesus.

The premonition of the approaching catastrophe brought Jesus into a state of deep depression; he begins to distrust the most trusted of his disciples.  His unhealthful fear produced hallucinations (Jn 12,28ff).  This fear reached its highest point in Gethsemane where Jesus had a vision; *the consciousness of his mission, in which he had believed so long and to which he had sacrificed the best of his life, was strong enough to overcome the fear of death* (S. 82).  In his words at his arrest (Mt 26,51ff) Jesus' *Wahnsystem* suddenly broke forth again with all its former force and he regained his earlier composure.  He did not seek to detain his disciples in their desertion; he knew that he must fight the battle alone and he entered the conflict with a royal dignity and bearing which enabled him to greet all charges during his trial with a stony silence.  Pilate did not regard Jesus as a dangerous person, *rather as a visionary, a fanatic, a morbid mind;* his sympathy for Jesus' pitiable plight is expressed in Jn 19,5.  If Lc 23,43 are genuine words of Jesus, it is certain that he died on the cross without his faith in his own Messiahship being broken and without being shaken from his happy delusion.

In conclusion de Loosten says: *Suffering from birth on under hereditary burden Jesus was probably a half-caste, who as a born degenerate attracted attention even in early youth by his exceedingly pronounced self-consciousness which was combined with a highly gifted intelligence and a meagerly developed sense for family and sex* (S. 90).

These elements of degeneration determined the course of Jesus' public career; first subjectively; later objectively. *His intelligence enabled him to recognize the mistakes of the religious conceptions that controlled his time and to give to the precepts of the law an interpretation that was new in form, freer and capable of development.*

*His self-consciousness was aggravated in a slow process of development that ended in a fixed system of delusions, the particulars of which were determined by the intense religious bent of the time and his own one-sided preoccupation with the Scriptures of the Old Testament. The physiologic genial and the pathological elements in his nature influenced each other strongly and were intimately combined* (S. 90).

In the course of his public career the more pathological element in Jesus' person smothered out the more healthy element. Jesus' psychic disturbance manifested itself in hallucinations in more than one field of sense, and their character and content always corresponded to the nature of his delusion. Jesus' end came as the result of the inevitable clash between *Wahn und Wirklichkeit* (S. 91).

There is a seriousness and conscientiousness in de Loosten's book that we missed in Rasmussen's *Jesus*. The very fact that Dr. Lomer wrote under a pseudonym is evidence enough that he was not seeking notoriety, a charge from which Rasmussen would have difficulty in freeing himself. Over against the others who have figured in the contention against the psychic health of Jesus de Loosten stands alone in his recognition and high estimate of the remarkable intellectual abilities of Jesus. He classes Jesus among the great geniuses of history.

Although de Loosten states that his purpose is not to write a life of Jesus, his book is in fact a pathography of Jesus for he comments in one way or another upon nearly every important word or incident in Jesus' public career. De Loosten is really the first pathographer of Jesus. He makes no definite diagnosis in the case of Jesus, but his conclusions fit paranoia only.

The chief weakness of de Loosten is his complete lack of orientation in the field of New Testament criticism. He rejects the canonical birth stories of Mt and Lc, and places considerable confidence in the slanders of Celsus and the Talmud. He cites the apocryphal Gospels of Thomas, Hebrews, Ebionites, Egyptians and Peter. The Fourth Gospel furnishes him the greater bulk of his materials. The petty character of many of his criticisms is illustrated by his remark on Jesus' word in the contention concerning the washing of hands (Mc 7,1-23): *Is not one rightly accustomed to judge the stage of any people's culture by its use of soap?* (S. 68). But when de Loosten tells us that Jesus opened his ministry in Nazareth, that he subordinated his message to his miracles, that his own ego was the theme of his parables, and that Jesus experienced a vision on the mount of transfiguration, we need only to reply that de Loosten would do well to read the Gospels again.

### William Hirsch, M. D.

Hirsch's book, *Religion and Civilization: the Conclusions of a Psychiatrist* (Truth Seeker Company, N. Y., 1912, 610 p.) appeared in German in 1910 under the title, *Religion und Civilisation vom Standpunkte des Psychiaters* (E. W. Bonsels & Co., Muenchen, 652 S.) Hirsch is a doctor of medicine in New York, a specialist in mental diseases, and a free-thinker. His general view of religion corresponds more closely to that of Washburn than to that of any other writer who has pronounced a psychiatric judgment against Jesus. His reasoning is characteristically free-thinking. He knows that there is no God, no son of God, no soul, and no such thing as immortality. *Religion is a remainder of barbarism* (p. 599, Ger., 648). *No matter what form religion took, it has always been an evil; it has either kept mankind ignorant and stupid, or made them hypocrites...... Religion of the present is like a poisonous hydra, whose venomous tooth has been drawn by civilization* (p. 593, Ger., 641f). *Christianity was the greatest hindrance, the most persistent obstacle that civilization has had to overcome* (p. 592, Ger., 640). *Christianity, from its very beginning, was a curse and blight to the human race* (p. 453f,

Ger., 487). *It has kept mankind in a state of stupidity and superstition for nearly two thousand years* (p. 526, Ger., 566). *The Christian religion has always exerted an exceedingly unfavorable influence on the morals of mankind. Hard as this may seem, it is nevertheless true......the less Christianity, the higher the morals* (p. 542, Ger., 583).

It is only the psychiatric portions of the book, particularly those in reference to Jesus, that are of interest to us here. Hirsch finds that the science of psychiatry is not yet sufficiently appreciated as furnishing a correct account for certain historical phenomena. *Since the earliest times mental diseases have exerted an enormous influence on the development of mankind, and there are many great historical events which cannot be understood at all without a psychiatrical explanation* (p. III, Ger., I). This is especially true in giving an historical account of the rise and history of Old Testament religion, as well as the beginnings of Christianity. *Biblical phenomena are given a complete and exhaustive explanation by the assumption of mental diseases* (p. IV, Ger., III).

The biblical accounts in their entirety are to be taken as strict historical facts. The undeniable proof that all the prominent personages from Abraham down to Paul actually lived and that all that is related about them actually happened is as follows: *Mental diseases, like all the other phenomena of nature, have quite a typical, unmistakable character to the expert. To invent a psychical condition, corresponding in all its details to the actual course of a well-known mental disease, is just as impossible as to describe the course of typhoid fever or malaria without ever having seen or heard anything about these diseases. The description given in the Bible of the persons in question corresponds so accurately to a certain form of insanity which we have occasion to observe every day that the proof that these people must have existed has hereby been presented beyond any doubt* (p. V, Ger., IIIf).

The mental disease in question, which has played such an important role in the domain of religion, is paranoia. This form of insanity is as old as the human race, but it was only during the last century that it began to be understood. The remarkable thing about this mental disturbance is that it does not necessarily involve an impairment of the intellect. Paranoiacs often manifest an unusually high degree of intelligence and are often gifted and talented. They do not present the ordinary symptoms of insanity, such as incoherent speech, chattering, absurd acts, attacks of fury, etc. Apparently they are healthy, well-bred persons and not infrequently make a decidedly favorable impression by their charm of manner and speech. Their judgment seems clear and correct, and their emotions normal. Yet a whole multitude of morbid psychical phenomena lies hidden behind this seemingly normal mental state. (On paranoia see below pages 257ff).

For Hirsch, all the Old Testament personages, Abraham, Isaac, Jacob, Moses (the most ingenious of them all about whose paranoia whole books could be written), Gideon, Samuel, Saul, all the prophets from Isaiah down to Malachi, whose *writings represent nothing but the confused and incoherent manifestations of an unbalanced mind,* are nothing other than typical clinical cases of paranoia such as are found in our hospitals for the insane today. The three chief figures connected with the beginnings of Christianity, John the Baptist, Jesus, and Paul, were also paranoiacs. All the biblical characters from Abraham down to Paul suffered with delusions of grandeur and persecution and with hallucinations in every field of sense. The psychiatrist can account for these phenomena, so well known to him, only by the assumption of paranoia.

Hirsch repeats the position of Rasmussen to the effect that the old alternative, that Jesus was either the one he professed to be or he was the greatest swindler that ever lived, is false. There can be no question about Jesus' sincerity: *Christ was thoroughly honest and was convinced himself of the truth of every word he uttered* (p. 94, Ger., 89). The whole of his conduct, his attitude toward his contemporaries, and the accounts of him handed down to us prove that he was neither an adventurer nor an impostor. Some of his contemporaries did him a great injustice in this respect. There is a third possibility which saves Jesus' sincerity and frees him from fraud, that is, he was a paranoiac.

Regarding the sources Hirsch takes the same position as Binet-Sanglé, as we shall see, and accepts all four Gospels as literal history down to the last detail: *Every sentence in the Gospel rests on the solid foundation of a historical fact* (p. 98, Ger., 95). *What, in our estimation, forms a much stronger proof of the truth of the Gospel than anything else, is the fact that the entire psychical manifestations of Jesus Christ represent a certain mental condition, to be analysed at once, which is so characteristic and typical in every respect, that it seems utterly impossible that these utterances could have been invented by any one* (p. 99, Ger., 95).

Jesus, for Hirsch, offers in every respect an absolutely typical picture of paranoia. *All that we know of him corresponds so exactly to the clinical aspect of paranoia, that it is hardly conceivable how anybody at all acquainted with mental disorders, can entertain the slightest doubt as to the correctness of the diagnosis* (p. 103, Ger., 99). Jesus was one of those cases of paranoia that remain quiet and self-engrossed during youth. He could be called a prodigy in view of his unusual mental ability manifested at the age of twelve. The seeds of the delusion that later possessed him were sown in his youthful brain by his arduous study of the prophets. *Anyone acquainted with the writings of the insane Prophets, anyone who has been able to read through this endless chaos of delusions, these incoherent products of a hallucinatory delirium, must be able to realize what a pernicious influence the eager study of them must have exerted on a juvenile mind, predisposed itself to psychopathic conditions* (p. 103, Ger., 99).

The first developments of his delusions were slow and imperceptible to Jesus' friends. The obscurity that shrouds the life of Jesus before the time of his public appearance makes it impossible to determine when these delusions first appeared and began to systematize themselves. They were probably more or less latent and had not come into permanent possession of his self-consciousness. Otherwise they would have forced him out of his seclusion. *He obviously constituted one of those cases, where the isolated and disconnected delusions required an external stimulant and a strong emotion to systematize them-*

*selves into a typical paranoïcal structure* (p. 104, Ger., 100).
This stimulant was furnished by John the Baptist and his
preaching. Jesus' baptism by John aroused him to a condition of intense emotional excitement; his long cherished delusions were converted into hallucinations of sight and hearing.
*The hallucinations of paranoiacs are always materialized delu-*
*sions* (p. 105, Ger., 101).

The subsequent sojourn of forty days in the wilderness is
of greatest interest, for these forty days lie between two fundamentally different periods in the life of Jesus. Jesus returned
from the wilderness a different person; an enormous change had
taken place in his psychic condition. *The delusions, until then*
*isolated and disconnected, had expanded and combined and*
*formed themselves into a great systematized structure* (p. 106,
Ger., 102). This transition corresponds to the regular course
of this psychosis; it is the transition from the latent to the active stage of paranoia. During the rest of his life Jesus was
possessed with *immeasurable, perpetually increasing delusions*
*of grandeur.* All of his thoughts and words culminated in the
one word "I." Jesus' *I ams* are as typical chatter of a paranoiac as could be found. Most of his parables have reference
to his own person (Hirsch cites Jn 10,7f). *Everything revolves*
*solely and alone about his "Ego," and the delusions that center*
*on this "Ego" know no limit.* Jesus' prayer in Jn 17,1ff *fur-* ✓
*nishes proof of his paranoia in every word. His very relation*
*to "God" as his "Father" is gradually obliterated in his delu-*
*sions, and he begins to consider himself God* (p. 110, Ger., 107).
*Like a long drawn out crescendo in a Beethoven symphony, be-*
*ginning with the faintest pianissimo and gradually expanding*
*more and more, growing in intensity with every movement until*
*it reaches, in a thundering fortissimo, its highest climax, so*
*Jesus Christ's delusions of grandeur began slowly, developing*
*step by step, until they finally assumed such dimensions that*
*further intensification became impossible* (p. 111, Ger., 108).
*No text book on mental diseases can give a more typical de-*
*scription of delusions of grandeur, gradually developing and*
*infinitely increasing, than is offered by the life of Jesus Christ*
(p. 112, Ger., 109).

Jesus not only suffered with delusions, but also with hallucinations; he *saw* and *heard* the creations of his own morbid imagination (the baptism, temptation, and transfiguration). We have record of at least one illusion (Jn 12,28f), which is psychologically closely akin to the hallucination.

Jesus' diseased mental condition showed itself in most every thing he did. His selection of the twelve is evidence enough of his *Groessenwahn*. His acclamation in Mt 11,25ff (Lc 10, 21ff) is his paranoiacal interpretation of the fact that he was rejected by the élite among his contemporaries and was accepted by the proletariat; his words in Lc 10,19 and Jn 9,3— How typical of paranoia! No one but a paranoiac would curse a barren fig tree for its failure to bear fruit out of season, or undertake such a foolhardy entrance into the capital.

Jesus' miracles are not at all remarkable; they are to be explained by suggestion and auto-suggestion. Jesus did not really cure; his supposed cures were cases of suffering from *imaginary health. It is almost pathetic how he smeared saliva and earth into the eyes of a blind man, believing that thereby he had cured him* (p. 121, Ger., 119). The miracle at Cana is a slight-of-hand trick to which no self-respecting God would stoop. Jesus deluded himself, as did his disciples, into thinking that he miraculously multiplied food and fed the multitudes; the litter left in a New York park after a Jewish picnic will explain the basketsful of fragments.

That the apostles, headed by Peter, asked Jesus why he called himself the *Son of God*, in that he was really the son of Joseph and Mary, and that this subject was frequently discussed in detail with him is a matter of absolute certainty for Hirsch. Jesus evidently answered that God was his father, and not Joseph, and that he had been born of a virgin mother by divine miracle. For Hirsch, Jesus is the originator of the legends of the wonderful events that attended his birth as related in the narratives of the nativity by Mt and Lc. These fanciful creations were constructed by him after he had become obsessed by the delusion of grandeur that he was the son of God. That Jesus was one of those cases of paranoia that ascribe to themselves a distinguished ancestry is clear from his fabrication of the fictitious paternal genealogies.

Jesus' paranoia is further clear from the eccentric and absurd character of his teaching. His words concerning *the other cheek* and *the mantle also* are ridiculous. Jesus is indifferent to the moral and ethical considerations in the living of life as long as his disciples will only continue to believe on him. If his instructions regarding labor and provision for the future were followed it would mean a *retrogression to the prehistoric condition of man! A negation of all civilization!* (p. 132, Ger., 132). Jesus did not conform his conduct to his own teaching regarding love for one's enemies; no one could be more intolerant toward his enemies than Jesus. He cursed cities *neck and crop*, yet in his last moments on the cross he could promise Paradise to a criminal; and all because the one believed and the other disbelieved in him. Jesus' whole code of ethics rests upon blind faith. In view of such utterances as Mt 10,37 and Lc 14,26 the diagnosis of a mental disease is charitable. Mental derangement is the only excuse for his inconsiderate words and haughty attitude toward his mother.

Like all paranoiacs Jesus harbored hatred for those who did not agree with him or humor him in his delusions. His attitude toward the rich is absurd. He had not the slightest notion of a social system of any kind. The point to his parable of the rich man and Lazarus is a demoralizing and pernicious doctrine. Jesus' mental condition led him to the crassest contradictions. In the parable of the pounds he advises us to become Shylocks. In his own conduct he did not manifest the indiscriminate mercy which he idealizes in the parable of the good Samaritan, for in Mt 10,5 he instructs his disciples to avoid the cities of Samaria and the ways of the Gentiles.

Jesus' habit of expressing himself in superlatives was the result of his psychic degeneration. His passion for self-mutilation is abominable and grossly immoral. *As is so frequently the case with psychical degenerates, Christ was sexually impotent* (p. 530, Ger., 571). His commandment *Thou shalt love thine enemies* is *another of those psychological impossibilities which originated in the morbid desire to outdo the existing law*

(p. 531f, Ger., 572).  All his proposed changes in the Mosiac laws actually sound like persiflage.

Jesus replied to the Pharisees in Lc 13,31f in a genuine paranoiacal fashion, for he saw in their advice only a new conspiracy against himself.  During his trial Jesus conducted himself in the same insane manner; *at that time the High-Priest who knew nothing of mental diseases, there being no chair of psychiatry in Jerusalem, could naturally see only a blasphemy in Jesus' utterances* (p. 155, Ger., 157).

Hirsch concludes his study of Jesus in the conviction that any one not forcibly opposed to admitting the truth cannot longer be in doubt concerning Jesus' paranoia.  *He represents as typical a case of this disease as can be imagined.  All the symptoms are fully represented, and the development as well as the course of this case corresponds in every respect to the well-known description which modern psychiatry, based on many years' clinical experience, has given of this peculiar psychical affection* (p. 129, Ger., 128).  The whole Christian world worships an insane Jew who was crucified two thousand years ago.

The average Christian believer who reads Hirsch's book will without doubt receive a severe shock.  But the student of Biblical literature takes his work much less seriously.  Hirsch's book is too full of back-ally mud-throwing from the religious point of view to make any real impression.  Even from the psychiatric angle it has nothing of the serious scientific character that one has a right to expect of a doctor of medicine.  Along with the others who diagnose paranoia Hirsch is absolutely indiscriminate in his use of sources, drawing most of his material from the Fourth Gospel, and he shows himself absolutely unacquainted with the conclusions of Biblical criticism.

### Dr. C. Binet-Sanglé

Dr. Binet-Sanglé, Professor in the School of Psychology in Paris, tells us near the close of the fourth volume of his work, *La Folie de Jésus*, (4 *Tomes*, Paris, 1908—1915; 1914 p.) that he read the canonical Gospels for the first time in 1898.  Prior to that time he had known *Ieschou bar-Iossef* (*Jesus, son of Joseph*.  Throughout his work Binet-Sanglé in-

sists on using the transliterated form of Biblical names.) only
as presented in works such as that of Renan, and he was sur-
prised beyond measure to find the great disparity that existed
between the portrait by Renan and the actual model furnished
by the Gospels themselves (1).    On the very first reading of the Gospels he was convinced that Jesus was an
alien and that the Christian religion had for its founder
a psychopath whom five hundred millions of men worship as
divine.   Provoked by these first impressions he began his study.
In 1902 he published an article, *Les cures miraculeuses de Jésus,*
in the *Revue Blanche* (June 15 and July 1).   In 1903 he wrote
a lecture on *Les hallucinations de Jésus* which he revised in 1905
and now comprises part IV of volume II of his finished work.
In January 1907 he began a series of lectures on *La Folie de
Jésus* in the School of Psychology in Paris which he gave on
Saturdays and continued through three winters before students
of medicine and philosophy.   The first volume of his work appeared in 1908 and the fourth and last in 1915.   (See bibliography for the editions of the various volumes from which
quotations are made.)

   Before examining the contents of Binet-Sanglé's work it
is necessary to state briefly his general view of religion and his
philosophical position in order to comprehend the ease with
which he pronounces such harsh judgments against Jesus.   In
his atheistic confession he says that belief in either God or devil
seems to him absurd, and, since the world at present is enjoy-
ing the age of reason, he is completely delivered from all need
of faith.   *No religious idea seems to me to merit the inquiry of
an intelligent person* (IV 323).   Religious devotion is a mark
of psychic degeneration.   Philosophically Binet-Sanglé is a
determinist and materialist.   Psychology is merely a branch of
physiology and biology.   There is no ego, no free will; both are
delusions.   *The free will, the spontaneity of the ego, autonom-
ous volition are only illusions.   I is only a word.   It designates
the conscious element of our being, infamous element, governed*

---

   (1)   *Quelle différence en effet entre le charmant philosophe de la "Vie
de Jésus" et le vagabond hautain, farouche et incohérent des évangiles!*
IV 321.

*by subconsciousness, the organism, and the outside world......
Man is a machine partially endowed with consciousness; and he
imagines that he has within himself the power and direction of
his acts, but who in reality is acted upon by all the forces of
the universe.   Irresponsible for his constitution, his temperament, his character and the environment in which hazard has
placed him, man is the plaything of events as the planet on
which he lives is the plaything of the stars.   All acts, mental,
muscular and moral, draw their energy from the depths of the
organism and are as rigorously determined as the rebounding
of a ball thrown against a wall.   Ethics has only an illusory
efficacy.   It should be replaced by eugenics and social hygiene
(IV 72f).   The ignoramus, the hypocrite, the liar and the criminal are as little responsible for their feelings and acts as the
electric machine is responsible for its sparks and flashes, the
injuries and deaths which it can cause (I 5).*

In his previous studies in morbid religious psychology (1),
Binet-Sanglé expressed his judgment to the effect that, if the
prophets had lived in our day, many of them would have been
interned in our asylums for the mentally diseased, for they, with
all the religious by vocation, belong to the family of the psychopaths.   *The same is true of this Jesus, son of Joseph, of
this Jesus Christ of whom we have made a god* (I 4).   The
scholar has the right to study the founders of the great religions without entertaining for them a special sentiment of reverence or love which their work does not justify.   As a psychologist he intends to employ the method of all natural sciences,
since human psychology is merely a branch of anthropology.
As the naturalist, the psychologist must observe, compare, gen-
eralize, and infer.   *Il ne doit jamais employer la pétition de
principe* (I 9).   He regards almost all the writers who have
studied Jesus as having employed this false method.   He does
not intend to study Jesus as would a Catholic or a Protestant
theologian, nor as a mythologist, but as an anthropologist, and
to prove that for 1900 years occidental humanity has lived
under the ban of a mistaken diagnosis.

(1)  *Les prophètes juifs*, 1905; *Le prophète Elie*, 1904; *Le prophète
Élisée*, 1905; *Observations de religieuses de vocation.*

Regarding the trustworthiness of the sources (I 20-71) Binet-Sanglé says that the evangelists were not inventors of fictions, but historians and biographers. If they were inventors, they were admirably instructed in nervous and mental pathology; but this science was not yet born when they wrote. The Gospel writers were honest men who saw develop before their eyes, without knowing its nature, a case of theomegalomania, a case of religious paranoia, and they naïvely described what they saw. He will prove his position step by step in a detailed examination of the canonical Gospels, the fourth being of equal historical reliability and value as the first three. He will not employ the apocryphal gospels, but merely cite them in the foot-notes as a kind of superfluous sub-support to the abundant psychopathic materials found in the four Gospels as they at present stand in the New Testament.

### Son Hérédité (I 73-200)

Concerning Jesus' father we know very little. His affection for his son is perhaps reflected in Jesus' parable in Mt 7,9 (Lc 11,11). He probably did not live to see the insanity of his son enter upon its active phase. It is certain that he did not live to witness the death of the theomaniac, for Jesus consigns his mother to the care of the beloved disciple (Jn 19,26f). Jesus' mother was very devout, yet, as all the women of the time, very ignorant. She was not slow in perceiving the demented state of her son; it is this painful realization that she hid away in her heart (Lc 2,51). Nevertheless she manifested a true mother-love for her son; this he did not return. She remained in the shadow where Jesus relegated her, sharing with him his joys, fears, and sorrows. *Pity the mothers who give Jesus as an example to their sons!* (I 114). Mary did not abandon her son, but followed him throughout his errant life. She believed in his divine mission and was a member of the *secte ieschouite*.

Jesus' family was one of those of which Billod says: *Il doit y avoir ou y avoir eu des aliénés dans la famille* (quoted by Binet-Sanglé, I 131). The brothers of Jesus can be divided into two clans: the Messianic which believed in his divine mission, and the anti-Messianic which disbelieved.  Mc 3,21 makes it clear that the brothers of Jesus who were still of sound mind were under no delusion as to the true nature of their brother's words and acts.  Judas (Mc 6,3) belonged to the second clan, and Jacob (James) to the first.  Jacob was a mystic temperament; he believed in Jesus' messianic mission and shared in the resurrection hallucinations (I Cor 15,7).  He was later the fanatical, yet vacillatory head of the Jerusalem community. Jesus and Jacob constitute a psychopathic pair, a case of *folie religieuse à deux*, in which the active subject (Jesus) communicates his delirium to the passive subject (Jacob).  Jacob was a psychic degenerate, *un régressif hypersuggestible* (I 153). Jacob was younger than Jesus, as is usually the case in the communication of mental contagions, and possessed essentially the same personal characteristics, and shared common conditions of life; he was *l'aliéné par reflet, l'aliéné par induction, un demi-fou* (I 156ff).  This religious epidemic which first affected the mind of a blood-brother has spread over the whole western world and we call it Christianity.

In the less immediate family of Jesus Binet-Sanglé reckons Simon, son of Clopas, as the blood-cousin of Jesus (his mother, Mary, being the sister of Joseph, Jesus' father) and as identical with the Cephas of I Cor 15,5 who shared in the resurrection visions thus adding a third psychopath to the group. The family of Jesus, composed of thirteen members according to Binet-Sanglé's calculations, forms a psychopathic group, which he calls a *hierosyncroteme* (sacred group), in which there are found one *fou religieux*, two *demi-fous religieux*, and four *dévots*, all seven mystics (I 198).  Thus Joseph and Mary engendered a theomegalomaniac, *un fou*, and the head of the sect in Jerusalem, *un demi-fou* (I 186).

This phenomenon of two aliens in one family of seven children Binet-Sanglé says is due to heredity.  Jesus' hereditary burden probably came from the paternal side of the family, for his father's precocious death seems to suggest a weakness on the paternal rather than on the maternal side.  This hereditary burden was due to alcoholism.  Jesus was born and brought up in a land and family that consumed a great deal

of strong wines and where the alcoholic habit was wide-spread
and deep-seated. In such lands and families psychic degeneracy is specially frequent. The incident at Cana is very instructive, for it gives a clue to the excessive quantities of wine
consumed on such occasions. A family in which mental degeneracy is so advanced soon becomes extinct; it is, therefore,
probable that the family of Joseph did not survive beyond the
fourth generation.

### Sa Constitution et sa Physiologie (I 201-366)

,Though the canonical Gospels furnish no precise information concerning the physiological constitution of Jesus, yet
Binet-Sanglé believes that certain biographical details do give
some approximate indications. Jesus was not taller than the
average person, for Zachaeus was compelled to seek a vantage
point in order to get a view of him. His entry into Jerusalem
on a colt of an ass (Mc 11,7) shows that he could not have been
either tall or heavy in weight. That Jesus did not differ much
in appearance from his companions is clear from the fact that
Judas must identity him with a kiss. (These remarks are characteristic of the profundity of most of Binet-Sanglé's criticisms). Jesus cannot have been robust, but was rather delicate
of constitution. Mental degeneracy most frequently corresponds to physical degeneracy. The alien's constitution is
*mediocre or bad; he appears younger than his age; he mani-
fests elements of infantilism, juvenility or feminism. Child,
adolescent or woman in mind, he is the same in body* (I 210).

The change in Jesus' countenance at the transfiguration
was an attack of ecstasy. This experience was but a variety
of cataleptic attack, a vesanic syndrome. As the majority of
ecstatics, who usually have a vague consciousness of the pathological nature of their attacks, Jesus demanded secrecy of the
three witnesses. (Here Binet-Sanglé strikes upon one of Rasmussen's chief points). The author of the Fourth Gospel respected this request of his master and omits all mention of the
transfiguration (Compare Wrede, CTJE, S. 56 on Jn 12,28ff).
Peter was less discreet and makes mention of this extraordinary spectacle in one of his letters (II Peter 1,17-18).

Binet-Sanglé even finds materials in the Gospels which make possible an approximate analysis of the condition of Jesus' digestive, vasomotoric, respiratory and genital organs. That Jesus was voracious and, as many paranoiacs, abused his stomach is clear from Mt 11,19 (Lc 7,33). The same passages show that Jesus, predisposed by hereditary alcoholic inclination, was an oenophilist. Wine figures prominently in his teaching (Mc 2,22; 14,23f; Lc 5,39). The scene at Cana is specially instructive concerning Jesus' alcoholic habit (Jn 2, 1ff). His mother, having learned by experience that this drink multiplied Jesus' deliriant attacks, said, *They have no wine*, in order to distract her son, but his irritated reply, *Woman, what have I to do with thee?*, forced her to concede in order to avoid a scene.

Sitiophobia is a further pathological trait in the personal habits of Jesus (Mt 6,16ff; 17,21; Mc 9,29). It is to sitiophobia that we are to ascribe the forty days fasting in the wilderness. This experience of Jesus corresponds exactly to the typical clinical cases, for this long period of fasting aggravated his delirium and gave rise to hallucinations which clinical psychiatry confirms as usually demonomaniac in character and content. Jesus' words in Jn 4,31ff and their impression on the disciples is *the impression which certain aliens make on the crowd* (I 246).

Jesus' agony in Gethsemane is of greatest importance in the diagnosis of his vesania. Jesus' emotions on this occasion are morbid. It is a vasomotoric attack accompanied by facial hematidrosis (Lc 22,44) which appears only in cases of mental malady, neuropathology and hysteria. This attack was brought on by exposure to the chill of the early spring night and prostration on the damp ground. The state of affairs with the Jerusalem authorities contributed to the favorableness of the conditions for such an attack by the emotional upheaval in which Jesus found himself. As is often the case, this attack was attended by visual hallucinations (Lc 22,43). *Nothing further is required for declaring that the founder of the Christian religion was a psychic degenerate* (I 288).

The pathological condition of Jesus' respiratory system

is evident from his inability to carry the cross to the place of execution. *I am sure that the theomaniac was fatigued; I am sure that he had not slept the night before* (I 290). If he had been strong and robust as were his two fellow victims, he would have been able to carry the cross the few hundred meters distance. But this natural feebleness was complicated with a graver malady. Jesus' loud cry on the cross proves that he did not die of exhaustion. The surprising rapidity with which death overtook Jesus on the cross has its special reason which the spear-thrust and the issue of blood and water make clear, and for which we are specially indebted to the author of the ✓ Fourth Gospel (Jn 19,34). The issue of water and blood is a serofibrinous effusion due to pleurisy which Jesus had acquired. Legué says that this is certainly the first example of thoracentesis. Jesus was afflicted with pleuritic tuberculosis which is a disease often concomitant with religious paranoia. Jesus' habit of nocturnal retreats to solitude with frequent exposure to the damp and chill of the night air was the chief contributing cause to this pleuritic tubercular complication.

Mental degeneracy is often accompanied by an arrestment of the genital system. Jesus' attitude toward women, his exaltation of sterility (Lc 23,29) and eunuchism, his general attitude toward the institutions of the family and marriage, and his supersexual conception of the kingdom of God (Mc 12,25) confirm this in his case. His recommendation of automutilation, the enucleation of the eye and the ablation of the hand, seems to be directed against sexual perversion, a common phenomenon among psychopaths.

### Ses Connaissances et ses Idées (II 3-167)

Jesus was profoundly ignorant of Aryan science. The exploration of the brain of the son of Elohim from this point of view ends with lamentable results; *his scientific conceptions reduce themselves to a few errors* (II 9). Jesus shared the Old Testament supernaturalistic view of the world and life, and with it its scientific ignorance. From the angle of religious erudition Jesus fares better: his brain, *poor in learning, is rich in beliefs and religious conceptions drawn from the Bible and other lucubrations of mystic Jews* (II 21). Gifted with a good

memory, as are most of his race, Jesus' arduous reading of his
people's scriptures resulted in his retaining a great number
of passages, particularly those which nourished his reveries and
deliriant dreams.  His ideas of God, the Holy Spirit, angels,
demons, sheol, the resurrection and the last judgment Jesus
borrowed from the Old Testament and Jewish tradition, both
of which were saturated with the religious myths and beliefs of
the peoples of the Near and Far East.  *Le lecteur n'a pas été
sans remarquer ce qu'il y a de sombre dans ces élucubrations*
(II 124), but all of these ideas simply aggravated Jesus' vesania for he believed that all of these traditional teachings centered upon himself.  Jesus thus came to stipulate exclusively
egocentric conditions for entrance into and participation in the
kingdom of God; *faith in Jesus is such an essential condition
for entering into the kingdom that good and bad are admitted
without distinction, if they have only believed and followed him*
(II 158).

### Son Délire (II 169-327)

By *son délire* Binet-Sanglé means the problem of Jesus'
self-consciousness.  Jesus' self-consciousness corresponds closely to the historical and clinical type which is designated as
theomegalomania.  *Megalomania is a psychic affection characterized by a pride out of all proportion to the social worth of
the subject; I mean by theomegalomania a psychic affection
where this excessive pride is combined with an extreme piety*
(II 219).

How did Jesus come to identify himself with the Messiah
of the Old Testament?  Binet-Sanglé replies, *By a purely pathological process.*  The first step in this process is furnished by
Lc alone (2,41ff).  This early incident in the temple at Jerusalem marks a hebephrenic crisis which usually appears in
youthful psychopaths of this type, and is due to puberal auto-
intoxication.  Jesus' remarkable discussions with the teachers
and his rude reply to his anxious parents are simply a fit of
intellectual excitation and an exaggeration of self-consciousness resting on a purely pathological physiologic state.  Outside circumstances also made their contribution to Jesus' case

of theomegalomania. The consciousness of this psychosis is usually very sensitive to predictions, particularly those of a prophetic type. The prophetic preaching of the Baptist was a prime stimulus to Jesus' delirium. John himself appears as a member of the great family of asthenic and melancholic degenerates. He was a victim of the Messianic suggestions of the epoch and an alien who made a great impression upon the general public. His message confirmed Jesus in his delirium. Jesus and John, for a time at least, as Elijah and Elisha, as Jesus and his brother James, constituted a psychopathic pair. *John was the spiritual father of Jesus whose servile imitations attest, in default of other proofs, an intellectual infirmity* (II 255). On Lc 3,23 Binet-Sanglé comments: *This precious bit of information, furnished by the gospel according to Luke, accords with the data of psychopathology*, for the psychiatrist sees here the vesania of Jesus entering upon its active phase which usually comes about the thirtieth year.

But the one element that seems to have convinced Jesus of his Messiahship more than any other was the cures he effected. They played an etiological role in the delirium of the Nazarene through the influence of auto-suggestion. The sick that were cured made their contribution by direct suggestions regarding his identity. The realization of his ability to divine the thoughts of both friends and foes still further added material to the fire that burned within Jesus' soul. Jesus was further strengthened in his vesania by the fact that he could win and retain disciples whose confessions corroborated the contents of his own consciousness.

Binet-Sanglé distinguishes three stages in the development of Jesus' theomegalomania. 1) *L'erreur fixe primordiale* of Jesus was the conviction that he was the Messiah, king, son, confidant, sole agent, and interpreter of Jahweh. 2) *La transformation de la personalité.* This transformation seems to have been well under way in Jesus' case when he was twelve years of age. *At the age of twelve perhaps, his personality* n°1 *(son of the village carpenter) gave place to a personality* n°2 *(Messiah, Son of God)* (II 284). It was completed when Jesus said, *I and the Father am one.* 3) *La systématisation du délire* appeared in Jesus' case when he begins to speak of his resurrection and cosmic triumph as supreme judge of human fate and the sole expiation for sin.   Each stage is definite and distinct, and each marks an aggravation of Jesus' vesania.   On page 307 of volume two Binet-Sanglé assures us, *there is not in the history of science a case of theomegalomaniac delirium that manifests itself in a more evident fashion.*

## Ses Hallucinations (II 329-394)

The hallucination is a sensation without a real object in the outside world, a sensation central in its origin.   Three periods are to be distinguished in religious paranoia: 1) the period of conception and systematization 2) the hallucinatory period; 3) the period of the transformation of the personality. *Jesus, the son of Joseph, does not escape this law of pathology* (II 345).   It is probable that the theomegalomaniac of Nazareth had had hallucinations prior to those recorded by the evangelists.   His word to his parents (Lc 2,49) betrays a consciousness won without doubt by hallucination.   The evangelists actually report seven hallucinations of Jesus.   The first is at the Jordan; it is visual and audative in character.   The temptation, *the post-Johannic crisis* (II 355), with its scene and circumstances, furnished the most favorable subjective and objective conditions for hallucinations: the solitude and silence so favorable to meditation, contemplation, reveries, concentration of the attention on a fixed object of thought, and the rumination of certain fixed ideas, the monotony of the desert, the heat, the fatigue and hunger prepared a very fertile soil for numerous and various hallucinations.   Four hallucinations follow one upon the other in rapid succession.   The first was an hallucination of abstinence and nurture brought on by long fasting and was attended by visual and audative-verbal demonomaniac appearances so frequent in clinical religious paranoia. The second and third hallucinations in the desert were panoramic and "aeroplanic," and not less classical in clinical psychiatry.   The fourth hallucination, the appearance of the angels and the wild beasts, is common to mystics and arose from successive emotional reverses between comfort and fear.   These four hallucinations in the desert constitute a psychic syndrome known as *le ragle*. *Plus que tout autre, Ieschou devait être atteint de ragle au désert* (II 381).

Lc 10,18 is Jesus' sixth hallucination; it is *haute* and luminous in character, and with Jesus seems to have had a *religionsgeschichtlichen* origin based upon the Assyrian legend and the book of Enoch. The last specific hallucination is also reported by Lc alone in 22,43, the appearance of the angel in Gethsemane. To the kinesthetic verbal hallucinations of Jesus Binet-Sanglé reckons the transfiguration and certain Johannine words in which Jesus disclaims his words as his own and ascribes them to the *Father* who speaks directly through him (verbal automatism).

From the point of view of hallucinations the life of Jesus is to be divided into two distinct periods: the first in which the hallucinations are frequent and follow rapidly one upon the other (the first five belong to this period); the second which includes the remainder of Jesus' life, but during which only two specific hallucinations are reported, and by Lc alone (10,18; 22,43).

The hallucinations of Jesus, such as they are reported to us by the evangelists, permit us to conclude that the founder of the Christian religion was a victim of religious paranoia. Such hallucinations aggravate the delirium of the paranoiac, exercise a strong reaction on his spirit, and confirm the unfortunate soul in his errors and delusions. *The hallucination at the Jordan marks the entry of Jesus, son of Joseph, into the ranks of the incurables. Henceforth nothing is able to restrain him in the expression of his delirium, neither the injuries of the priests and the soldiers nor the majesty of the Sanhedrin and the Praetorium, not even the suffering of the cross* (II 394) (1).

### Ses Facultés intellectuelles (III 11-153)

Jesus' faculty of memory was abnormally developed and fits the state designated as hypermnesia. His memory special-

---

(1) Part V of volume II, 385-510, Binet-Sanglé devotes to citing sixty-one instances of megalomania and theomegalomania from the time of Jesus' death down to the present.

ized particularly on rural and mystic objects. On the least occasion passages from the Old Testament were pertinently placed in his addresses and contentions. The normal subject forms most of his associations upon the meaning of words; purely verbal associations are extremely rare. In the case of Jesus these verbal associations are very frequent; he seemed fond of a play on words. (Binet-Sanglé cites seven instances of this type of association: Mt 4,3f; 4,9ff; 16,18; Lc 9,60; √ Mc 1,17; Jn 3,3ff).

Jesus had also acquired the psychopathic habit of ego-echolalia, of which Binet-Sanglé cites fifteen instances (*Verily, verily; Blessed; Ye have heard it said of old; Woe unto you;* etc.) These instances in the form of Jesus' address are of real value from the clinical point of view, for they show that Jesus had entered in upon the third stage of religious paranoia; besides, they resemble closely the characteristic type of address of theomegalomaniacs. Jesus' language is often incoherent; he expresses himself in abrupt sentences without endeavoring to bind them together in thought (Binet-Sanglé finds six such instances). Jesus' thought itself is often incoherent (five instances), and particularly toward the close of his life where his reasoning powers seem to have weakened.

A further sign of intellectual inferiority is Jesus' inclination to allow his thought to revel in a dream world rather than in the real world. He was interested in the real world of men and things only in so far as it furnished him parable and metaphor for the illustration of the facts and processes in his imaginary scheme. *These images turned about his primordial delusion* (III 103). His imaginative creations, the parables, are vague, inconsistent and without color; the person who composed them was neither an observer nor a thinker. This feebleness of Jesus' creative imagination accords, on the one hand, with the simplicity of his hallucinations; on the other hand, with his attitude toward his critics. *A man of vivid imagination, in evoking the suffering that awaited him, would have chosen other words* (III 103) (1). It is very doubtful

---

(1) When Binet-Sanglé finds the parables of Jesus inferior to those of the Indian Scriptures he reminds us of the position of Von Hartmann.

if Jesus composed all the parables found in the Gospels;
those that we can with certainty ascribe to him are the products
of an ignorant and debilitated mind and are uninteresting from
the literary point of view. They simply illustrate his delirium
and are all inspired by his vesanic passion. Most of them fall
within the earlier period of his career and would suggest a decline, or even a loss, of his mnesic and imaginative faculties
during his Jerusalem days. The Fourth Gospel, the biography
of the decline, contains no parables. As weak as it was Jesus'
imagination was his predominant intellectual possession. It
probably explains his taste for retreat to solitude where in the
silence of the night and the mountains he loved to build up his
illusory kingdom, and where in the intimacy of his own consciousness he played the role of king and God and surrendered
himself to the contemplation of his work and self-adoration.

In the words of Jesus there does not exist a single example of correct reasoning. His argumentation is weak and its
method is Talmudic. Its theme and point is his own delirium.
In seven out of nine instances he goes out from false premises;
his discourses contain but three complete syllogisms. His reasoning is by enthymeme in which one proposition of the syllogism is omitted, the usual logic of aliens. The purpose of his
logic is to convince, and not to attain to the truth. As is usual
with paranoiacs, Jesus' mind worked by stops and starts, by
a kind of intellectual spasms or fits. The first instance of this
that has come down to us is the incident of the twelve year old
boy discussing and disputing with the doctors in the temple.
The frequency of these spasms was augmented during his
Jerusalem days. It is during these *accès intellectuels* that
Jesus narrated his parables and preached the kingdom of God
in such terms and manner as filled his hearers with astonishment
and admiration. There is nothing in the Gospels to explain
this popular admiration; it must have been in the emotions that
Jesus manifested in his public address and which do not register themselves with pen on paper. Mt. 6,25-29 is about the
only passage in the Gospels of any literary value or importance. It was less what Jesus said that captivated the multitudes, more the manner in which he said it. *It was the fire of*

*his look, the tension of his features, the arrogance of his atti-
tude and bearing, the vehemence of his manner, the inflections
of his voice, the conviction that emanated from his whole being,
a total eloquence, of which there remains nothing for us because it was purely sentimental and temperamental* (III 150).
From the intellectual point of view Jesus was an inferior mind
and manifested many traits in common with aliens.

### *Ses Sentiments* (III 152-348)

Jesus was an emotional and passionate individual, abnormally temperamental. *We shall see in him, following one upon
the other without cessation, attacks of joy, sadness, fear, love,
anger, eruptions diversely colored and emanating from the same
volcano, from the same furnace, from the same central fire that
had consumed him from youth: admiration, love and passion for
self, inextinguishable pride* (III 167).

The experience of joy was rare for Jesus. The Gospels
record not more than four hedonic experiences: the voice at the
Jordan, the confession at Caesarea Philippi, the remonstrance
of the centurion against Jesus coming under his unworthy roof,
and Jesus acclamation (Lc 10,21ff—Mt 11,25ff). All these
bore directly upon his delirium and added fire to his vesanic
passion. *These egocentric joys show how the psychic life of
the theomegalomaniac was strongly systematized, how its various wheelworks were closely geared. The whole system revolves around the same fixed idea, everything rests upon the
adamant of pride* (III 172).

Jesus did not escape the psychopathic law of temperamental depressions. He was subject to longer and shorter attacks
of melancholy which were often attended by demonomania.
They are regularly scattered throughout his public career beginning with the temptation and ending with the desolate cry
on the cross (Binet-Sanglé cites nine such instances of depression). Jesus' depression and melancholy is pathological in that
it was in no way able to alter his fixed idea.

Fear was a prominent determining factor in the life of
Jesus. It forces him to flee beyond the borders of Galilee, re-

sort to retreats, to travel and work incognito.   Jesus often
confesses his fear; Jn 12,27 is a precious notice for the psy- ✓
chopathologist.   His fears would have caused him to lead an
obscure life, but the aggravation of his vesania would not permit him.   He must materialize his dream; *but it was with extreme prudence that he undertook its realization*  (III 197).
This caution is seen clearly by his commands for silence to those
whom he had cured.   He never confessed his identity even to
the most intimate disciples until the close of his Galilean ministry.   His employment of circumlocutions in referring to himself is a precaution motived by fear.   *Thus, in designating himself as the Son of man, the theomegalomaniac fully satisfied his
own pride and abandoned himself completely to his vesania without risk; he made himself understood to his confidants and left
his adversaries in uncertainty*  (III 205).   The employment of
this singular expression, *Son of man*, which neither Jesus nor
his disciples ever explain and which does not occur in the narrative portions of the Gospels, concords completely with the
observations of clinical psychiatry.   *In fact chronic aliens
often condense in a word, which they forge with the aid of elements borrowed from ordinary language, or in an expression,
the sense of which they pervert, the essential and characteristic
element of their delirium*  (III 206).   Jesus' parables are simply
a veil which he elusively drapes about his identity and intentions.

When questions concerning his identity became too direct
and pointed, he either remained silent or gave an ambiguous
reply.   As is frequent with megalomaniacs, Jesus dissimulated
his delirium, but as he came to lose his sense for the real world
of social relations and his dementia grew this dissimulation was
less indirect.   *What a difference between the imaginative enig-
matic addresses at the beginning of his career and the rash discourses during his last sojourn in Jerusalem*  (III 224f).

Jesus' fear turns his ministry into one eternal hegira, a
series of escapes and flights.   In spite of the peril which lurked
for him in Jerusalem he could not distance himself from it.
The holy city had an invincible fascination for him, but in this
grave period of his vesania with the fading away of his dis-

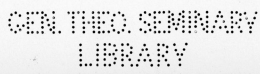

criminative faculties it was to be the beacon-light against which he was to suffer shipwreck.

Jesus' affections were pathological. Two emotions dominated all others, his love for himself (*l'amour propre*) and his love for those who believed in him. His affection for children was equally egocentric in character. He loved the docile, the obliging, and those who showed affection for him. This autophilism is the predominant affection of megalomaniacs, but it is not their only affection. At certain times they are capable of altruism, but this affectivity follows the fluctuations of their delirium. It is in Jesus' occasional manifestations of pity for the oppressed and the social outcasts that we find the thing that has contributed more than anything else to the success of Christianity. But even the most selfish egoist is now and then capable of a touching altruistic word or deed.

Sexually Jesus' affections were inverted, if not perverted. This is characteristic of psychopaths. On the parable of the prodigal son Binet-Sanglé comments, *it seems that Jesus, son of Joseph, conceals within this parable some incident of his sentimental life* (III 287); it tells the story of the flight of a beloved disciple, his repentant return, and the great scandal created by another jealous disciple. It was jealousy, so frequent among homosexuals, that provoked the betrayal of Judas. *Le suicide de l'homme de Kérioth était un suicide par amour* (III 293).

Jesus' admirers loved to portray him as a God of love, but he was possessed with a violent hatred that was anything but sane. *Blinded by his vanity, convinced that the world would be effaced before him, the theomegalomaniac was constantly wounded, offended and humiliated by those with whom he came in contact* (III 300). Jesus' impatience, his rude replies, threats, woes, and violence furnish abundant evidence of the irritated state of his mind. His kindness toward others was limited to the earlier part of his career and made only occasional fitful appearances toward the end of his life. He vented his wrath against innocent objects (the sea and the fig tree), even against his disciples when they were specially dull or would turn him from his perilous path. His rebuke to Peter (Mc 8,33) is *in-*

*comprehensible from a man of sound mind, but this anger is admirably accounted for in a theomegalomaniac* (III 307).   He shared the usual zenophobia of his race and turned to the Gentiles only when such a turn served the ends of his delirium because he had been unsuccessful with his own people.   His hatred was uncompromising toward rival prophets (Mt 7,15ff) and the incredulous for whom, as have paranoiacs of all times, he depicted disaster.   Jesus knew only hatred for the family and its ties; *this perversion of affective sentiment Jesus, son of Joseph, desired to instill in his disciples, all for the satisfaction it would afford his pride,* Lc 14,26 (III 333).   Jesus' animosity against wealth and the wealthy was only a reaction of his pride; the parable of the great supper is only a reflection of his failure to win them and a veil for his rancour.

## Son Procès (III 349-528)

The accounts of Jesus' trial Binet-Sanglé finds of capital importance both from the historical and the psychological point of view.   Historically the Gospel records of Jesus trial are confirmed by the Talmudists in their outlines of Jewish legal procedure.   From the point of view of the alienist the account of Jesus' trial is interesting and instructive, for Jesus' attitude toward his judges is that commonly observed among paranoiacs.   The judges of Jesus committed the judicial error which has become classic in the treatment of such aliens.   At the time of his trial Jesus' personality was completely transformed in accordance with his delirium and he identified himself with the God of the Jews.   His confession of his identity before the Jerusalem authorities definitely consigns Jesus to the dissimulating group of paranoiacs, who under the impulse of a momentary passion divulge their long guarded secret.   Jesus' silence before his judges is nothing other than a paranoiac stupor from which the high priest could evoke him to answer only by adjuration (Mt 26,63).   Pilate was a poor psychologist, for he did not discern the nature of the case before him, unless his words, *Behold the man,* can be understood as his plea for Jesus' life in view of his demented condition.   Jesus' condemnation to death by the Jewish and Roman authorities is the symbol of the lamentable judicial error that civil authority has always been guilty of in its treatment of aliens to whom it has meted out so-called justice. The centurion's confession at the cross (Lc 23,47) can serve as the conclusion to the history of this legal mistake.

## Sa Morale (IV 1-57)

The majority of Jesus' moral precepts were inspired by his vesanic pride (*Sa morale n'est que l'expression de sa vésanie; IV 12*). His deification of his own ego does not deserve the name of morals. The one precept that dominated all others was the duty of admiring him. To secure this, he taught the duty of humility, accord, mendicity, sobriety, continence, and subvention. Other moral precepts were provoked by his hatred for the Jewish and his fear of the Roman authorities. Duties toward the poor, parents, wife, and widow may have rooted in a genuine feeling of pity, but it was not an unselfish pity. Jesus' moral teachings that are worth while are not original with him, for most of them are merely reproductions of earlier Biblical rules of conduct.

What one usually calls the morals of Jesus are only an Asiatic chrestomathy. *The son of the carpenter of Nazareth only chose in keeping with his temperament, character, feelings, pride and the demands of his vesania from among the ethical precepts which were current in his land and time, above all from the Bible whence he drew with full hands* (III 53). Of the sixty-three different precepts which Jesus expressed only eleven are original with him, and ten of these eleven center upon himself. Jesus was not an original moralist; in fact, he was not a moralist at all. He did not possess the true moral sense, for his choice is never determined by observation and reason, but by his delirium which is usual with aliens.

## Son Activité (IV 61-293)

Jesus' public career was vagabond and only one long series of peregrinations. As is frequent with paranoiacs Jesus was taken with ambulomania; this explains best his attitude toward labor, possessions, and the family, all of which require

permanent residence. Jesus entered the ranks of the incurables
when he began his itinerary in Galilee. This regular restlessness was often interrupted by frequent and fitful flights; this
is merely *un accident dans le cours de sa vésanie* (IV 119). His
chronic vagabondage and fits of flight began at twelve years
when he escaped the attention of his parents and was found
again in the temple.

In his reconstruction of Jesus' public career and its chronology Binet-Sanglé finds eight flights and retreats, four propaganda campaigns about the lake of Tiberias, one shift in the
scene of his ministry from Nazareth to Capernaum, two attempts on Galilean cities, and five attempts on Jerusalem. Jesus
was driven by the same spirit, *la Rouah d'Elohim*, which drove
Elijah and Jonah. Summary notices of preaching tours in the
Gospels evince the chronic character of Jesus' ambulatory affliction. The oscillations of his itinerary between Galilee and
Jerusalem were provoked by two emotions, fear and pride. His
Messianic pride drove him to the capital in the south, but his
morbid fear drove him north again to Galilee, *son pis-aller.*
*He is the feather on the wind of his delirium. He is the wreck
on the tide of his insanity. He is the stone that dislodged the
avalanche of his thoughts and passions* (IV 183). This errant
type of life was full of privations and prepared the way for
the pleuritic tuberculosis which caused his precocious death on
the cross.

Among the vesanic acts of Jesus is to be reckoned his
stilling of the storm during which he had fallen into a morbid ✓
sleep. His writing on the ground (Jn 8,8) is a deliriant preoccupation. His aggravated mental state vented itself particularly during the passion week, during which Jesus commits
five vesanic acts: 1) the entry into Jerusalem, *la manifestation
la plus éclatante de sa folie*); 2) the cursing of the fig tree,
(an act *qui est telle qu'il ne s'en trouvera pas une semblable
dans la vie d'aucun homme raisonable*); 3) the cleansing of the
temple, (*de tels acces ne se rencontrent que chez les aliénés*);
4) the washing of the disciples' feet, (*le fétishisme de pied est
le plus commun des fétishismes chez le homosexuels*); 5) the

celebration of the last supper where his words are comprehensible only in view of his delirium.

The *curriculum vitae* of Jesus is identical with that of other theomegalomaniacs; this type of insanity first appears in the form of fantastic thoughts and ideas, later in extravagant words, and finally breaks forth in vesanic acts.

Jesus' language was anomalous in character, as is the case with aliens who usually experience difficulty in expressing themselves. Medically Jesus' type of expression is to be designated as logorrhea (Mc 4,2; 6,34). Jesus' need of expressing his surging thoughts satisfied itself by indulging in monologue, at first apart in private prayer but later in public. His farewell address in the Fourth Gospel is one thematic paralogy: *it is so manifestly deliriant that I have never been able to read it without asking myself whether I am the first alienist to open the Gospels* (IV 244). Jesus' language can further be described as embolophasia and auto-echolalia. He abused the personal pronoun "*I*" and loved auto-designation in the third person. His authorative word is again *one of the characteristics of the psychosis he had attained* (IV 253). Jesus' verbal explosions were provoked by his pride, joy, fear, sadness, and hatred (Binet-Sanglé lists twenty-eight such explosions). Jesus' silence before the Sanhedrin and Pilate was an attack of mutism. His designation of his words as not his own but as those of another is to be described as verbal automatism. The voice at the transfiguration *émanait du larynz de Ieschou bar-Iossef* (IV 266). *In reality the language of Jesus, son of Joseph, is identically that of theomegalomaniacs in our present-day asylums* (IV 239).

Jesus presents anomalies of sleep. Insomnia is habitual with neuropaths and is one of the first symptoms of insanity. That Jesus was afflicted with insomnia is clear from the frequent retreats at night for prayer. His sleep during the storm which he stilled is paroxysmal and morbid.

### Diagnostic de sa Folie (IV 295-461)

In his diagnosis of the insanity of Jesus Binet-Sanglé proceeds as follows: Jesus was a Jew (the race particularly predisposed to insanity), a bachelor, a degenerate, an alien, a paranoiac, a megalomaniac, a theomegalomaniac, an hysterico-theomegalomaniac (religious paranoia).

Binet-Sanglé concludes his work with the remark: *I have reached the end of the task which I set for myself and I believe that I can say that for alienists, medical men, for all learned and sincere persons, the insanity of the founder of the Christian religion is a demonstrated truth* (IV 462).

Binet-Sanglé's work is the most extensive and thorough-going pathography of Jesus that has appeared, four volumes with a total of 1914 pages. Its very voluminousness speaks against it. Among the pathographers of Jesus none finds Jesus so thoroughly demented as Binet-Sanglé. Hardly an incident or word in the Gospels does he leave unturned toward the support of his contention. No pathographer of Jesus is more uncritical and indiscriminate in his use of the sources. The Fourth Gospel is his fortress. One would judge from the character of his conclusions that he had never read a standard critical work on the Gospels.

His work is written from the purely medical and technically psychological point of view, and is chiefly interesting because of his electro-chemical theory of psychic phenomena. He explains psychic pathology by 1) *phénomènes de circuit interrompu* and 2) *phénomènes de court-circuit* (III 1ff). Binet-Sanglé sometimes seems more interested in the airing of his psychological theories than in the subject under treatment. His work is full of its *selon moi*. His collection of historical and clinical cases of mental alienation of various types is interesting for comparative psychopathology, but medically of no special value.

For the student of the life of Jesus Binet-Sanglé's four volumes are practically worthless.

### 4)   Jesus—A Case of Nerves
#### Julius Baumann

Baumann, Professor of Philosophy at the University of Goettingen, in his book, *Die Gemuetsart Jesu: nach jetziger wissenschaftlicher, insbesondere jetziger psychologischer*

*Methode erkennbar gemacht* (Leipzig, 1908, 80 S.), deals only incidentally with the question of Jesus' psychic health. He chooses as his historico-critical guide the New Testament work of Wellhausen, Bischoff and Dalman; his psychanalytic position he bases on Werner's *Der religioese Wahnsinn* (1890). Baumann is far from analysing the mentality and mind of Jesus as a case of religious paranoia. Ascetic habits of life, insomnia, and frequent or protracted fasting, usual in religious paranoia, have no counterpart in the life of Jesus. But Baumann does find two of the stigmata of this disease in Jesus' personality, namely, *the concentration of mind on certain ideas and the thereby aggravated imagination* (Werner). The family of Jesus regarded him as beside himself; that is what we would term inflicted with religious paranoia. *We could content ourselves with excessive nervousness* (Nervenueberreizung) (S. 7).

The fixed ideas, upon which Jesus came to concentrate his thought so completely, were furnished to him in the person and preaching of the Baptist. Jesus' strongly stimulated fancy accounts for his hallucinations of sight and hearing at the Jordan and his hallucinations and illusions in the desert. His Messianic consciousness was suddenly suggested to him at his baptism. This consciousness was reinforced by the demoniacs who recognized and proclaimed him as the very one he believed himself to be. It is to be understood only *in the light of excessive nervousness* (S. 40).

The excited state of mind, in which he found himself after the experience at the Jordan, drove him into the desert for prayer. From this retreat to solitude we may conclude that Jesus was easily fatigued and exhausted. This fact is further confirmed by Jesus being too weak to carry his own cross and his surprisingly sudden death on the cross which was unusual in cases of this manner of execution. Even his withdrawal with his apostles upon their return from their mission *into a desert place to rest for a while* (Mc 6,31) shows that Jesus presupposed, *that the apostolic vocation (just as his own) was fatiguing* (S. 16). In II Cor 12,10 Paul manifests an emotional make-up similar to that of Jesus.

The transfiguration is a group-vision in which all four present participate. The cursing of the fig tree was the work of an ill-humor (*Unmutswunder*), which expressed itself independent of moral considerations, *even the considerations of good sense* (S. 28). Moreover, Jesus' conduct and words during his Jerusalem days are marked by a climax in the excessive nervous overtension in which he found himself. His word concerning mountain-moving faith is an expression of his fitful nervousness. In his eschatological address (Mc 13,3-37) Jesus manifests that greater or less degree of nervous excitement so frequent in the history of religion and in cases of religious paranoia. The willing spirit in Mc 14,38 is the same *Nervenueberreizung*.

Jesus was a poetic nature fond of rural surroundings as is clear from his parables. He possessed a romantic and one-sided optimism. He saw only the blessing of the rain and sunshine; he did not think of the floods and droughts. He saw the hand of God in the life of the bird that must neither sow, nor reap, nor gather into barns without thinking of the millions that perish each season. He saw the flowers that must neither toil nor spin, yet surpassed any acquired glory, without thinking of their struggle for existence and their being at the mercy of their environment. *The concluding of facts from sentiments of a desirable nature is the work of imagination through and through.* But it is just this that constitutes the charm of Jesus' character: *He was a disposition that would help all, bodily and spiritually, and that with its demands holds itself to the practically important phases of morality (10 commandments) and besides inspires men with a great hope (the imminent kingdom of God), to which it itself gives demonstration to a certain extent, and at the same time gathers about itself simple but heroic souls, i. e., men whom, like himself, suffering imbues all the more with lofty sentiments and expectations* (S. 47).

Thus Baumann accounts for Jesus' self-consciousness, conduct, character, and teaching by the state of nervous excitement in which he so often found himself.

For Baumann there is much in Jesus' temperament and

thought which must be rejected under the test of modern and strictly scientific methods of psychanalysis. His personal return prophesied for his own generation has never fulfilled itself. He ascribed a power to prayer which it does not possess. His miracles are to be rejected in so far as they have no parallels accomplished by modern medicine without the aid of religion. Critical and empirical science cannot accept his resurrection. Jesus was over-tolerant with too much of the world and preferred suffering instead of labor as the way of progress. He had not the slightest idea of science and his knowledge was restricted to the few erroneous conceptions of his times.

From the modern point of view Jesus is problematic in his ethics and eschatology. His conception of and attitude toward life was morally practical and eschatological. His ethics were probationary and provisional (*Interimsethik oder -moral*), analogous to the special measures enacted in a besieged city. A test of his character and temperament according to present-day scientific methods makes it impossible that we respond to his summons, *Repent ye, and believe the gospel.* It is just this first message of Jesus that betrays *an inclination toward an excessive nervousness that breaks forth perhaps suddenly* (S. 56). Pronounced piety is often characterized by an overtense nervous excitement in which it seats (Mohammed, Luther, Swedenborg). As Peschel says, *Certain ideas that are common throughout the world are the consequence of a natural intellectual weakness, of an untamed and still unbridled imagination similar to that to be observed in the undeveloped child* (Quoted by Bauman, S. 57).

Baumann concludes his pamphlet to the effect that, although Jesus has much to say to us today, his *Gemuetsart* prevents him from becoming an infallible guide in matters of religion for the modern man. A freer path must be cleared for a more human and yet a more serious conception of religion. Knowledge must displace faith. The modern man must be a moral Christian and a friend of science. As such his religion will bear the sharpest criticisms of thought and yet prove itself in life.

It is interesting to note just here that among the pathographers of Jesus, Rasmussen, de Loosten, Hirsch and Binet-
Sanglé, not one knows or refers to the work of any of the
others. Each looks upon himself as doing pioneer work in this
particular field. It is quite understandable that Rasmussen and
de Loosten should not know each other, for their works appeared close together; both appeared in German in 1905. But
it is surprising that neither Hirsch nor Binet-Sanglé know of
their works, nor of the work of each other.

## 5)   Jesus in Fiction

In recent times fiction writers, particularly in Germany,
Denmark and Sweden, have taken a distinct pathographic turn
and seem specially fond of presenting psychopathic characters which often constitute psychopathic parallels to the career,
character, and personality of Jesus. This is clear in Rasmussen's character *Fausto* in his four act passion play, *Der Zweite
Heiland* (1906); in Gerhart Hauptmann's character *Emanuel
Quint* in his novel, *Der Narr in Christo* (1910); and in Bengt
Berg's character *Virole Skind* in his novel, *Genezareth* (1912)
(1). These three writers of fiction make it clear that Dr.
H. Schaefer is fully justified in speaking of *the psychiatry of
fiction writers*.

Two writers of fiction in particular, Gustav Frenssen and
Rudolf von Delius, have undertaken character studies of Jesus
which are specially interesting in our present survey.

Gustav Frenssen in his *Das Leben des Heilands* (Berlin,
1907, 109 S.; a separately published extract from his novel
*Hilligenlei*) writes of Jesus, *He lived as all his people and time
in a charmed world. For him the angels of God descended his
whole life long. He saw Satan fallen as lightning* (S. 15). The
experience at the Jordan was *a moment of being beside himself,
a rapturous ecstasy* (S. 24). There was often the danger
that Jesus would betray his heavenly Father, and that he must
return to his native village as a simple hand-worker, but as a

---

(1)   For the presentation of psychopathic parallels to Jesus in recent
fiction see Leipoldt's *Vom Jesusbilde der Gegenwart,* S. 177ff.

man whose soul would be torn, tormented and laid waste by pangs of conscience. But with Peter's confession at Caesarea Philippi and his premonition of the parousia his soul was exalted to the very heights of heaven and expanded until it compassed within itself the whole of humanity. *His soul spun monstrous thoughts and painted pictures of extravagant splendor. His soul mounted to the very limits of the finite, even to the verge of a sublime insanity* (S. 57). *He was the noblest of the children of men* (S. 84), *but he was mistaken, particularly in his fine and fervent childish faith* (S. 101).

Particularly psychological in its pretentions is the little book by Rudolph von Delius, *Jesus: sein Kampf, seine Persoenlichkeit, und seine Legende* (Muenchen 1909, 182 S.) Von Delius gives a prominent place to ecstasy in the experience of Jesus. At the transfiguration Jesus is again *profoundly one with the Father, caught away in ecstasy* (S. 66). At the cleansing of the temple *a sudden rage seizes him* (S. 78). In tracing the various features in Jesus' personality von Delius writes, Jesus was *a fighting heroic person, a master of debate, a ruthless extreme paradoxical spirit, a heart brimming over with its thirst for love. He was a terrible demolisher and yet a mighty lover. Still his hate never found a worthy foe, nor his heart a worthy friend. He perished before the callousness of the commonplace, the spiritlessness of the sluggish masses. (The eternal indolence of the human soul killed him)* (S. 107).

In Jerusalem *the shrewd general in him saw the battle lost. Then his fanatic-ego hurled itself desperately into the bright glow of a fantastic hope* (S. 108). *His temper flared up quickly, but his fine mind promptly subdued it again* (S. 109). *He must retreat to the loneliness of solitude again and again to wrestle down released powers of soul. . . . . . Sexual ferment resolved itself into passion of heart and ardor of soul. He required all his strength for his struggle. He was a fighter through and through; the very giftedness of his intelligence was combative. His mind possessed a ghastly fleetness of thought, a fearfully keen penetration of every other mind, a splendid accuracy in singling out the essential. In a few minutes in the midst of a contention he found words that bear the golden stamp of eternity* (S. 110). Jesus was master of his own ground, ethics, but weak in metaphysical debate. He often without doubt regretted what he had said in harsh haste. *We see in Jesus the contrasting states of soul of every called man*: *complete confidence alongside most dejected depression* (S. 116).

Jesus' impatience with the dullness of his disciples on various occasions *zeigt ihn fast nervoes-ueberreizt* (S. 123). Jesus' soul was rich in vision (the temptation, the baptism, Lc 10,18; Mt 18,10), but *pathological states never had decisive influence on him* (S. 120).

### 6) The Defense of Jesus' Psychic Health

The attack against the psychic health of Jesus has called forth none of the commotion that followed upon the lives of Jesus by Strauss and Renan, or that attended the historicity debate. (For the long list of literature called forth by Strauss' *Leben Jesu* see A. Schweitzer, GdLJF, S. 643ff; by Renan's *La Vie de Jésus*, S. 647ff; in the historicity debate, S. 498ff). The imminent conflict which Naumann foretold in 1906 did not come. Only four (to the writer's knowledge) separately printed replies, all pamphlets, have appeared in defense of the psychic health of Jesus. Otherwise all discussion of the question has been confined to brief replies, reviews, and mention in theological works of an historical character and various religious, psychological and medical periodicals. This all goes to ✓ show that not only the Christian world, but even its theologians have not taken the question at all seriously. In fact, the number of believing Christians who know that the psychic health of Jesus has ever been questioned at all is to be reckoned within the few thousands.

We begin with the separately printed replies. These have come from theological, both Catholic and Protestant, and medical circles.

Hermann Werner, Pastor Emeritus, in his pamphlet, *Die psychische Gesundheit Jesu* (*Biblische Zeit- und Streitfragen*, *IV. Serie*, 12. *Heft*, 1908, 64 S.), undertakes to meet de Loosten and Rasmussen on their own ground. He is well qualified for this in view of his extended experience with cases of mental alienation and his observations during his years as Pastor at the Hospital for the Insane in Andernach on the Rhine.

On the basis of the New Testament sources and general psychiatric principles he refutes de Loosten's claim that Jesus suffered under some hereditary burden and was infected by his milieu. Against de Loosten's position as a whole, Werner writes that it is not psychiatrically permissible to speak of a partial dementia, for once a mind is affected in one phase of its activity, say the emotions, it soon brings about a derangement or collapse of the other faculties, say the intellectual abilities, which de Loosten maintains remained unimpaired in the case of Jesus.

Against the diagnosis of epilepsy, Werner points out that Rasmussen bases his diagnosis on purely psychic symptoms, which is poor psychiatry. The Gospels furnish positively no instances of the classic epileptic attack, either in the form of *petit* or *grand mal*, in the case of Jesus. There is, further, no trace of a decline in Jesus' intellectual abilities which, almost without exception, overtakes epileptic victims.

In reply to the question, *Was Jesus Insane?*, Werner writes, *One will never be able to demonstrate with tenable reasons that Jesus was an alien* (S. 21).

Against O. Holtzmann and Bousset, Werner urges that nowhere in the canonical accounts of Jesus do the characteristic marks of ecstasy appear. Repeated lapses into states of ecstasy would have broken down the equilibrium of Jesus' personality. Werner does admit manifestations in Jesus of, what he calls, *uneigentliche Ekstase*, which in no sense is pathological, but merely the concentration of thought to its highest degree and power; such ecstasy would only be natural to Jesus with his extraordinary God-consciousness (1).

In reply to the question, *Was Jesus a fanatic?*, Werner finds that Jesus' sense for the real world of men and things, his sobriety and prudence, the natural, moral and religious restrictions which he set upon himself, his tolerance and patience,

---

(1) Weber remarks that Werner's distinction between a *major* and a *minor* ecstasy is artificial (Sp. 234).

the privations and hardships which he promised his followers, his inwardization, moralization and deepening of social and personal ethics, are all the exact opposite of what is naturally expected of a fanatic; *even in general Jesus nowhere leaves the impression of a fanatic* (S. 45). However, Werner feels that Jesus can be saved from fanaticism only by the elimination of eschatology from his thought and teachings, and allowing it at best to serve only as a dim background scarcely discernible behind him.

Was Jesus abnormal? Werner sees in Jesus, judged absolutely, the only really normal person that ever lived. But judged by our usual standards of normality, Jesus is neither normal, abnormal, nor subnormal, but supernormal. At this point, Weber says, the psychiatrist cannot follow Werner, but he does concede that according to the Gospel picture Jesus is *the most perfect representative of the human species* (Sp. 234).

Werner undertakes to demonstrate the positive proof of Jesus' psychic health by the harmonious functioning of his intellectual, emotional, and volitional powers. *Indeed this soul life presents an incomparable example of the complete harmony of all psychic powers...... To him, the one without sin, we are compelled to extend the palm in matters of psychic soundness* (S. 64).

From the psychiatric point of view Werner's defense of the psychic health of Jesus is well to the point. Historically, however, in spite of all the fine and forceful appreciations which he knows so well how to express of Jesus' personality and work, his pamphlet is unsatisfactory. For the problem of Jesus' self-consciousness he has only a supernaturalistic solution. He entirely ignores the egocentric words of Jesus, which are psychiatrically the most problematic element in the Gospels. He meets the question of eschatology only by rejecting it. On the whole he tries to solve historical and critical problems by apologetics and homiletics.

The pamphlet, *Moderne Leben-Jesu-Forschung unter dem Einflusse der Psychiatrie: eine kritische Darstellung fuer Gebildete aller Staende (Mainz, 1908, 76 S.)*, by Dr. Philipp Kneib, Professor of Apologetics at the University of Wuerzburg, is written from the Catholic and purely apologetic view-point. It is directed against the modern *Willensrichtung* which makes the questioning of Jesus' psychic health possible. He laments, *How many false judgments the exalted person of the savior of the world must suffer patiently even during his earthly life, and still more in the course of history!* (S. 5).

Kneib proceeds against particular points in the positions of de Loosten, Rasmussen, Baumann, and Holtzmann. In a characteristic apologetic way, he points out that what is a symptom of one mental malady for one is a symptom of some other psychic disease for the other. He devotes seventeen pages to the metaphysical possibility of miracle in general, the historical necessity of miracle in the career of Jesus in partic-ular, and the historicity of Jesus' miracles *in toto*. The rais-ing of Jairus' daughter must be a real raising from the dead, otherwise the physician Luke would not have reported it. The cursing of the fig tree should not be taken with such tragic seriousness, *for the "defenseless" tree felt nothing* (S. 50).

Eschatology is to be explained by the symbolic and figur-ative character of Oriental thought and language. The par-ousia came in the form of the descent of the Holy Spirit and the destruction of Jerusalem in definite fulfillment of Mt 10,23. In all of the 76 pages Kneib cites less than a score of verses from the Gospels in support of his position; such is the extent of his historical criticism.

It suffices to say that Kneib's pamphlet in no way con-stitutes a contribution to the solution of the problem of the psychic health of Jesus. A. Schweitzer passes over Kneib's work with the sole remark, *Kneib must be left out of considera-tion entirely* (GdLJF, S. 365).

Dr. H. Schaefer, Head-Physician at the Friedrichsberg Hospital for the Insane in Hamburg, directs his little book, *Jesus in psychiatrischer Beleuchtung. Eine Kontroverse* (Ber-lin, 1908, 178 S.), against de Loosten. Baumann and Holtz-mann, he says, cannot come into consideration, for their respec-tive diagnoses of *Nervenueberreizung* and ecstasy are too inde-finite designations to furnish a starting point for scientific refu-tation. Rasmussen deals with epilepsy in such an amateur way that the psychiatrist cannot follow him in his conclusions. Therefore, Schaefer devotes only a few pages in his introduction to Rasmussen, his chief criticism being that the morbid prophetic type, of which Rasmussen makes so much, is not found in epilepsy but in cases of religious paranoia.

Schaefer finds that, in the case of Jesus, the psychiatrist must obligate himself to the most careful scientific conscientiousness. He proposes to go directly to the sources themselves and investigate the ancestry and childhood of Jesus, his baptism, miracles, alleged lack of natural human feelings, particularly in regard to the family, his morbid emotions and hallucinations, the judgment of his contemporaries, his consciousness as the Son of God and the Messiah, and his work as a reformer.

Schaefer finds no basis in the sources for the assumption of an hereditary burden. There is no evidence, which psychiatry could accept, of the Baptist's paranoia. At twelve years Jesus manifests the first signs of his future greatness as have many other great personages at a much earlier and more unnatural age. Jesus' miracles are to be explained by suggestion, auto-suggestion, group- and mass-suggestion (the miracle at Cana and the feedings). The demoniacs were hysterics, Jairus' daughter a case of catalepsy, and Lazarus a premature burial. *Jesus was a fascinating therapeutist who cured by suggestion, thoroughly optima fide* (S. 68).

A defect in the affections for one's own family, Schaefer says, the psychiatrist regards as a sign of degeneration, but by this he means something entirely different from anything that Jesus manifested. Pendulum-like swings of the emotions from one extreme to the other are normal as long as there exists a stimulation sufficiently strong to explain their intensity; we find no unoccasioned emotional eruptions in the case of Jesus. It is rather an unbroken and uninterrupted emotional monotony that is to be regarded as morbid. Regarding any reference to illusions or hallucinations of Jesus, Schaefer reminds his readers that both pathological in themselves, can and do appear isolated and occasionally with persons of unquestionable mental soundness and are not *per se* manifestations of mental morbidness.  On the temptation he remarks that a psychopath, who had withheld himself from food for forty days during which he had undergone a psychosis, would hardly have emerged alive, to say nothing of entering upon a public career soon after.

The harsh judgment of Jesus' contemporaries against him is, for the most part, to be understood as slander and insult which was inspired by hatred and hostility.  Mc 3,21 is only an expression of the care and concern for Jesus' safety on the part of his friends and family, even perhaps a ruse to rescue him from a feared fate.

The content of Jesus' teaching, the product of his own psychic activity, is a good criterion of his mental health; for this clinical psychiatry can furnish no parallels.  His conception of man and his mission is the highest accomplishment of human intelligence.  As a reformer and genius, who created a religion of greater moral power, Jesus is without paranoiac or other parallels.

A point of particular strength in Schaefer's work is that he sees in the problem of Jesus' self-consciousness the crux of the whole question of his psychic health.  On this point he furnishes some interesting and instructive clinical contrasts of paranoiac self-consciousness which clear Jesus of all symptoms of psychic degeneracy in this respect.  Historically he leaves the problem of Jesus' self-consciousness untouched.

Schaefer's book is a specially valuable psychiatric contribution to the problem of the psychic health of Jesus because of the light which he throws on it by the comparative psychopathic materials (As Dr. Weber remarks, some of these materials are too anecdotal to be valuable) he assembles and his observations on morbid psychology.  Though he strikes out the right path by turning to the investigation of the sources, his chief weakness is historico-critical.  He is not well oriented in the results of historical criticism.  All Jesus' miracles have a natural explanation.  The dove at the baptism was a real dove that fluttered for a moment about the head of Jesus and gave rise to the illusion.  The voice was an hallucination on an apperceptive basis of Jesus' previous mental preoccupation, or he might have faintly overheard a whisper of some one present. Schaefer interprets Jesus' words regarding the parousia, his role in the final judgment of human fate, and the resurrection as symbolic and figurative; the kingdom of God was a purely abstract notion in the thought of Jesus.

Albert Schweitzer's pamphlet, *Die psychiatrische Beurteilung Jesu. Darstellung und Kritik* (*Tuebingen*, 1913, 46 S.), is his dissertation for the Doctorate of Medicine which he published in keeping with his promise in his *Geschichte der Leben-Jesu-Forschung* (S. 367, Anm. 1) in defense of the psychic health of the Jesus of eschatology as attacked by H. J. Holtzmann, Werner, Theobald Ziegler, Juelicher, and Wellhausen. Holtzmann finds that in reading Schweitzer's purely eschatological interpretation of Jesus' self-consciousness that he cannot forget the words *idée fixe* (MBJ, S. 80). Ziegler writes, *Those who are acquainted with Schweitzer's eschatological picture of Jesus will have to concede that Strauss was right when he said that such is not the thought world of a healthy, but of a pathological, alienated mind* (II 609). Werner, in his pamphlet already reviewed, says that Schweitzer's Jesus *is so consistently controlled in all his acts, teaching and suffering by eschatological expectations that there is nothing left to do but assign him a place in the ranks of the psychopaths* (PGJ, S. 13). In 1911 he again writes, *the Danielic-apocalyptic Messianic consciousness of the historical Jesus of liberal theology was by no means as harmless as one thought, and is thoroughly incompatible with psychic soundness* (NKZ, S. 369). Concerning the parousia Wellhausen writes, *According to the opinion of not a few even orthodox theologians Jesus himself is said to have been the fanatic who emphatically held out the prospect of his parousia...... Recently Albert Schweitzer has followed in the footsteps of Strauss, although the fanaticism of Jesus does not repel him as it did the latter, but attracts* (Einl. S. 150f). Juelicher sees in Jesus' self-consciousness as interpreted by Schweitzer only *an insane conceit which no eschatological enthusiasm excuses* (Quoted by H. J. Holtzmann, MBJ., S. 81). It is in the light of these criticisms that the polemic character of Schweitzer's pamphlet is to be understood.

Schweitzer finds that pathography has recently fallen into serious discredit because its methods, which in the hands of specialists and with proper restrictions can render valuable service, have been applied by amateurs with insufficient psychiatric experience and with little knowledge of the sources they undertake to investigate. The one who undertakes to investigate the case of Jesus must be able to pass both expert historical and psychiatric judgment; this he believes that he is able to do since he has studied both theology and medicine (Schweitzer has his doctorate in both philosophy and medicine; he was for a time Professor of Theology in Strassburg in Alsace).

It is against the pathographic literature that Schweitzer proceeds: de Loosten, Hirsch, and Binet-Sanglé (Schweitzer is the first to take up a refutation of Binet-Sanglé). He merely mentions O. Holtzmann and Baumann; to Rasmussen he devotes two pages at the close of his pamphlet and finds that the comparative study by Rasmussen is medically worthless. These three fall naturally into the same group because of their common diagnosis of paranoia. Further, Schweitzer must refute them in particular, for the chief psychiatric charge against the Jesus of eschatology must be paranoia.

Schweitzer regards Mt and Mc as the only reliable sources, but even they contain here and there later misunderstandings and disfigurations, and report the public career of Jesus as at most a year in length.

Jesus' message from the first to the last was, *the kingdom of God is at hand.* This kingdom is Messianic; it is a supernatural order which in the near future is to displace the present order by cosmic catastrophe. In Jesus' thought is completed, for the first time, the identification of the Messiah and the Son of man.

This supernatural dignity Jesus does not possess on earth, it is reserved for him at the parousia; Jesus' own conviction of his identity does not figure in his message, but is a secret which he carefully guards. For the general public he is only and always the prophet of Nazareth.  At the transfiguration three of his disciples learn his secret which Peter betrays to the twelve at Caesarea Philippi and Judas to the authorities in Jerusalem.  But Judas was the sole witness, and Jesus could be condemned to death only by the testimony of a second witness, which came in the form of his own confession during his trial. Jesus could have saved himself by silence, but it was his set purpose to die and thus force the kingdom of God to appear.

Jesus' determination upon his death arose out of the course of the events themselves.  Jesus did not spend the entire period between his first public appearance and his death in public activity.  He expected the appearance of the parousia before the disciples returned from their mission (Mt 10,23).  In this Jesus was disappointed, for the disciples returned and he resorted to the north with them where he seeks to remain incognito during the fall and winter.  Here he comes to the conclusion that the parousia will be indefinitely delayed unless he suffers and dies.  This thought was suggested to him by the death of the Baptist which had intervened and in whom he sees the promised Elias.  He, therefore, proceeds to Jerusalem in order to compel the parousia by his death on the cross.

A chief point of strength in Schweitzer's critical contribution to the solution of the problem of Jesus' psychic health is his rejection of the Fourth Gospel as a reliable historical source concerning Jesus and which makes the pathographic position possible.  He further points out that the later Judaic apocalyptic world-view explains Jesus' striking picture of the future; of this the pathographers take no consideration.

From the psychiatric point of view, Schweitzer calls attention to the fact that a diagnosis of a *Wahnidee* depends much more upon the rise and development, the manner and way in which it expresses itself, than upon the content of the idea itself.  The sources furnish us no materials for tracing the rise and development of a psychosis in the case of Jesus; this is difficult enough in a living subject where repeated and extended observation is possible.  If Jesus had been an ordinary paranoiac, he would have hardly been able to win and retain disciples.  That Jesus could not have had repeated hallucinations is seen from the fact that paranoiac subjects are usually rendered incapable of subsequent occupation and their acts seldom correspond to the contents of their *Wahnidee*. Paranoiacs seldom draw practical conclusions from their illusions or *Wahnideen*. Jesus' self-consciousness of being the Son of God is not clinical in character, but is the same as that which the old Jewish kings claimed for themselves and the people ascribed to them as God's representatives. Schweitzer regards Jesus as actually of Davidic descent. Insight into the career of Jesus delivers him from the alleged delusions of persecution. There is no transformation in Jesus' *delusion* that is not objectively motived and logically consequent. Jesus showed himself influenceable in a way and to a degree that forms a direct contrast to the paranoiac. He further lacks the unmotived and mistaken antagonistic aggressiveness of the active paranoiac type, and the restricted resistance or resistlessness of the more passive type.

In conclusion Schweitzer sums up the weaknesses of the pathographic position of de Loosten, Hirsch, and Binet-Sanglé: they employ, for the most part, unhistorical material; they have no historical appreciation of the thought of Jesus' times and people and no insight into the problems of Jesus' public career; from these false presuppositions and with the aid of highly hypothetic symptoms they manufacture a diagnosis that is by no means psychiatrically faultless. The only possible historical material for an eventual pathographic study is Jesus' high estimate of himself and the hallucinations at the baptism, which are insufficient for the confirmation of a mental malady.

In spite of its brevity and exclusively eschatological emphasis Schweitzer's reply is the best, for he leaves the contention where it belongs, on historico-critical ground. However, his eschatological exposition of the cursing of the fig tree is as unsatisfactory as any of the pathographic interpretations of it.

The problem of Jesus' psychic health has found brief mention and review in works which aim at an historical presentation of the various estimates, past and present, of Jesus' work, person, and character.

Johannes Leipoldt, Professor of Theology in Kiel, in his work, *Vom Jesusbilde der Gegenwart* (*Leipzig* 1913, 445S.), devotes chapter three to *Die Aerzte* (S. 141-204) (1). He knows O. Holtzmann's book which, he says, presents little material that is valuable from the medical point of view. He finds that every person is an ecstatic in the sense of Holtzmann's use of the word *ecstasy*. He regards Holtzmann's understanding and interpretation of Jesus as an ecstatic in the pathological and morbid sense. The effect of the ecstatic element in Jesus upon his whole personality, that of calming down rather than stimulating, which Holtzmann constitutes, is so unnatural and unusual that the medical expert would not call it ecstasy at all. Leipoldt reviews briefly the works of Rasmussen, de Loosten, and Baumann; he knows only the first two volumes of Binet-Sanglé. Specially interesting is Leipoldt's review of the recent presentations in fiction of characters created as psychopathic parallels to Jesus (see above p. 111ff). Among the refutations Leipoldt knows Kneib, Werner, and Schaefer.

Hermann Jordan, Professor at the University of Erlangen, in his little book, *Jesus und die modernen Jesusbilder* (*Biblische Zeit- und Streitfragen, V. Serie, 5/6. Heft*, 1909), devotes pages 42-55 to *Der kranke Jesus* (*The Morbid Jesus*). He mentions only Rasmussen and de Loosten, and their opponents, Werner and Kneib, also F. Moerchen and J. Naumann. Jordan remarks very pertinently that the question of the psychic health of Jesus is chiefly historical and critical, and that the sources furnish no adequate basis for a pathological study of Jesus, for in them cannot be traced any psychological developments or changes from one phase to another. He finds nothing morbid in the impression which Jesus made upon his contemporaries, in the reported visions which are, for the most

(1) The writer is indebted to Professor Eduard Riggenbach of Basel University for calling his attention to this interesting chapter and for the gift of a copy of this work from his private library.

part, literary creations, nor in Jesus' exalted self-consciousness *eo ipso*.

H. Weinel in his *Jesus im 19ten Jahrhundert* mentions Rasmussen and the psychiatric problem in only one brief paragraph (S. 283).

G. Pfannmueller in his *Jesus im Urteil der Jahrhunderte* merely mentions O. Holtzmann and de Loosten, and devotes a brief section to Rasmussen (S. 408f).

A. Schweitzer in his *Geschichte der Leben-Jesu-Forschung* devotes pages 362-367 to the psychiatric studies of Jesus; here he mentions Rasmussen, de Loosten, Binet-Sanglé, and Baumann with their opponents Werner, Kneib, and Schaefer.

G. Stanley Hall in his two volume work, *Jesus the Christ in the Light of Psychology*, devotes pages 157-172 of the first volume to the psychiatric problem. He briefly reviews the works of Rasmussen, de Loosten, Holtzmann, Hirsch, and Binet-Sanglé (only the first volume); among the replies, Werner and Schaefer.

Mention has already been made of Loofs' review of the psychiatric problem in his book, *Wer War Jesus Christus?* (See above p. 39ff).

The problem of Jesus' psychic health has naturally found its way into religious periodicals in the form of reviews and criticisms of the works of Rasmussen and de Loosten who are the most generally known.

F. Niebergall of Heidelberg reviews Rasmussen's book in the *Zeitschrift fuer Religionspsychologie* (*Band I., Heft 5.*, 1907, S. 223-226) with the remark that confessed Christians have little to fear and psychiatrists have much less to learn from it than is commonly supposed.

G. Hollmann in the *Theologische Rundschau* (*9. Jahrgang, Heft 7, Juli* 1906, S. 270-275) reviews briefly the works of Rasmussen and de Loosten. (See his conclusion above p. 40f).

H. Windisch, in the same periodical (*17. Jahrgang, Heft 12.*, 1913, S. 439-441), reviews Schweitzer's dissertation and finds it pertinent at points but not thorough enough.

Mention has already been made of Werner's article in the *Neue Kirchliche Zeitschrift* (see above p. 42f).

J. Naumann, in discussing the books of Rasmussen and de Loosten comforts the readers of the *Christliche Welt* (No. 12, Maerz 22., 1906, Sp. 266-271) with the remark, *Vagaries are a part of the progress of science.* Against Rasmussen he alleges a false and superficial method born of textbooks on psychiatry rather than of concrete clinical observations; he has gone through the psychiatric problem as an enslaved rather than as a free man. His chief criticism of de Loosten is his indiscriminate use of sources. At the close of his article he again consoles his readers to the effect that Jesus has stood in judgment, not only before the High Priest and Pilate, but before the courts of philosophers, statesmen, historians, and scientists, and he will again return victorious from before the seat of the psychiatrist.

Dr. Fr. Moerchen's article, *Zur psychiatrischen Betrachtung des ueberlieferten Christusbildes* (*Monatsschrift fuer die kirchliche Praxis, Oktober* 1906, 10 *Heft,* S. 422-26), is written from the medical point of view. Dr. Moerchen emphasizes the difficulties in the way of a psychiatric diagnosis of the mind of Jesus. The sources he finds inadequate for a definite diagnosis; such materials as they do contain can lead modern medical science to no definite results. *A scientific expert judgment of the psychic status of Jesus is so impeded that the attempt to establish a definite diagnosis must from the very start be designated as hopeless* (S. 424). He does say, however, that the striking self-consciousness of Jesus furnishes a real subject for psychiatric discussion. This feature of Jesus' personality he designates as *abnormal,* but hesitates to describe as *pathological.*

The best periodical review and criticism in the psychiatric discussion is that of the works of Werner and Schaefer by Dr. William Weber in the *Theologische Literaturzeitung,* 1911, Nr. 8, Sp. 232-36.

Karl Beth's article, *Jesus in psychiatrischer Beleuchtung,* in the bimonthly *Maerz* (4,18; 16. Sept. 1910, S. 459-467) and

E. K. Zelenka's article with the identical title in the *Deutscher Merkur* (42,24) were not accessible to the writer.

---

In conclusion we may say that the replies and refutations of the works of Jesus' pathographers have been either too apologetic or too academic in their interests and intentions to be adequate. None has undertaken a serious and systematic sifting of the sources. Binet-Sanglé has received practically no attention and he, more than all others, pronounces Jesus insane in every word and act that is ascribed to him in the written sources that have come down to us.

We turn, therefore, to a systematic sifting of the sources in quest and investigation of the materials that have been exploited in support of the pathographic contention against Jesus.

# CHAPTER IV

### The Sources from the Pathographic Point of View

The literary sources of our knowledge concerning Jesus, the only sources that we possess, are not all that could be wished for. In the first place, we have nothing from Jesus' own hand. So far as we know, Jesus wrote only upon one occasion and that was on the ground (Jn 8,6). If we possessed something from Jesus' own hand, as we do in the case of Paul whose letters contain numerous valuable personal confessions and reminiscences that we would never know if we had only the accounts of him and his missionary enterprises as found in the book of Acts, we would be much more fortunately situated. For it is often the personal confessions and reminiscences of the great personages of history that give us our best and most reliable knowledge of them, and, in connection with our present problem, furnish the materials which make a pathographic diagnosis possible. But Jesus has left us no diary, no autobiography, no personal confessions and reminiscences, no correspondence of any kind.

In the second place, we see Jesus as he is presented in the Gospels only through the eyes of admiring and devoted disciples whose records of him were written with a pure propaganda purpose in the interests of the spread of the Christian faith, and only after the elapse of at least three decades after his death on the cross. These Gospels, documents of faith rather than of history as we today conceive it, often manifest clearly the highest idealization of their hero, and the historical facts which they report are often so colored by the fervent faith that inspired their recording that some (Wellhausen and Wrede) can entertain only the most sceptical attitude toward them as historical documents. The records of Jesus' words and deeds as they stand in the New Testament have been strongly

127

christianized.   This christianization of Jesus' words, in particular, and deeds was only a most natural process which is at
once understood when we begin to realize the vitality of the
early Christian faith out of which these records of him organically grew.

Over against all of these historical limitations and handi-
caps, we can say that we nevertheless possess as full and reliable information concerning Jesus as we do of any other great
man of that early date.

### 1)   The Fourth Gospel

From Strauss (*Leben Jesu* 1835; I 483-518, 700-745; II
134-175, 221-237) down to Wernle (*Quellen*, S. 17-31; Engl.
trans., p. 25-57) the Fourth Gospel has been consistently rejected by liberal theologians as a source of reliable knowledge
concerning what Jesus said and did; that is, with the exception of certain chronological data concerning the date of Jesus'
public appearance and his death.

We are now interested in the Fourth Gospel only as it
concerns our present task of sifting the sources.   (For a concise summary of the historical grounds on which the Fourth
Gospel has been rejected see L. Jackson's book, *The Problem
of the Fourth Gospel*, Chapter V, pp. 49-82; for a more elaborate treatment see P. W. Schmiedel's book, *Das vierte Evangelium gegenueber den drei ersten*).

It is not for historical and critical reasons that we here
make a separate treatment of the Fourth Gospel, but it is the
fact that the pathographers, those who diagnose paranoia,
have drawn most of their materials from the Fourth Gospel.
As Schweitzer has pointed out, three-fourths of the materials
employed by Hirsch, de Loosten and Binet-Sanglé are taken
from the Fourth Gospel (1).   These three writers all
agree in their diagnosis of paranoia, and it is the Fourth
Gospel that furnishes them their materials for this conclusion.
It is at this point that the liberals can throw a destructive
bomb into the conservative camp occupied by Loofs and Wer-

---

(1)   See abundant references to the Fourth Gospel in Hirsch, Chapter
VII; throughout de Loosten's book; in Binet-Sanglé's work, II 5ff.

ner, for, if the liberals by their attempt to construe the consciousness of Jesus in purely human terms have prepared the way for the questioning of the psychic health of Jesus, the conservatives have made possible a definite diagnosis of paranoia by the retention of the Fourth Gospel as an historical source of information concerning what Jesus said and did. Binet-Sanglé openly calls the Fourth Gospel *la biographie du déclin* (III 114). It is only by the rejection of most of the Johannine words, and some of the Johannine acts, of Jesus that his psychic soundness can be saved.

Hollmann writes, *the picture would be changed in many respects if the Fourth Gospel were excluded* (S. 274).

Schweitzer writes, *the exclusion of the Fourth Gospel is of the greatest importance. This source alone enables the pathographers to assume that we can trace the development of the mind of Jesus through a period of three years; it alone permits them to delineate a personality that was constantly occupied with its own ego, that sets it in the foreground of all its discourses, that claims for itself divine descent and demanded a corresponding belief on part of the hearers* (PBJ, S. 24).

Even the most casual reader of the Fourth Gospel must have the impression that here Jesus' words are exclusively egocentric. The word "I" occurs six times as often in this Gospel as in the Gospel of Mt. The seven *I ams* of Jesus are found only in the Fourth Gospel (6,35 48 51; 8,12; 10,7 9; 10,11 14; 11,25; 14,6; 15,1). The kingdom of God, the permanent theme of Jesus' message and teaching in the Synoptics, has disappeared, except in 3,3 5. In the Synoptics we see Jesus absorbed in the great cause of the kingdom of God, but in the Fourth Gospel he is engrossed in his own ego. Except for 8,7 the pointed and piercing replies of Jesus are gone. The short pithy, pregnant, sententious utterances are displaced by long drawn-out pointless discourses about his own person and his relation to his Father. Dialogues drift off into monologues and we know no longer who is speaking (3,11ff; 3,31ff). Except for a very few instances like 12,24f; 13,16; 15,20 and 16,21 the Johannine words of Jesus have no parallels in the Synoptics. The parables, the characteristic form of Jesus' address in the first three Gospels, are missing or have degenerated into unclear allegory (10,1ff; 15,1ff), the theme of which is not the kingdom of God but the indispensability of the position of the person of Jesus in the scheme of salvation. The consciousness of his identity, which is gained only by personal struggle in the Synoptics and once gained is most carefully guarded by him and revealed at Caesarea Philippi only to his most intimate disciples and only a few hours before his death to the Jerusalem authorities, Jesus possesses in the Fourth Gospel from the very beginning. It is never problematic for himself. He makes no effort to conceal his identity and employs no circumlocutions in the Synoptic sense. The Baptist recognizes him and announces his identity to the public. His disciples know who he is from the very start; it is this knowledge that wins them. Instead of guarding his secret he discloses it freely to the wanton woman at the well (4,26 Messiah), to the blind beggar to whom he has restored sight (9,37 Son of man), and to his enemies (10,36 Son of God). The points of Jesus' contentions with his enemies are no longer questions of the Jewish law, except incidentally (5,16; 7,22f; 9,14), but disputes regarding Jesus' claims for himself. In the Synoptics Jesus does not directly identify himself with the Son of man, but he does freely and frequently in the Fourth Gospel (3,13 14; 6,27 53, 62; 12,34), however, no longer in the apocalyptic but in the Christian sense. In the Synoptics it is surprising that Jesus has so little to say of himself. The conditions for entrance into the kingdom of God are moral and ethical, but in the Fourth Gospel Jesus is represented as setting purely egocentric stipulations. In the Synoptics all emphasis is laid upon the doing of the will of God, and what Jesus means by this is sun-clear; in the Fourth Gospel Jesus never explains what he means by it, although he speaks repeatedly of doing God's will.

In the Fourth Gospel the moral motive for miracle has disappeared. Jesus no longer heals and cures out of sympathy, pity, and compassion. The desire to help has degenerated into a desire to arouse belief in the divine dignity of his own person. Jesus' words to his disciples concerning the affliction of the man born blind (9,3) and the death of Lazarus

(11,4 15) are expressions of a morbid heartlessness that contradicts all that the Synoptics tell us of his character. Faith is no longer the prerequisite of the cure but the result. Faith in the Fourth Gospel is no longer the confident personal faith of the Synoptics, but a cold confessional faith or belief. The miracles of the Fourth Gospel are *signs* (2,11; 4,54; 6,2; 6,14; 6,26; 9,16; 12,37; 20,30) and proofs that would compel confession. Without realizing the terrible indictment that he brings down upon the Johannine miracles Kneib writes, *It contradicts the dignity of faith as well as the dignity of the miracle-worker to compel belief* (S. 28).

It is upon the above enumerated egocentric elements in the Fourth Gospel that de Loosten, Binet-Sanglé, and Hirsch base, for the most part, their diagnosis of paranoia. Here we cannot help being reminded of a statement of Strauss in his 1864 *Leben Jesu* to the effect that whoever ascribes to Jesus the egocentric words of the Fourth Gospel *renders him a perilous service* (see above p. 5f).

Further when we read Jn 5,19; 8,19 29; 10,38; 14,23c; 17,21 we cannot but think of those cases of double or coexistent personality of which Ribot writes: *In demented subjects the disorganization is organized: they are double, believe themselves double and act as double personalities. There is not the least doubt about it in their minds . . . . . . To them it seems as natural to be double, as to us it does to be single. There is no scepticism on their part as regards their state, nor do they tolerate it in others. Their mode of existence, given to them by their consciousness, appears to them so clear and evident as to be above all doubt, or the supposition of it. It is important to note this point, because it proves, in these morbid forms of personality, that spontaneity of affirmation and action which is characteristic of all natural states* (DP, p. 127).

As stated above, it is not our purpose here to make a complete catalogue of the historical and critical objections to the historicity of Jesus' words, either in their form or content, as found in the Fourth Gospel. It is further not our intention to discuss the character and purpose of the Fourth Gospel as a whole. For such a treatise the writer would refer the reader to Wrede's pamphlet, *Charakter und Tendenz des Johannes-evangeliums*, which in spite of its brevity, is the best general characterization of the Fourth Gospel that has appeared in the recent life-of-Jesus research.

Our present purpose is to show that the egocentric words placed in the mouth of Jesus in the Fourth Gospel are not words of Jesus at all, but really the christocentric confessions of the fourth evangelist. And as such they cannot be used as pathographic matter for the diagnosis of paranoia. Strauss wrote that the words of Jesus in the Fourth Gospel are merely *an uninterrupted Doxology, only translated out of the second person into the first* (see above p. 5). Strauss would have been nearer the truth had he made it from the t h i r d to the first person.

In the Fourth Gospel we do not hear Jesus speaking, but we hear the early Christian preacher addressing the early Christian community, or at times those who do not believe, or even those who oppose the Christian faith (3,11; 4,22; 5,38). For the convenience of making this point and position clear the discourse material of the Fourth Gospel is divided into three groups: 1) those passages in which the author is directly addressing himself to his readers; 2) those passages in which the words and thoughts of the early Christian preacher are put into the mouth of Jesus in the second and third person; 3) those passages in which the words and thoughts of the early Christian preacher are put into the mouth of Jesus in the first person.

1)   To this group belong such passages as follow. 1,16 *For of his fullness we all received, and grace for grace.* 8,32 *Ye shall know the truth, and the truth shall make you free.* 9,4 *We must work the works of him that sent HIM, while it is day: the night cometh when no man can work.* In these passages, as well as in 6,27; 19,35-37, etc., we hear the early Christian preacher directly addressing himself to the early Christian community in the first and second persons.

In the following passages we hear this early Christian preacher addressing the early Christian community in the third person. 3,14-16 *For as Moses lifted up the serpent in the wilderness, even so must the Son of man be lifted up; that whosoever believeth may in him have eternal life.  For God so loved the world, that he gave his only begotten Son, that whosoever believeth on him should not perish, but have eternal life.  6,40 For this is the will of the Father, that everyone that beholdeth the Son, and believeth on him, should have eternal life.  7,18 He that speaketh from himself seeketh his own glory: but he that seeketh the glory of him that sent him, the same is true, and no unrighteousness is in him.  15,13 Greater love hath no man than this, that a man lay down his life for his friends.* The same is true of 1,1-5; 1,9-14; 3,31-36; 6,58; 20,30-31; etc.

2)   This group divides itself into two sub-groups.   a) Those words of the early Christian preacher addressed to the early Christian community in the second person, but put into the mouth of Jesus; 6,29 *This is the work of God, that ye believe on him whom he hath sent;* also 5,35 37b-39; 12,35-36; etc.  b)  Those words of the early Christian preacher addressed to the early Christian community in the third person, but put into the mouth of Jesus; 10,1-5 *Verily, verily, I say unto you, He that entereth not by the door into the fold of the sheep, but climbeth up some other way, the same is a thief and a robber.  But he that entereth in by the door is the shepherd of the sheep.  To him the porter openeth; and the sheep hear his voice: and he calleth his own sheep by name and leadeth them out.  When he hath put forth all his own, he goeth before them, and the sheep follow him: for they know his voice.  And a stranger will they not follow, but will flee from him: for they know not the voice of strangers;* also 5,19-23; 5,25-29; 10,11b-13; 11,9-10; 13,31-32; 16,2; etc.

3)   This group includes the greater portion of the discourse material in the Fourth Gospel: 5,43 46-47; 6,48-51 55-57; 7,16-17 37-38; 8,31 42 51; 10,7b-11a 14-18 27-30 37-38; 12,32 44-50; 13,13-15; 14,1-4 6-7 11-21 25-27; 15,1-12 14-27; 16,1 3-6 7b-15 23-24 27-28 33; 17,1-2 4-26; 18,37b; 19, 11; all the *I ams.*  All the above words the fourth evangelist puts into the mouth of Jesus in the first person.  Why he has done this we do not know.  It is doubtless the fact that Jesus has so little to say of himself and the identity of his person in the Synoptics that has prompted the fourth evangelist to con-

vert these early Christian convictions and confessions into words of Jesus in the first person. It is perhaps an attempt to bridge over the gap that existed between what Jesus actually claimed for himself and what the early Christian community and its faith claimed for him.

A concrete confirmation of this change from the third to the first person by the author of the Fourth Gospel is seen in the Johannine account of the baptism of Jesus, 1,32-34, where the whole narrative of the Synoptic scene at the Jordan is put into the mouth of the Baptist in the form of a confession in the first person.

That these egocentric words ascribed to Jesus in the Fourth Gospel are only early Christian convictions and confessions, originally in the third person, set in the first person in the mouth of Jesus is clear from the ease with which they can be reset from the first into the third person. The *I ams* are not words of the historical Jesus, but early Christian convictions and confessions of faith put into his mouth to augment their authority. They should read in the third person: *HE is the bread of life; he that cometh unto HIM shall not hunger, and he that believeth on HIM shall never thirst (6,35). HE is the light of the world; he that followeth HIM shall not walk in darkness, but shall have the light of life (8,12). HE is the door; by HIM if any man enter in, he shall be saved, etc. (10,9). HE is the good shepherd; the good shepherd layeth down his life for his sheep (10,11). HE is the resurrection, and the life; he that believeth on HIM, though he die, yet shall he live; and whosoever liveth and believeth on HIM shall never die (11,25-26). HE is the way, and the truth, and the life; no one cometh unto the Father, but by HIM (14,6). HE is the vine, WE are the branches (15,5).*

Thus all the words ascribed to Jesus by the fourth evangelist in this group can be readily reset into the third person, which resetting makes them historically understandable. The farewell prayer, 17,1-26, is to be understood only as a prayer of this early Christian preacher as verse three clearly betrays, *And this is life eternal, that they should know the only true God, and him whom thou didst send, even Jesus Christ;* only

historical violence can ascribe this word to Jesus. In **10,10b**
we hear the early Christian preacher addressing his hearers:
*HE came that WE may have life, and may have it abundantly.*
All of these egocentric words ascribed to Jesus in the first person in the Fourth Gospel should read in the same person as that
great verse in which is concentrated and crystalized all that is
essential in Christian confession, Jn **3,16**, *For God so loved the*
*world, that he gave his only begotten Son, that whosoever be-*
*lieveth on him should not perish, but have eternal life.* Does
this chief of all Christian confessions lose any of its force or
appeal because it stands in the third person and has not been
converted into the first person and set on the lips of Jesus to
read, *For God so loved the world, that he gave ME, his only*
*begotten Son, that whosoever believeth on ME should not perish,*
*but have eternal life?* Not in the least. Such is the case with
all the egocentric words of Jesus, particularly in the first person, in the Fourth Gospel. We understand them only when they
come from the heart of this great disciple of Christ who wrote
the Fourth Gospel, and not from the lips of Jesus. It is the
stipulation of this source that accounts for the popularity and
appeal of the Fourth Gospel to personal Christian piety down
through more than eighteen centuries.

One of the greatest misunderstandings in the critical research of the Gospel literature has been the notion that the rejection of Johannine words of Jesus as historical means the
complete rejection of the Fourth Gospel. As Wrede has pointed
out, the work of the fourth evangelist is one of the most
significant and remarkable documents of primitive Christianity.
The Fourth Gospel is the greatest of all Christian confessions.
It is its confessional character that has won for it the chief seat
in the Christian conscience and consciousness. This view brings
the Fourth Gospel into that great group of the confessional
literature of Christianity which has always meant the most to
personal Christian faith. Here it rightly belongs. Here it
occupies a place second to none.

We must remind ourselves constantly that historically the
Gospels contain vastly more of what others thought about
Jesus than what he thought about himself. Regarding the first

we are quite sure.  Regarding the second we have only confusion and controversy.

We must further keep in mind that the thought and religion of the early Christian community were distinctly and decidedly christocentric.  This should help to the realization that the resetting of the egocentric words of Jesus in the Fourth Gospel into christocentric confessions and convictions on the lips of a beloved disciple is our gain and not our loss.  Why read them as words on the lips of Jesus when they do not belong there, and when they mean much more on the lips of an early Christian disciple, perhaps an eye- and ear-witness of Jesus' public career?  That any early Christian disciple, whether or not he had seen and heard Jesus as a man among men yet who stood historically at most but a few decades removed, could confess such things with such conviction as the author of the Fourth Gospel confesses about Jesus still awaits its parallel in esteem accorded to any person of history.

From the viewpoint of historical criticism we can put the Fourth Gospel on a parity with Paul's epistles, which are not the less valuable because we cannot reconstruct *a little life of Jesus* from them as Renan thought he could.  The early Christian confessions of the Fourth Gospel are even more exposed and accessible to the average Bible reader than are the epistles of Paul.  For the Fourth Gospel is free from the abstract theological phraseology and complications found in Paul's letters, and from the Fourth Gospel radiates constantly a magnetic mysticism and glowing warmth of faith that are only occasional in Paul.

### 2)   The Synoptics

### A)   Discourse Matter

From the viewpoint of the pathographic contention the Synoptic materials fall into two main groups:  A) Discourse Matter; and B) Biographical Incidents.  The biographical incidents are listed and discussed in the last part of the present chapter.  The discourse matter falls into three classes: a) Egocentric Words of Jesus; b) Eschatological Elements; c) Social Teachings.  We begin with

a) Egocentric Words of Jesus in the Synoptics.

i) In the preceding pages we have discussed the egocentric words of Jesus as found in the Fourth Gospel, and it is our first duty here to search out any words of Jesus in the first three Gospels that have a clear Johannine character. In this search we are not disappointed, for we find two such instances; the first is found in both Mc and Q, the second in Q only.

```
Mc 9,37b Whosoever        receiveth me, receiveth not me, but
Lc 9,48b Whosoever shall receive   me   receiveth
him that sent me.  Mt 10,40 He that receiveth you receiveth me,
him that sent me.  Lc 10,16 He that rejecteth you rejecteth me;
and he that receiveth me receiveth him that sent me.
and he that rejecteth me rejecteth him that sent me.
```

The specially Johannine feature of these words is the idea of Jesus being sent, and that the reception or rejection of him is identical with the reception or rejection of him that sent him. Mc 9,37b and Lc 9,48b is a word of Jesus spoken in connection with his setting a little child in the midst of the disciples. Mt 10,40 and Lc 10,16 are from Q; both cite this word as addressed to the disciples on sending them out, but in Mt it is to the twelve, in Lc to the seventy. Mt and Lc are identical in thought, but manifest their characteristic difference in the choice of vocabulary in their reproductions of Q (Compare Mt 10,37 and Lc 14,26).

```
Mt 11,27 . All things have been delivered unto me of my Father
Lc 10,22  All things have been delivered unto me of my Father
and no one knoweth     the Son      save the Father; neither doth
and no one knoweth who the Son is, save the Father;      and
any know the Father,    save the Son, and he to whomsoever the Son
who      the Father is, save the Son, and he to whomsoever the Son
willeth to reveal him.
willeth to reveal him.
```

Both the language and thought of this passage are Johannine and are without other Synoptic parallels (See Mt 28,18b). "Me" and "my" should be changed to read "him" and "his" in order to fit in with the third person of the second half of the passage, for it is simply an early Christian confession set in the mouth of Jesus in the first person. Mt 11,27 and Lc 10,22 have been commonly regarded as the conclusion of Jesus' acclamation, or prayer, in Mt 11,25-26 and Lc 10,21, but Jesus' acclamation proper is confined to Mt 25-26 and Lc 21. These verses express a completed thought and have no essential connection with Mt 11,27 and Lc 10,22. Jesus' acclamation in Mt 25-26 and Lc 21 is simply a figurative address, in no sense Johannine, confirmed by Jesus' actual experiences of success and failure with the various classes of his contemporaries.

In the above cited passages we discover slight Johannine invasions of Synoptic matter, one of Mc and two of Q. This is not at all surprising. The surprising fact is that the Johannine invasions of Synoptic matter are not more extensive. Those who cannot find a single reliable historical datum in the Fourth Gospel, nor a single Johannine expression in the first three Gospels, draw a hard and fast line that does not exist in the sources themselves. The New Testament canon cannot be treated so mechanically, for the Gospel literature sprang too vitally and organically out of the life and faith of the early Christian community. The distinction between the Fourth Gospel and the Synoptics is modern, a nineteenth century distinction dating from Strauss. Such a distinction never occurred to the Gospel writers. As Wrede says of the fourth evangelist, *Wie der vergleichende Kritiker von heute hat er ja doch den Unterschied seiner Erzaehlung von der der andern nicht gemessen* (CuTdJE, S. 70).

ii) We come now to those egocentric words of Jesus in the Synoptics which are not Johannine in character, but reflect rather the conceptions and convictions of the early Christian faith concerning the significance of Jesus' person. For the most part, these words are distinguished by the expressions *for my sake, for my name's sake, because of me*, etc.

We notice first those passages found in Mc, many of them also in Q, and reproduced by either Mt or Lc, or both.

Mt  16,24  If any man would come after me, let him deny himself,
Mc   8,34  If any man would come after me, let him deny himself,
Lc   9,23  If any man would come after me, let him deny himself,

and take up his cross,         and follow me.
and take up his cross,         and follow me.
and take up his cross daily, and follow me.

Mt 10,38   And he that doth not take his        cross, and follow after
Lc 14,27   Whosoever  doth not bear his own cross, and  come  after
me,  is not worthy of me.
me, cannot be my disciple.

This word ascribed to Jesus is a doublet in both Mt and Lc. It is written in the light of the death of Jesus on the cross, and is a metaphor of early Christian homiletics rather than a real word of Jesus. If it does go back to Jesus at all, its present form was given it by the early Christian community when the cross had become the common Christian symbol (Compare Wellhausen, Marci, S. 66; J. Weiss, SdNT, I 151). Besides Mc is grouping topically here, for he introduces this word immediately after the first prophecy of the passion.

```
Mt 16,25  For whosoever would save his life shall lose it; and who-
Mc  8,35  For whosoever would save his life shall lose it; and who-
Lc  9,24  For whosoever would save his life shall lose it; but who-
soever shall lose his life for my sake                          shall
soever shall lose his life for my sake and the gospel's         shall
soever shall lose his life for my sake             the same shall
find it.
save it.
save it.
```

```
Mt 10,39    He that         findeth      his life shall lose it; and
Lc 17,33    Whosoever shall seek to gain his life shall lose it; but
he that         loseth his life for my sake shall    find    it.
whosoever shall lose   his life          shall preserve it.
```

Lc 17,33 preserves the more original form of this word of Jesus. Its form in Jn 12,25 confirms this. "For my sake," ἐμοῦ καί, is missing in D a b i (k) sy[s] arm aeth Or texts of Mc 8,35, (Huck, S. 101).

```
Mc 8,38  For whosoever shall be ashamed of me and my words in
Lc 9,26  For whosoever shall be ashamed of me and my words
this adulterous and sinful generation, the Son of man also shall be
                                      of him shall     the Son of
ashamed of him.
man be ashamed,
```

```
Mt 10,33  But whosoever shall deny    me        before     men,
Lc 12,9   But  he that        denieth me in the presence of men
him will I also deny        before     my      Father who is in
shall be    denied in the presence of the angels of God.
heaven.
```

Mt 10,33 completes the identification of Jesus with the Son of man, and is therefore christianized and less original than the single form in Mc and the double form in Lc, where this word is less egocentric and the supernatural role is ascribed to the unidentified Son of man. Wellhausen writes, *This utterance is out of the same metal as 8,35 but it is of a different stamp. The demand is by no means so extreme; "I and my words" is something entirely different from "I and the gospel"* (Marci, S. 67). Mc 8,38a is more in the tone and theme of

Mc 13,31 (=Mt 24,35=Lc 21,33), words which no one is willing to take from the mouth of Jesus.

```
Mt 18,5   Whoso        shall receive one    such little child     in my
Mc  9,37  Whosoever shall receive one of such little children in my
Lc  9,48  Whosoever shall receive     this       little child     in my
name receiveth me.
name, receiveth me.
name  receiveth me.
```

```
Mt 18,3    Except ye turn, and                             become
Mc 10,15                            Whosoever shall not receive  the
Lc 18,17                            Whosoever shall not receive  the
                  as   little children ye shall in no wise enter into the
kingdom of God as a little child,   he shall in no wise enter
kingdom of God as a little child,   he shall in no wise enter
kingdom of heaven.
   therein.
   therein.
```

The original form of Mc 9,37 and parallels is to be found in Mc 10,15 and parallels. Here the child represents that model of modest mentality to which alone is destined the participation in the kingdom of God. But in Mc 9,37 and parallels this conception is christianized, and the child as such is Jesus' personal representative on earth and the objective occasion by which loyalty to his person is tested. The original meaning is still retained in the preceding verses, Mc 10,14= Mt 19,14=Lc 18,16 (Compare Mt 18,10; 18,14; Lc 15,7). A still further elaboration of this thought is found in Mt 18,6 and Mc 9,42 where "the little ones" are no longer real children, but disciples who believe on Jesus. Lc 17,1-2 is the more original form of this word; here there is no reference to "the little ones who believe on me." Many texts of Mc 9,42 omit "on me"; εἰς ἐμέ is found in A B L Θ Σ . . . min c f l q vg sy$^s$ $^{vg}$ sa arm go (Huck, S. 110). Nestle omits it, as do Westcott and Hort.

```
Mt 10,42  And whosoever shall give to drink unto one of these
Mc  9,41  For  whosoever shall give                       you
little ones a cup of cold water only         in the name of a disciple,
         a cup of     water     to drink   because ye are Christ's,
verily I say unto you, he shall in no wise lose his reward.
verily I say unto you, he shall in no wise lose his reward.
```

Some ancient authorities add "in my name" after "water" in Mc 9,41. Tischendorf retains this expression in its full form. Nestle omits μου, as do Westcott and Hort. μου is found in Aleph* D X Δ Θ . . . . . min lat bo aeth go; it is missing A B C L Σ  1 238 435 579 . . . . . sy arm (Huck, 110).

The omission of "my" results in the English translation "because" ("in name that ye are"). Mt cites this word as the conclusion of the address to the twelve. Mc cites it in connection with a reminiscence by the disciple John of an incident doubtless experienced during the mission of the twelve. In Mc "the little ones" are not only disciples but the twelve.

```
Mt 19,29    And  every  one  that hath  left  houses,                              or
Mc 10,29    There is no  man  that hath  left  house,                              or
Lc 18,29    There is no  man  that hath  left  house,  or wife,  or
brethren,  or sisters,  or father,  or mother,  or children,  or lands,  for my
brethren,  or sisters,  or mother,  or father,  or children,  or lands,  for my
brethren,              or         parents,      or children,
name's sake,
        sake, and for the        gospel's       sake,
              for the kingdom of God's sake,
```

Lc's conclusion in 18,29 is unquestionably the more original form, for it corresponds most closely to what was central in Jesus' thought and message. Both Mt and Mc present the early Christian point of view regarding sacrifice rather than that of Jesus.

Mc 13,9 ("for my sake") and Lc 21,12 ("for my name's sake") are a part of Jesus' eschatological address. Mt omits the egocentric conclusion in this connection, but unadvisedly reproduces this verse of Mc in the address to the twelve (Mt 10,17-18) and closes with "for my sake." That we have in Mc 13 perhaps the only written source of the second Gospel which was circulated at a very early date as an apocalyptic fly-leaf (thus Wernle, SF, S. 213) is very probable, but that before or with its incorporation in Mc it has undergone a change and thorough revision is clear from the following verse (Mc 13,10) which breaks off the eschatological point of the address itself. The original address centered upon the great cosmic catastrophe and the sudden appearance of the unidentified Son of man. If the man on the housetop has not time enough to go down, nor the man in the field to return for his cloak, how shall the disciples ever be delivered up to councils, beaten in synagogues, or stand before governors and kings, to say nothing of preaching the gospel to all nations? Mc 13,9 (=Lc 21,12) and 13,13 (=Mt 24,9b; 10,22a=Lc 21,17), as well as 13,10 (Mt 24,14), are written in the light of already experienced persecutions and the delay of the parousia.

We now turn to one or two egocentric words of Jesus not found in Mc but common to Mt and Lc, peculiar to Q.

Mt 5,11 Blessed are ye when men shall          reproach you......
Lc 6,22 Blessed are ye, when men shall......reproach you......
for     my       sake.
for the Son of man's sake.

That Lc's conclusion in 6,22 is the more original is clear from the fact that the texts of the passage in Lc are constant in this reading while the texts of Mt 5,11 vary strongly.  sy[s] [c] read "for my name's sake," τοῦ ὀνόματος μου; D a b c g k read more impersonally "for righteousness' sake," δικαιοσύνης, which is the logical continuation of the identical expression in the preceding verse, Mt 5,10.

A second egocentric word from Q is Mt 7,22-23; here Jesus is represented as anticipating his role as decider of destinies in the final judgment.  A glance at Lc 13,25-27 shows that Mt's word is an early Christian corruption of this parable where these words belong in the mouth of the "master of the house."  The introduction, Lc 13,25, Mt has tacked on to his parable of the wise and foolish virgins (Mt 25,1-13), which parable should end with verse 10.  Juelicher clamorously contends for the originality of Mt 25,1-10 (GRJ, S. 458f).  Wellhausen protests in favor of the priority of Lc 13,25-27 (Matthaei, S. 122f).

Mt 10,32 and Lc 12,8 stood in Q as a counterpart to Mt 10,33 and Lc 12,9.  Mt's form is much more strongly christianized and confessionalized than that of Lc.

To matter peculiar to Mt bearing the coloring of early Christian confession and conviction belongs 11,28-30 which contrasts too strongly with 8,18-22 (=Lc 9,57-60) to be pure. In Mt 12,6 the American Revised Version follows the minority readings, (C) L Δ. 13-346-788 118-209..lat.  Tischendorf, Westcott and Hort, and Nestle agree in retaining μεῖζον of Aleph, B D[gr] Θ.. . . . . min ff q sy[s] bo instead of μείζων of the minority readings (Huck, S. 54).  Mt 18,19-20 is not a word of Jesus but an instance of *Gemeindetheologie*.  In Mt 23,10, not Jesus, but the author of the first Gospel is speaking.

The above comparisons of the readings of the first three

Gospels and various readings of the same Gospel in its different texts and translations show that Jesus did not set egocentric stipulations for entrance into and participation in the
kingdom of God as Binet-Sanglé and Hirsch represent. Such
expressions as *for my sake, for my name's sake, because of me,*
etc., are to be eliminated, for the most part, by a comparison
of the first three Gospels or an examination of the varying
texts of the same Gospel. In order to correspond to what was
central in the thought, teaching and preaching of Jesus, these
egocentric words should read *for righteousness' sake, for the
kingdom of God's sake, for the Son of man's sake,* etc. In the
few cases where the different readings will not make this possible such expressions are to be assigned to the thought and
theology of the early Christian community, for they represent
rather the significance attached to the person of Jesus by the
early Christian community than any significance which Jesus
himself attached to his own person. In such passages, as Wellhausen says of them in Mc, Jesus is no longer *the proclaimer,
but the substance of the gospel itself* (Marci, S. 67).

The egocentric expressions, *for my sake,* etc., are least frequent in Mc and most numerous in Mt. This frequency in
Mt is due to the fact that Mt has strongly christianized and
confessionalized his second source Q. That Mt has done this
is clear from a comparison of the first beatitude and the Lord's
Prayer in Mt and Lc (Mt 5,3=Lc 6,20; Mt 6,9ff=Lc 11,2ff),
further by a comparison of Mt 7,23 and Lc 13,25-27; Mt 10,33
and Lc 12,9. The egocentric words ascribed to Jesus are specially lacking in Lc which fact is easily understood by his conception of Jesus' person in 5,17b where he speaks of Jesus'
miracle power as an intermittent and inconstant endowment and
equipment; besides in his peculiar matter Lc regularly refers
to Jesus as a prophet (See 7,16; 7,39; 24,19). That Lc does
not consider Jesus as egocentric in his thought is clearest from
that incident peculiar to Lc in 11,27-28.

That these confessional conceptions of Jesus' words are
more frequent in Q than in Mc is only natural in view of the
catechetical principle and purpose of the Q collection (see
Wernle, SF, S. 227). Harnack designates Q as exclusively

intended for the use of the early Christian community (SuRJ, S. 163). Castor even goes so far as to say, *the conception of Jesus' person here* (in Q) *is the same that we find in the speech of Peter, Acts* 2,14-36 (p. 209).

No student of the Gospels can deny that in them we see Jesus only through early Christian eyes and hear him speak only through early Christian lips. The Synoptics from beginning to end are permeated with the conceptions, convictions and confessions of the first Christians, and these are, for the most part, put into the mouth of Jesus. The expositions of Jesus' parables (Mc 4,13-20=Mt 13,19-23=Lc 8,11-15; Mt 13,37-43 49-50) are only early Christian homilies; they are unnecessary for the parables themselves are sun-clear. Lc is specially homiletic in his presentation of Jesus' preaching; Mt tends towards confessionalism and ecclesiasticism (16,17-19; 18,16-17). Even Mc has his theology. This christianization and confessionalization, from which no one of the Synoptics is entirely free, is the cause of Wellhausen's source-scepticism which he condenses in the remark, *We cannot get back to him, even if we would.* (Einl., S. 104).

The egocentric words of Jesus in the Gospels can furnish no support to the pathographic contention. In the Synoptics we do not see Jesus consumed with his own ego as the megalomaniac or the paranoiac, but we see him so completely consumed in the great cause of the kingdom of God that he entirely forgets his own self except as that self can serve and sacrifice for the cause that he champions even to the cross. Not his own person, but the kingdom of God, its coming, its nature, the conditions of entrance into it, and the winning of men for it, is the constant thought and theme of Jesus' every parable, preaching, prophecy, and prayer. Never once is Jesus in doubt about this kingdom; it is only the personal part that he is to play in its realization that is problematic for him and presses him apart for petition and prayer. As Carpenter writes of the picture of Jesus in the second Gospel, *The Jesus of Mark is a man, with a man's wrath and disappointment. He cannot do everything, he does not know everything...... Difficulty cannot overpower him, or danger daunt, or opposition suppress him.  He may perish, but his cause is eternal.  The kingdom will triumph! the Son of Man will come!* (p. 217).

b)   The Eschatological Elements in Jesus' thought and teaching from the pathographic point of view are to be a matter for special discussion in the following chapter (see below p. 215ff).

c)   The Social Teachings of Jesus

Nietzsche was the first to malign Jesus' individual ethics and morals as morbid.  Von Hartmann was the first to condemn the social teachings of Jesus as dangerous and destructive to the institutions of society.  It is Rasmussen and Binet-Sanglé who see in Jesus' social attitudes and recommendations a sure symptom of morbid mind.

It is not our intention here to go into a discussion of Jesus' social teaching and its agreement or disagreement with modern social estimates and viewpoints.  This field has already been fairly well covered by men like Peabody, Rauschenbusch, Shailer Mathews, Kent, Soares and Horne.  We, therefore, urge only a few general considerations pertinent to our present problem which are in need of special emphasis.

For Jesus the solution of social situations is not one of method and mechanism but of morals.  Social justice is to be the result of principles, not of precepts.

Jesus did not take a mechanical view of the world and man, but a personalistic view.  Man and the world in which he lives are not finished products, but are still in the process of making. Both are improvable.

We live in a very different world from that of Jesus.  A whole new world of civilization and culture has appeared since his day.  The centers of civilization and culture have shifted to the north and west, and this shift has brought with it its own special and peculiar problems.  These problems never confronted Jesus in the modern sense.  Their solutions he naturally left unformulated.

Jesus did not prescribe all the details of conduct for any particular situation for the world since his time and for all time to come.  But he laid down certain general principles for living life, both as individual and as group, and has left the individual or group, as the case may be, to determine the type of conduct that is in harmony with his spirit of living life.

Jesus has little to say to our modern day, but he has a great deal to communicate.  His contribution to the solution of the social problem is not a system or scheme, but the gift of a spirit.  Men are to live together in all the aspects of social contact, not according to a set system or scheme, but in a spirit, the spirit of the Golden Rule, sacrifice and service.

On detailed solutions of modern social problems Jesus is silent for clear historical reasons.  Standards in the social scale, wage adjustments, sharing the profits of production, ownership of natural resources, rights and responsibilities of capital and labor, etc., are problems that did not exist for him.

We cannot modernize Jesus and force him to speak our language and think our thoughts after us.  We must leave him in his own historical setting.  Jesus was born in Bethlehem of Judea in the days of Herod the king, and not in the twentieth century.  We must leave him to think his own thoughts and express them in the idioms of his own language in his own way.  He often does not say just what we would like to have him to say, but we must not and cannot compel him to speak otherwise.  Our task is not only to understand Jesus' thought and teaching but his person, and to translate both into the idioms of our own day.

We must learn to understand Jesus in the light of his own historical background.  Thereby we shall find that much that is foreign, or even repulsive, to us today in the thought and teaching of Jesus belongs to the local color of Jesus' historical background and day.

We cannot expect from Jesus a reply to a particular question that is peculiar to our present stage of development and culture.  Jesus speaks to no one age alone, but to all ages.

It is only the neglect of such historical considerations as are above outlined that can lead to the notion that the social ethics and morals of Jesus are sickly and morbid.

## B)  Biographical Incidents

We now come to those biographical incidents in the Synoptic life of Jesus which, almost without exception, have figured in one form or another in the pathographic contention to the effect that Jesus was an ecstatic, an epileptic, or a paranoiac.

### a)  Jesus at Twelve Years   Lc 2,41-51

Whether we are here dealing with an actual historical incident in the life of Jesus is open to such serious question that many New Testament scholars reject it as legendary, or apocryphal.  It is not related by either Mt or Mc; this of course weakens its literary basis.  Voelter rejects the historicity of Lc 2,22-51 for two reasons: 1) this section of Lc's narrative of the nativity and boyhood regards both Joseph and Mary as the real parents of Jesus in contradiction to the representation in Lc 1,26-38; 2) Lc 2,33 and 2,50 represent both Joseph and Mary as absolutely without understanding for the words of Jesus, or words spoken about him by others, which is not reconcilable with the representation in Lc 1,26-38 where Mary seems fully cognizant of the future greatness of her son (S. 57ff; 75ff).

The fact that this incident in the temple at Jerusalem is the only one that has come down to us from the boyhood and youth of Jesus would naturally raise the question as to just why this particular incident and no other has been preserved from this obscure period.  Reasons can be given for  1)  its invention, if apocryphal, 2) its preservation, if historical.  If apocryphal it would be invented to exhibit the remarkable intellectual ability of the youthful Jesus which enabled him to confound the old doctors in the temple.  This is a theme of which the apocryphal gospels are very fond.  Strauss saw in this incident a myth modelled after the Old Testament accounts of the boy Samuel and other Old Testament characters (*Leben Jesu*, 1835, I 335ff).  If historical, the chief motive for the preservation of this incident from the early Christian point of view would be the extraordinary God-consciousness that Jesus manifested so early in life.

Neither of these considerations is of special interest to us

today. That Jesus at the age of twelve should show such a
marked development of the consciousness that fully possessed
him in later life is not at all remarkable when we read in Rein-
ecke's *Meister der Tonkunst* (Berlin & Stuttgart, 1903, S. 9),
that Mozart began to compose at the age of five, and his father
before him at the age of eight, (S. 5). Our difficulty with the
incident is moral, in that Jesus gives such an indifferent, if not
improper, reply to his anxious parents. It could be argued
that this answer of the boy Jesus is historical for it corresponds
exactly to the attitude which he seems to have entertained
toward his family in later life. For, while Mc 3,31-35 is less
direct, Jesus' words are identical in tone with Lc 2,49 and
betray exactly the same content of consciousness. But it must
be remembered that we know not how many of the words of
Jesus we possess as he actually spoke them, and that many
of them bear the colorings of early Christian thought.

The early Christians in their preservation and transmission of the words of Jesus did not subject them to all the modern moral proprieties that we demand. They rather took delight, and not offense, in Jesus' rebuffs, not only to his enemies,
but to his most intimate disciples, and even to his immediate
family. Neither Mt nor Lc takes offense at Jesus' words in Mc
3,31ff, for Mt reproduces Mc almost verbatim; Lc abbrevi-
ates, but the import of Jesus' words concerning his true kinsmen is identical with that of Mc. The offenses that Mt and Lc
feel in their reproductions of Mc are theological rather than
moral. In his revision of Mc 10,18 Mt (19,17) feels a theological and not a moral difficulty. This lack of moral offense at
the words of Jesus goes to its greatest extreme in the apocryphal gospels where whole incidents are created to the end
of calling forth from the boy Jesus the most insolent acts and
the rudest replies.

The most important thing in the understanding of the
words and incidents in the life of Jesus as we have them now is
historical orientation. If the incident under consideration is legendary, it cannot figure in the pathographic contention. If
it is historical, it can be paralleled by many and still more
remarkable incidents in the lives of great men historically less

removed from us and of whom we know a great deal more than
we do about the life of Jesus, yet whose mental health remains
unquestioned. (For such instances see Werner, PGJ, S. 55).
The moral offense is modern and not original, otherwise the
incident would have undergone revision somewhere in the process of the transmission of tradition. It is the lack of historical orientation that enables Binet-Sanglé to speak of this incident in the temple at twelve years as a hebephrenic crisis due
to puberal auto-intoxication, and de Loosten to speak of a premature intellectual development and a strongly exaggerated
self-consciousness that was perhaps not free from ethical defect.

### b)   The Baptism   Mt 3,13-17=Mc 1,9-11=Lc 3,21-22

That the baptism of Jesus should figure prominently in
the pathographic position is only natural because the incident
is inaugural in the place it occupies in the evangelical life of
Jesus and because it, not only historically, but psychologically
marks a high point in the life of Jesus. The rupture of the
heavens, the descent of the dove, and the assuring voice are
psychic phenomena uncommon and unusual to the average run
of healthy-minded persons and are quite common and usual
in the experience of psychopathic subjects.

Holtzmann (WJE, S. 35ff) sees in the experience at the
Jordan the ecstatic beginning of Jesus' public ministry. Here
in a state of ecstasy Jesus wins his Messianic consciousness in
a vision. This moment is the only possible one in the earlier
part of Jesus' public career that could furnish a stimulus sufficiently strong to bring him into this ecstatic consciousness.
Henceforth Jesus knows himself to be possessed by a spirit
foreign to his own ego. At the Jordan Jesus gains that enthusiastic and ecstatic faith which later expresses itself in his
words and acts. Rasmussen speaks of the experience at the
baptism as an hallucination which figured prominently in Jesus'
subjective life (S. 142). De Loosten tells us that the experience at the Jordan was the culmination of a long process of
psychic incubation that had long been stirring the soul of Jesus.
Here Jesus had a vision, an hallucination in the visual and auditory fields of sense, which is to be explained by the abnormal
emotional upheaval in which Jesus came to John (S. 35ff).

Binet-Sanglé speaks of Jesus' baptism as the hallucination at the Jordan (II 346ff).  The striking certainty of the tone in the Baptist's message and the contagious exaltation of the multitude threw Jesus into an emotional state most favorable to the appearance of hallucinations.  The experience at the Jordan has all the marks of a genuine hallucination; it is inaugural, rural, *haute*, and encourages Jesus in his delusions of grandeur.  The voice is distinct, definite and imperative as is usually the case in religious paranoia.  Hirsch too finds Jesus at the Jordan in a *condition of intense emotional excitement;* the hallucination is paranoiac in character and represents only the materialization of the delusions that had long possessed him (p. 105; Ger. S. 101).

This representation of Jesus' experience at the Jordan has been met in various ways.  Schweitzer reckons with the probability of a vision or hallucination at the Jordan, but he throws doubt upon the historicity of the whole scene since Jesus enters upon the stage of history only with his appearance in Galilee (Mc 1,14-15) and all that transpires before that time belongs to unclear and uncertain tradition (PBJ, S. 38f).  Against this view of Schweitzer it suffices to say that for Mc the scene at the Jordan is as historical as any scene in the whole of his Gospel.  In fact, this inaugural incident is indispensable to the whole of Mc's narrative, for in it we have Mc's christology, his view of Jesus' person.  For Mc the baptism is the moment of Jesus' election and selection as the Son of God in the fullest sense by virtue of his endowment and equipment with the Divine Spirit.

Others have tried to meet the difficulty by ascribing the vision to the Baptist (Thus Beyschlag, II 110; B. Weiss, I 325).  They point out that the whole scene at the Jordan is presented as the personal and private experience of the Baptist in the Fourth Gospel (1,32-33), and is further supported by the voice in the third person in Mt 3,17.  To omit critical evidences and to cite only historical considerations, it is to be replied that the vision at the Jordan cannot have been that of the Baptist for his later conduct does not correspond with the view that he here recognizes Jesus as the Messiah.  The Baptist does not voluntarily retreat or resign in favor of Jesus. He does not become Jesus' disciple as he naturally would have become if he had received at the Jordan the assurance that the Messiah he had been announcing was now before him. It is only later when Jesus' activity is at its height that the Baptist comes to reflect upon the possibilities of Jesus' person. If the experience at the Jordan was the private vision of the Baptist he does not seem to have been enlightened or benefited by it. (For pertinent points in this connection see Rev. G. W. Wade's article, *Does historical criticism imperil the substance of the Christian faith?* Hibbert Journal, XVIII 2, January 1920, p. 329).

Still others urge that the vision and voice at the baptism were public, and not private and personal for either Jesus or John. This they find in the voice in the third person in Mt and Lc's notice in 3,21, *when all the people were baptized,* as though the bystanders were witnesses and hearers. Apart from the psychological difficulties of a mass vision, this view makes impossible the subsequent public and popular attitude toward Jesus which seems to have regarded him as a great teacher and healer; it would render senseless Jesus' own commands to the demoniacs and to his disciples for silence and secrecy, and would make unnecessary the transfiguration scene, as well as the confessions at Caesarea Philippi and before the Jerusalem authorities.

The experience at the Jordan, whether it be classed popularly as a religious vision or psychologically as an hallucination, is the private and personal experience of Jesus. This is clear in the Synoptic text itself. Mt and Mc distinctly say that *he saw,* and Lc, though he omits this notice, adds the equally favorable psychological motive that Jesus was *praying.* Further, Mc and Lc represent the voice as directly addressed to Jesus in the second person. Mt's voice in the third person contradicts his previous notice, *he saw.* In D a sy$^s$ $^c$ of Mt the voice speaks in the second person as in Mc and Lc. Irenaeus cites the words of the voice in Mt 3,17 in the second person. The texts of Mc and Lc are constant in their readings in the second person, the only variation being that D a b c ff$^2$ have the voice quote Psalms 2,7, which version of Lc 3,22 was known to

Justin Martyr, Clement of Alexandria, Origen, and Hilarius (Huck, S. 13; Resch, 3. Heft, S. 21f).

That the Baptist had made a profound popular impression by his appearance and message is clear from the reluctance of the chief priests and scribes to pronounce an unfavorable judgment regarding his baptism (Mc 11,32=Mt 21,26= Lc 20,6). Upon presenting himself for baptism Jesus must have shared fully in this popular impression made by John, and his emotions must have run considerably higher than those of the average pious person. Here it suffices to recall the statement of Holtzmann in his *Leben Jesu* (See above page 55) to the effect that Jesus' experience at the Jordan betrays no psychopathic elements, for Jesus proves the clearness of his judgment and the strength of his will too unmistakably in his subsequent life to deduce his vision here from any morbid mental state; besides, no religion has ever been founded by a personality whose imagination did not transcend the ABC of the experiences of the average run of men.

Case is dubious about the ecstatic element in Jesus' experience at the Jordan, *This picturesque description—the rending of the heaven, the descending dove, and the audible utterance of God — shows the primitive Christians' fondness for vivid imagery, while the prominence given to the ecstatic element in their own lives easily led them to interpret Jesus' experience in terms of ecstasy.* In this same connection Case further remarks quite to the point, *All that can be inferred from Jesus' action in coming to John's baptism is that it marked a decisive step in his active life. It was the response of his own pious life to the religious ideals for which John stood. As a result of this action Jesus' religious experience would naturally be quickened and deepened* (p. 288).

The value of the psychopathic evidence deduced from the baptism can only be determined in connection with the determination of the role which visions, or any single psychic experience or moment, played in the life, more specially in the self-consciousness of Jesus (see below page 206ff).

c)   The Temptation   Mc 1,12-13; Mt 4,1-11=Lc 4,1-13

The account of the temptation of Jesus, especially in Mt and Lc, with its spirit that drives or leads, with its period of fasting, the appearances of the angels, wild beasts and Satan, the adventurous and spectacular shifts of scene, and the developments in dialogue has proved to be a veritable treasure house from which the pathographers bring forth things both new and old.

For Holtzmann it is just in the temptation that we come to recognize the true character of Jesus' ecstasy. The whole setting of the forty days of fasting and the shifts of scene are ecstatic. But here we see Jesus overcoming ecstatic excesses and setting restrictions and bounds to the activities of the spirit that drove him. De Loosten sees in the temptation a physiologic and psychic crisis through which Jesus passed and which was attended by visions and illusions corresponding to his delusions of grandeur and provoked by his weakened physical state after the long period of fasting. For Binet-Sanglé it was in the desert that Jesus attained that hallucinatory stage of paranoia in which the hallucinations follow rapidly one upon the other and constitute a mental syndrome known as *le ragle* (see above page 96f). Hirsch writes: *During the forty days in the wilderness he must have had hallucinations continually* (p. 112; Ger. 109). These forty days in the desert mark the transition from the latent to the active phase of Jesus' paranoia; it is the period of the complete transformation of the personality. The formerly isolated and disconnected delusions expand, combine and group themselves into a great systematized structure.

The critical treatment of the temptation in the course of the life-of-Jesus research has been extremely varied. Venturini presented this scene in the form of an elaborate dialogue between Jesus and the Pharisee Soddac (I 447ff). Many critics and biographers of Jesus have found in the temptation account only an allegory of the struggle that went on within the soul of Jesus; the Satan here is only an ego-Satan (*Ich-Satan* according to von Delius, S. 32). Strauss declared the whole account a myth created as a parallel to the experiences of Moses (Ex 34,28) and Elijah (I Kgs 19,8). Others have found in the temptation a legend, or a corruptly transmitted parable based upon some real inner experience in the life of Jesus. Case suggests that *the account of his temptation which tradition has placed in close connection with his baptism may have been framed to furnish scriptural authentication for Jesus' failure to display at once messianic prerogatives* (p. 288ff).

But that the threefold temptation in one form or another goes back to actual words of Jesus is clear from the pertinent and pointed use of Scripture which is thoroughly characteristic of Jesus' command of it. This repulse of the tempter by resort to Scripture has a pertinent pointedness and piercing power of which the evangelists do not show themselves capable, especially Mt who clumsily inserts his proof from prophecy at every possible occasion. As examples of the characteristic command of Scripture by Jesus and the clumsy inserts by Mt are to be cited Mc 2,25; 11,17; 12,26 36 over against Mt 2,15 18; 4,14ff; 12,18ff; 13,35. Apart from this characteristic command of Scripture, the threefold aspects of the temptation fit too vitally and organically into later incidents in Jesus' public career in Mc to be declared a mere literary or legendary product without parallel or occasion in the public ministry of Jesus. This we shall see presently.

The Gospel of Hebrews, as cited twice by Origen and three times by Hieronymus, puts the story of the temptation in the mouth of Jesus in the first person: *Then my mother, the Holy Spirit, took me (by one of my hairs) and carried me away to the top of Mount Tabor* (Huck, S. 15; W. Bauer, S. 142f).

The three temptations in one form or another go back to actual words of Jesus; Mt and Lc have taken them from Q and inserted them into Mc's order in connection with his general mention of a period of temptation, 1,12-13. They set the temptation immediately after the baptism, for they seem to regard Jesus as having gained his full Messianic consciousness at the Jordan. Most modern critics agree with this Mt-Lc point of view and they reinforce this position by pointing out that the temptation logically and psychologically must follow immediately upon the experience at the baptism, for moments of high exaltation are regularly followed by times, or even periods of deep depression. Baldensperger writes, *The tempt-*

*ation is to such a degree a psychological necessity and is so
well placed at the threshold of Jesus' public ministry that, in
its peculiarity, it would otherwise be hardly comprehensible*
(S. 170).

With this view regarding the proper place for the insertion of the threefold temptation we cannot agree. The variations of Mt and Lc in both their introductions and conclusions
and their close correspondence in the text of the dialogues
show that this threefold temptation stood in Q doubtless as
pure discourse material without historical setting and without
any connection with an initial retreat to the desert parallel
to Mc 1,12-13.

Mt and Lc have misplaced their account of the temptation
from Q. Then the question arises: Where does the threefold
temptation belong if not in connection with the general mention of a temptation in Mc 1,12-13? To answer this question
we must first determine the principal point which the temptation would seem intended to make.

In the first two temptations of Mt, the first and the third
of Lc, the proper place of miracle and the legitimate employment of miracle-power seem to receive special emphasis. But
if the temptation has to do with the place that miracle is to
occupy in the mission and ministry of Jesus, the question must
have arisen later for him when he is actually confronted with
the problem of his miracle-power. There is too much of surprise and solicitude in Jesus' mind at the success of his word
and touch in Mc 1,21-38 to suppose that the whole question
had been settled by a struggle in self and solitude as Mt and
Lc would have us believe. Mt omits the closing scene of the
day in Capernaum (Mc 1,35-38) and Lc modifies it to the
extent that the problem is less personal and pressing for Jesus
(Lc 4,42-43). The problem of miracle and miracle-power does
not, nor, we may add, do other specific problems of Jesus, figure
in Mc's general notice of the temptation. Mc sets Jesus' personal struggle regarding the relation of miracle and message
in his mission and ministry at the close of the first day of the
manifestation of Jesus' power to cure and heal, where it historically and psychologically belongs.

But the chief point to this threefold temptation according to Mt and Lc does not seem to be miracle-power and its legitimate employment, for all three temptations focus upon the question of Jesus' Messianic consciousness, its credentials, and course of conduct. The tempter will draw inferences from this consciousness of being the Son of God with the intention of rejecting them as false. The temptations are not moral in the ordinary sense of the word, but Messianic. But it is just because they are Messianic that they are moral for Jesus. However, Mc does not give us the least suggestion that the temptation was Messianic in content and character.

The insertion of the three specific temptations from Q by Mt and Lc in connection with Mc 1,12-13 is purely associational, and not historical and logical. This insertion contradicts the climax of Mc's narrative according to which Jesus gains clearness concerning his Messianic mission and role only very late in his Galilean ministry, shortly before Caesarea Philippi, and not during the first retreat to the desert. If Mc had known and used the threefold temptation, he could not have introduced it into his narrative at 1,12-13, but only after the rebuke and rebuff of Peter in 8,33, unless he had completely revised his present representation of Jesus' painful climb to the Messianic conviction or had crassly contradicted himself.

Mc regards neither the question of miracle-power nor the Messianic question as settled once for all with 1,12-13. If the question of miracle-power and its employment had been successfully settled in the desert, why should this same problem be so pressing and personal for Jesus in Mc 1,35-38? If Jesus became clear and convinced concerning his Messianic dignity at this early date, why must he pass through such conflicts of consciousness as Mc represents during the whole of his Galilean ministry? These questions cannot be answered by remarking that the temptation in the desert is a test in the abstract and the subsequent struggles are tests in the concrete. In fact, the process is exactly the reverse. The threefold temptation is an allegorical abstraction symbolizing the previous particular concrete conflicts in Jesus' consciousness.

That the temptation in the desert was not a final, once-for-all struggle with Satan is clear from the early morning flight from Capernaum, the repeated retreats to solitude during the Galilean days, which retreats suddenly end with Caesarea Philippi, and Lc's own notice to the effect that Satan departed from him *for a season* (4,13). Further we find peculiar to Lc Jesus' appreciative word to his disciples, *Ye are they that have continued with me in my temptations* (22,28).

That Mt and Lc have misplaced their temptation matter from Q is further clear from the fact that the three single temptations have their historical connections and points of contact only at later moments in the subsequent life of Jesus. (Compare the statement of H. J. Holtzmann in his HC, S. 46: *Die drei Versuchungen selbst haben ihre historischen Anhaltspunkte erst in spaeteren Momenten des Lebens Jesu*). They are as follows:

1) Mc 1,35-38 can easily be understood and ranged alongside as a parallel to the first temptation in Mt 4,3-4= Lc 4,3-4. In both Jesus appears in the same dilemma; both have to do with the ethical employment of miracle-power; both are alike seductive in that both appeal to the use of miracle-power in behalf of supplying natural and legitimate human needs.

2) The second temptation of Mt, the third of Lc, is a parallel to the demand for a sign in Mc 8,11-12=Mt 16,1-4 =Lc 11,29.

3) The third temptation of Mt, the second of Lc, has its logical and historical connection in Mc 8,32b-33 (=Mt 16,22-23) where Jesus hears the tempter speaking through the mouth of an intimate disciple. Peter's rebuke (Lc omits this rebuke by Peter and his rebuff by Jesus) would as completely turn Jesus from the divinely appointed path as if he were to fall down and worship Satan. Jesus' rebuff to Peter is identical in point with Jesus' parting parry to Satan in Mt 4,10 (Lc 4,8). D Z L it sy$^{di \, s \, c}$ of Mt 4,10 add ὀπίσω μου and Jesus' reply to the tempter then reads identically with his sharp words to Peter in Mc 8,33a (=Mt 16,23a ὕπαγε ὀπίσω μου, σατανᾶ (compare Huck, S. 16).

The threefold temptation, although it goes back to actual words of Jesus, is not to be understood as a single situation and struggle of soul in which Jesus found himself prior to his public appearance in Galilee.  This threefold test is rather to be regarded as a reflective and reminiscent review of conflicts in Jesus' consciousness which had been repeatedly repulsed in the past.  It is a symbolical summary of the subjective seductions that presented themselves to Jesus' growing Messianic consciousness with regard to which he gained clearness not later than Caesarea Philippi where he for the first time allows himself to be greeted as the Messiah by one of his disciples; also where he does not protest against the application of the title to himself (Mc 8,27ff), yet expresses his modifications and reservations in its use (Mc 8,31).

If anywhere in all the Gospels Jesus proves his psychic soundness it is in his decisions and choices as represented in the threefold temptation. In his replies to the suggestive seductions of Satan we witness a cutting criticism of current and contemporary Messianic ideals which corresponds exactly to Jesus' complete rejection of the Messianic title in the ordinary sense, and yet a devotion to the traditional precepts of a pure piety that is the diametrical opposite of what we would expect of a paranoiac.  We witness here a range of reflection, a clearness of moral and ethical conception, a soundness of judgment, a directness of dialectic, a decided and determined devotion to duty as interpreted and understood, a volume of wholesome volition, and a purity of piety that would send even the specialist in normal psychology on a fruitless search among the most select and the soundest of souls to produce a parallel, to say nothing of the hope of citing cases confined to the care of a clinic.

It is well for Holtzmann that he speaks of the temptation as an ecstatic experience of Jesus in which, contrary to what is commonly understood as ecstasy, Jesus ends the struggle by an *Ueberwindung der Ekstase*, for no psychological element in the account of the threefold temptation is more pronounced than that of choice and volition.  In genuine ecstasy, to speak with Ribot, there is a *minimum*, if not a *zero of will* (DW, p. 107).

### d)  Mc 3,21:  Jesus and his Contemporaries

The pathographers of Jesus feel that they are simply following in the footsteps of Jesus' friends and family. Binet-Sanglé traces the history of the discovery of the insanity of Jesus from Mc 3,21 down to his own work (IV 295-326). Not one of the pathographers fails to cite Mc 3,21: *And when his friends heard it, they went out to lay hold on him: for they said, He is beside himself.* On this particular notice of Mc Soury commented: *If Mary and the brothers of Jesus had brought him again into the house of the carpenter of Nazareth, the Galilean prophet would perhaps have ended his life obscurely in some cellar of the paternal dwelling, held by a chain as the Gadarene demoniac* (p. 74f). Binet-Sanglé remarks, *Thus we see them leaving Nazareth and setting out for Capernaum, where Jesus then resided, and doing all in their power to lay hands on him doubtless with the intention of sequestering him and binding him with chains as was the custom of the time in the treatment of dangerous aliens.....  Knowing what awaited him, he refused to disperse the crowd before him. They must then for the time being cease to trouble themselves about him and abandon him to his vesania* (I 126f).

The offense caused by Mc 3,21 is as old as the Gospels of Mt and Lc who both omit it. This offense is also evinced in many of the Latin translations in which this verse is omitted. It is as recent as the latest life of Jesus, which was written by J. Lepsius in 1917-18. For the most part, this offense has been out of all connection with the psychiatric problem. On two scores it has been a source of trouble to the Christian conscience: 1) that Jesus' own people, especially Mary, could make such a charge; 2) that such a thing could be thought or said of Jesus by anyone. In the course of the life-of-Jesus research Mc 3,21 has been treated along these two lines.

Venturini saw in Mc 3,21, not the opinion of Jesus' friends or family, but the exasperation of Jesus' host who had tried in vain to get him to come and eat. Hase ascribed the charge

in Mc 3,21 to the instigation of the Pharisees who appear in
verse 22 and who had *a mental murder in mind* (S. 592). Keim
insisted that the friends in Mc 3,21 are not Jesus' mother and
brethren, who appear in verse 31, but that verse 20f and verses
31ff are two separate and independent scenes. This method
of assigning the charge to Jesus' enemies can cite certain of
the Latin translations, (D* a b d ff² i q) which Wellhausen
quotes as reading καὶ ὅτε ἤκουσαν περὶ αὐτοῦ οἱ γραμματεῖς καὶ
οἱ λοιποὶ ἐξῆλθον κρατῆσαι αὐτόν· ἔλεγον γὰρ ὅτι ἐξέστατοι
αὐτούς (Marci, S. 25) and which throws Mary into a much
more favorable light and relieves Jesus of the charge of mental
alienation. But Wellhausen says that this reading is clearly
a correction (Marci, S. 26). Sir John C. Hawkins agrees with
Wellhausen and sees here *an attempt to avoid difficulty* (p.
119). Hoffmann regards this correction as very old (S. 148).
Volkmar, before them, was more out-spoken. He called these
variations in the Latin *clear attempts of Latin monks to expunge the scandal* (which he called *der Mutter-Wahn*) *from
the virgin mother* (S. 221, 257ff). οἱ παρ' αὐτοῦ is a rather
unusual and infrequent expression, but the consensus of critical
opinion sees in it a definite designation of some of Jesus' own
kin. Wellhausen finds the most original reading in the Syrian
versions where οἱ ἀδελφοὶ αὐτοῦ displaces οἱ παρ' αὐτοῦ.

Other critics leave these words in the mouth of Mary, but
seek to tone them down by the introduction of various motives.
Neander found it hardly conceivable that Mary could think
such a thing of her son; she came to Capernaum doubtless sol-
icitous for the safety of her son in view of the threatening
developments (S. 420). B. Weiss writes: *The whole account
does not exhibit the least trace of any mental alienation, but
plainly proves the easily understood care and anxiety which,
if somewhat limited, was exceedingly well-intentioned, bestowed
on the member of the family who had been too long removed
from the others* (II 284). Lepsius reminds us of the romantic
lives of Jesus when he finds Mary on this occasion to be an innocent tool in the plot of the chief of the synagogue at Capernaum to get Jesus out of the way.

B. Weiss further remarked that ἐξέστη does not neces-

sarily denote the state of being *beside one's self*, for Mc employs
this word elsewhere (2,12; 5,42; 6,51) with only conjugational
variations in describing the *amazement* of the multitudes (II
283); it would denote here then only the state of wonder or
awe in which Jesus found himself. But Volkmar had long before remarked: *Here amazement on the part of Jesus is not
to be thought of.' The absolute* ἐξέστη *can only mean for Mc*:
*he was beside himself, or insane* (S. 256). He finds the con-
notation of this word here to be identical with Paul's use of it
in II Cor 5,13. Still others avoid the difficulty by interpreting
ἐξέστη as meaning that Jesus was *exhausted*, or had *fainted*,
or *departed*. Bleek sees in Mc 3,21 not an expressed opinion
but rather the second evangelist's explanation of the action of
Jesus' family: *But it is not necessary to assume that Jesus'
family, or any member of it, used just this expression; it is
rather the evangelist who designates briefly in this way how he
believes they regarded the incident and how he thinks their
action is to be explained* (I 506).

But liberal criticism as a whole is more severe and less
careful for the character and conduct of Mary and concedes
the historicity of the scene in Mc 3,21 as representing the
actual attitude of Jesus' family toward him. Volkmar writes:
*There is perhaps no other sentence in Mc, or in the other gos-
pels, that in and of itself is as historical and credible as this
one* (S. 226). [It is only fair to say that Volkmar reckons here
with the possibility of a myth-formation patterned after the
visit to Moses by his family in Ex 18]. Emil Wendling ascribes
3,21 to *Urmarkus* (S. 21ff). P. W. Schmiedel sets Mc 3,21
at the head of the list of his nine historical ground-pillars for
a scientific life of Jesus (PJSMG, S. 7). O. Holtzmann conceives the whole scene as follows: Jesus' mother and brethren
were dissatisfied with Jesus' refusal to return home from the
Jordan and take up his previous occupation. Jesus' unconventional words and conduct in the meantime had reflected upon
them and they came to Capernaum convinced of his derangement and determined to take him back by force if necessary.
But their plan failed because Jesus was surrounded by his admirers and followers (LJ, S. 193).

Regarding the meaning of ἐξέστη liberal critics are also unanimously agreed that Mc intends here to tell us that, in the opinion of his friends or family, Jesus was in a state bordering on insanity.

Our effort here cannot be in the direction of explaining Mc 3,21 away, for it seems to belong to the bed-rock of earliest tradition. Nevertheless we can urge a general consideration drawn from Mc as a whole, and the other Gospels as well, which will throw some light on Mc 3,21 and help toward historical orientation and appreciation. The Gospel writers themselves, specially Mc, seem to delight in portraying a lack of understanding of Jesus' words and conduct on the part of not only Jesus' family, but of his own disciples whose dullness throws a not altogether favorable light upon them (See Wrede, MGE, S 101ff). In Mc the dullness of the disciples is almost inconceivable. Jesus' clearest words and parables they either fail to understand and must demand a private explanation, or they misunderstand them and must be subsequently corrected (see Mc 4,10 13 33f; 6,52; 7,17-19; 8,16-21; 9,10 32; 10,10). In spite of the simplicity of their origin and former surroundings historical probability is against Mc's representation of the inferior mentality of Jesus' intimate followers. That Mc is here exaggerating is clear from the fact that Jesus' opponents seem to gather, without the least hesitation, the import of Jesus' remarks and parables directed against them which are not less unclear and indirect than those addressed to the disciples. It is not historical exactness and completeness that causes Mc to faithfully report the situation in 3,21. It is rather his desire and delight to show that neither Jesus' friends nor family, those who knew him best, were equal to the task of fully understanding him. This constitutes an essential element in Mc's theology, namely, that Jesus, his person and his preaching as well, was and is incomprehensible. (This tendency is still more pronounced in the Fourth Gospel where Jesus is ceaselessly not understood or is misunderstood, and the disciples are so woefully weak of understanding that he must reserve many things that he would like to say to them until a later time. See Jn 2,20f; 3,4; 4,11 33; 6,42 52; 7,35; 8,22 27 57; 10,6; 11,13

24; 14,5; 16,17-18). This incomprehensibleness of Jesus' person Mc accomplishes not so much by the exaltation of Jesus himself as by bringing Jesus' disciples, friends, and family down to a level of intelligence that hardly does them historical justice.

But Mc 3,21 does not exhaust the New Testament contemporary judgment against the psychic soundness of Jesus. In the very next verse we read that scribes (Mt 12,24—*Pharisees*=Lc 11,15—*some of them*) say that Jesus was insane, that is, *He hath Beelzebub.* This scene is doubly attested in the sources; it is found in both Mc and Q. The subsequent Beelzebub address is a bit more elaborate in Q, but the charge is more severe in Mc. Mt and Lc avoid the direct charge of possession by modifying Mc's Βεελζεβοὺλ ἔχει, which is repeated in effect in verse 30 (πνεῦμα ἀκάθαρτον ἔχει) and both of which are employed elsewhere only in reference to cases of demoniacal possession encountered by Jesus, to ἐν τῷ βεελζεβοὺλ (Lc has the article follow) which would designate not more than an agency of or an alliance with the evil powers. It is possible that Mt and Lc found their form of the charge in Q. Volkmar found Mc 3,30 *a still worse surmise* than 3,21. A. Bollinger also finds the diagnosis here less mild, but sees the more original form of the charge in Mt 12,24, of which Mc 3,22 is only a secondary revision (S. 55ff).

This charge against Jesus on the part of the religious authorities is easily understandable in view of the conflict that went on between them. It was the habit of the religious authorities to brand as insane the prophets of a religion that would revolutionize their own. They pronounced a like judgment upon the Baptist (Mt 11,18=Lc 7,33) as did their fathers before them upon the prophets of their day (Jer 29,26; Hos 9,7; the prophets in general, I Sam 10 and 19; II Kgs 9,11; Zech 13). The nature of some of John's preaching, as well as that of Jesus, (Mt 3,7-10=Lc 3,7-9; Mt 23,13-36=Lc 11,37-52), with its direct denunciation of the religious authorities makes quite clear their charge of possession. It was not the eccentricities in the Baptist's habits of life (Mt 3,4=Mc 1,6), but his message that aroused them. To say nothing of

Jesus in this connection, John's practical advice to his inquirers in Lc 3,10-14 is hardly that of an unsound mind.

De Loosten alone sees in Lc 4,23, *Physician, heal thyself,* a taunt or insult which Jesus was forced to hear early in his ministry of healing (S. 62). But this is plainly a parable as Jesus designates it; it may be original with Jesus or a current axiom revised and employed by him (See Juelicher, **GR, II** 171ff).

To the contemporary charges and opinions concerning the soundness of Jesus' mind in the Fourth Gospel belong 7,19-20; 8,48-52; 10,19-21. The first and third passages are interesting parallels to Mc 3,22 30. The second may be a remote parallel. But the present form of all three is a Johannine creation. They figure too clearly in the author's elaborate system of the development of hostilities and sworn enmity between Jesus and the Jews (!), and in the staging of divisions of contemporary opinion concerning Jesus' person, of which the Fourth Evangelist is very fond (12,29). Jn 7,5 is perhaps an instructive parallel to Mc 3,21.

There is no need or purpose in trying to explain Mc 3,21 22 away. Both constituted a problem for Mt and Lc as they do for us. They solved the difficulty by omission or modification; this we cannot do. We may urge critical considerations concerning Mc's theology of Jesus' person as incomprehensible and his method of presenting his theology. Historical reconstruction may find reasons for an estrangement between Jesus and his family. We know further that a man's enemies are seldom, if ever, reliable and impartial judges of his mental soundness. But we must admit that some of Jesus' contemporaries, some of his family and friends as well as his foes, regarded him as an alien. But that these contemporary judgments passed upon Jesus are correct is quite a different question which can be answered only by our study as a whole.

Dr. F. Moerchen, Head-Physician in Ahrweiler, writes in his pamphlet, *Die Psychologie der Heiligkeit* (S. 13): *The champion of r e l i g i o n in particular is readily subjected to the adverse judgment of the crowd which feels the abnormal and striking element in his thought and action as something*

*foreign and unintelligible to it.* Concerning the scientific worth
of these contemporary judgments he says, *But critical judgment of the contemporary background, of the intellectual milieu
from which the saints and other religious heroes come, must
admonish us to apply to them with caution the measure of modern psychological and psychiatric methods of observation.*

Sommer writes: *Experience teaches that many men have
been regarded by their contemporaries as half or wholly paranoiac whom the historian looks upon as the pioneers of new
thoughts* (Quoted by Werner, PGJ, S. 6). Such was the experience of Luther, Goethe, and Bismarck. One nerve-specialist
diagnosed the case of the late and honored Theodore Roosevelt
as *paranoia reformatoria* (See Werner, PGJ, S. 7).

A. Schweitzer remarks to the point that such amateur
judgments of the remote past as are found in Mc 3,21 22 are
entirely without significance for modern psychiatry (PBJ, S.
25 Anm. 1). From the strictly medical point of view Dr.
Moerchen writes: *The contemporaries of Christ were not so
trained in psychology that we could utilize scientifically any
of their chance utterances concerning striking psychic phenomena* (MKP, S. 423).

e) The Transfiguration Mt 17,1-8=Mc 9,2-8=Lc 9,28-36

De Loosten finds in the transfiguration one of those occasional instances in which the disciples are witnesses of Jesus'
ecstatic experiences. Why Jesus selects just these three disciples is unclear; he probably felt the approach of an unusually
exalted state and would suffer only his most intimate companions as witnesses. The two prophets whom he sees and with
whom he speaks are hallucinated. Jesus' power of hypnotic
suggestion over the disciples enabled him to make them see and
hear what he saw and heard. That Jesus was fully aware of
the pathological character of the experience is clear from his
command for silence. But this was unnecessary, for the disciples realized the sad state of their master's mind and voluntarily held their peace, Lc 9,36b (S. 59ff). Binet-Sanglé
sees here an attack of ecstasy attended by facial transfiguration not unknown in certain varieties of cataleptic attack (I

211ff). For Hirsch, Jesus' hallucinations form the basis of
the story of the transfiguration (p. 112f; Ger. 110). Baumann construes the account as a vision common to all four present (S. 21).

The conclusions of modern research in the life of Jesus
have set the transfiguration, in one way or in another, in connection with the confession of Peter at Caesarea Philippi. A.
Schweitzer has it precede the confession of Peter, for it is at
Caesarea Philippi that Peter betrays to the twelve the secret
he had learned on the mount of transfiguration, (MLG, S.
60ff). J. Weiss and Wellhausen have the transfiguration follow Caesarea Philippi: the former finds the voice the first and
positive answer to Peter's confession (AeE, S. 228ff); the latter finds that the voice sets the divine seal upon this confession (Marci, S. 71). Baldensperger also finds the transfiguration scene in its correct chronological place as it now stands
in the Synoptics (SBJ, S. 188, Anm. 1). O. Holtzmann identifies the two incidents, the transfiguration being only the subjective side of the disciples' experience which is objectively
recounted as Peter's confession at Caesarea Philippi.

The problem of the transfiguration from the psychiatric
point of view is simply solved. One has only to read the accounts of it as it stands in the New Testament. Rasmussen
and Holtzmann do not employ it in their contentions. The latter writes: *In the transfiguration scene Jesus is the object, not
the subject of the revelation* (WJE, S. 39, Anm. 1).

The account of the transfiguration is rich in psychological
details which show, however, that the vision is not that of Jesus
but of the disciples:

| Mt | Mc | Lc |
|---|---|---|
| There appeared unto them | There appeared unto them | |
| | | Now Peter and they that were with him were heavy with sleep; but when they were fully awake, they saw.... |
| | Peter knew not what he said... | Peter, not knowing what he said...... |
| They were sore afraid ........ | They were sore afraid ........ | They feared............ |

(Spitta finds Lc's account the more original; S. 247f).

The voice in all three Gospels, as well as in the various texts of the same Gospel, speaks consistently in the third person. A C D N Δ Ψ... min b c e f q vg sy [s][c] of Lc 9,35 read ἀγαπητός instead of ἐκλελεγμένος ; further, C³ D M a add ἐν ᾧ ηὐδόκησα as in Mt 17,5 (Huck, S. 103). In the account of the transfiguration in II Peter 1,17-18 (*For he received from God the Father, honor and glory, when there was borne such a voice to him by the Majestic Glory, This is my beloved Son, in whom I am well pleased; and this voice we ourselves heard borne out of heaven, when we were with him in the holy mount*) the voice is addressed to Jesus, but the disciples are ear-witnesses for whom the message is really intended since it comes in the third person. In John 12,28-30 the voice seems addressed to Jesus, but is unintelligible to some of the by-standers for whose sake it is nevertheless uttered. But this Johannine account of the transfiguration is so radically revised that it is an almost unrecognizable remnant of the Synoptic account and does not deserve historical credibility.

Against Binet-Sanglé's description of a cataleptic metamorphosis is to be urged the fact that not only Jesus' face, but his garments and whole figure are transfigured. This makes it clear that the experience is that of the disciples and not of Jesus.

There is a further probability that we have here, not an incident from the historical life of Jesus, but a resurrection experience. J. Weiss finds it to be an anticipation of the resurrection appearances (AeE, S. 229f). Wellhausen says that it was originally an appearance of the risen Lord (Marci, S. 71). In common with the resurrection appearances we note that the transfiguration is in Galilee (Mc 16,7; Mt 28,7), is on a mountain (Mt 28,16), Jesus appears in glorified form, a cloud disperses the vision and the Syrian version of Mc 9,7 reads that the cloud envelopes *him* (αὐτῷ instead of αὐτοῖς) as in Acts 1,9 which Wellhausen considers the more original reading (Marci, S. 71).

Further the transfiguration seems to be the original resurrection appearance to Peter referred to in Lc 24,34 and I

Cor 15,5.  J. Weiss says that the transfiguration was originally a vision to Peter only (SdNT, I 155f).  Schweitzer speaks of it as an illusion of Peter (PBJ, S. 38).  Besides, the role of Peter in the incident is so predominant that the other two disciples could completely disappear without disturbing the scene.

### f)  The Cursing of the Fig Tree    Mt 21,18-20=
### Mc 11,12-14 20-22

In so far as our present problem is concerned, von Hartmann was the first to begin the quarrel with the cursing of the fig tree.  He saw in this incident the ease with which Jesus' anger could flash up even on the most harmless occasions and avenge itself most uncritically upon innocent objects, (S. 69). De Loosten speaks of the senseless cursing of the fig tree which is to be understood only in the light of the highly pitched nervous tension in which Jesus found himself during his Jerusalem days (S. 77f).  Binet-Sanglé cites and agrees with von Holbach in designating this act of Jesus as impossible to a man of sound mind.

The cursing of the fig tree was problematic as far back as the church fathers Origen and Ambrosius.  In the course of modern criticism none have left it untouched.  The naturalistic explanation began with Paulus who found Jesus' curse only a statement based upon his own observation of the fact that the tree was dying and could never bear again.  On Mc 11,13c he comments, *It was just a poor season for figs* (EHB, III 157).  Bleek followed in the footsteps of Paulus but refused to surrender the miracle.  Jesus' words only accelerated the process of corruption that was already at work at the tree's heart; Jesus destroyed no healthy part of the tree but simply hastened the inevitable issue.  However, he assures us that this miracle was not performed during Jesus' last Jerusalem days, but during his visit to the feast of the tabernacles (Jn 7,2) one year before (II 312).  Beyschlag followed Bleek in this chronological shift, (I 321).

However, the chief inclination in the course of the life-of-Jesus research has been to declare the incident unhistorical and assign to it a purely symbolic significance.  The offense at

its historicity was due to the lack of moral motive for such
an action; its physical possibility would require omnipotence;
it conflicts with Jesus' character; and Jesus' disappointment at
not finding figs out of season is too senseless to be taken seriously.  Volkmar, Neander (S. 636ff), Lange, Keim, etc., saw
in the incident only a symbol of the fate about to befall
the Jewish nation.  That Mc means it all as symbolic is clear
to Volkmar in the notice, *for it was not the season of figs.*
Beyschlag regards the cursing of the fig tree as symbolic of
the destruction about to fall upon Jerusalem; he cannot believe that Jesus came away hungry from the hospitable home
in Bethany (I 401).  Most recently A. Westphal is more homiletic in his symbolization of this *parabole en action* and remarks,
*It is a parable making clear to the disciples the fate reserved
for that portion of humanity which would disappoint the hopes
of the Creator* (I 352, note 3).

The chief argument against this symbolization of the
cursing of the fig tree is that the first two evangelists do not
seem to regard it as such, for they proceed to attach to it the
gnome concerning mountain-moving faith which does not in
the least suggest the imminent fate about to overtake either
Jerusalem or the Jewish people.  Lc's form of the gnome is
reported in a very different connection, 17,6, and is very interesting and instructive for he drops the figure of the mountain
and employs a variety of fig tree, συκάμινος.

The problem of the cursing of the fig tree has been solved,
for the most part, along textual-critical lines which lead back,
not to an actual act of Jesus, but to a corruption of or by
early Christian tradition.  Strauss was the pioneer in striking
out these lines which later criticism has followed rather consistently.  The two chief exceptions belong to the twentieth
century:  1) the eschatological exposition, represented almost
exclusively by Schweitzer; 2) the hard historicity of O. Holtzmann.  The latter writes, *This nature miracle stands firm as
an historical fact: the fig tree that Jesus cursed actually withered* (WJE, S. 93).  Jesus' curse is only the exasperated expression of the discomfort caused by the hunger he suffered.
In this act Holtzmann discovers fine (?) human features of

Jesus, for he hungers, is mistaken, disappointed, and curses a tree. He further reminds us that it was a tree, and not a person, that Jesus cursed.

Strauss admitted, by way of exception however, that no Old Testament parallels could be cited after which this miracle of Jesus was modelled, but he traced a New Testament development beginning with the figure used by the Baptist (Mt 3,10 =Lc 3,9), later employed by Jesus himself (Mt 7,19), still later formulated into a parable (Lc 13,6-9), and last of all corrupted into an act of Jesus by early Christian tradition; *Here we have before us one and the same theme in three different forms: first in its most concentrated form as a gnome, then elaborated into a parable, and finally converted into an historical incident* (Leben Jesu 1835, II 251). Bruno Bauer reverted this process and found that Lc had made a parable out of Mc's cursing of the fig tree (III 110ff). Just recently Spitta has urged that the themes of Mc 11,12-14 and Lc 13,6-9 are fundamentally contradictory; Lc omits the cursing of the fig tree because he did not find it in his sources (S. 306ff). Many, however, agree with the opinion of Wernle to the effect that Lc omits the cursing of the fig tree because he regards it as a doublet or parallel of 13,6-9 (SF, S. 6).

The conduct of Jesus in this Mt-Mc incident of the cursing of the fig tree is purely apocryphal. It is a miracle of punishment and destruction unparalleled in the canonical texts and it contradicts Jesus' character in the most flagrant fashion. Lc 9,52ff tells us that Jesus refused to allow fire to be called down from heaven upon an inhospitable Samaritan village and rebuked his disciples for such a suggestion which A C D X Θ ....min a b c f q sy vg hl aeth justify by adding *even as Elijah did.* D Fw K M Π Θ..... min lat syc vg hl add *and said, Ye know not what manner of spirit ye are of* to Jesus' reply which Fw K M Π Θ .... min a b c e f q r vg sy c vg hl bo arm further elaborate with *For the Son of man came not to destroy men's lives but to save* them (Huck, S. 114). As Strauss said in this connection it would have been much more like Jesus to restore and revive a barren or dying fig tree than to cause a green one to wither away to the very roots.

The variations in the incident as reported by Mc and Mt are very interesting and instructive. The course of the legendary process is still discernible in the canonical sources. Mc has the disciples discover and remark upon the withered fig tree only on the day following the curse pronounced by Jesus; but Mt has it wither away under the very breath of Jesus and before the very eyes of the disciples. Further Mc 11,12-14 20-21 is an interpolation by the evangelist which breaks the proper logical order and connection between Mc 11,15-19 and 27-33. Mt's manner of insertion accomplished by the contraction of the two separate elements of Mc is less disturbing.

As a critical conclusion on the cursing of the fig tree we can agree with the conclusion of Strauss: *In this case the prize belongs to the third gospel which has preserved to us, separate and pure, the parable of the barren* συχῇ *and the* συχάμινος *that can be removed by faith, each in its original form and meaning* (Leben Jesu 1835, II 253).

The cursing of the fig tree is apocryphal and legendary; as such it can not be ascribed to Jesus for historico-critical reasons and can furnish no support or matter for the pathographic contention.

g) The Cleansing of the Temple Mt 21,12-17=
Mc 11,15-19=Lc 19,45-46 (47-48)

For Rasmussen it would be difficult to find a more typical description of an attack of *grand mal* than is depicted in the Gospel account of the cleansing of the temple. The religious character of the act cannot save it, for it stands in open contradiction with Jesus' own teaching of forbearance. It is only an outbreak in action against the religious authorities of what had formerly confined itself to outbreaks in words. Here as nowhere else in the Gospels Jesus' awful affliction expresses itself in a classic and clinical manner (S. 140f). De Loosten speaks of the cleansing of the temple as a highly striking act of violence carried out in a bitter temper of wrath and hatred (S. 78). Binet-Sanglé sees here one of those dangerous acts frequent in mental alienation. Whether it was premeditated or spontaneous is not clear, but as all such dangerous acts it

stood in direct relation with Jesus' systematized delusion and
delirium. It was executed in an emotional state of maniacal
fury. *This was an impulsive action. It was sudden, abrupt,
explosive, executed like a flash and should have been followed
by a feeling of satisfaction, assuagement, relief and perhaps
by a feeling of deep depression* (IV 213).

Among the early church fathers Origen reckoned the
cleansing of the temple among the greatest of Jesus' miracles.
But modern criticism has rejected this view, however, without
escaping certain difficulties connected with the incident. These
difficulties have been twofold: 1) chronological; 2) moral.

The chronological problem arises out of the difference
between the Johannine and Synoptic accounts. In the Fourth
Gospel the cleansing of the temple is the inaugural act of Jesus'
public appearance proper; in the Synoptics it is among the
very last of Jesus' acts, being executed less than a week before
his death. Paulus met this chronological problem by accepting
two cleansings of the temple, one at the beginning and one at
the very close of Jesus' public career (LJ, I 1 172ff; I 2 86f).
Since Strauss the alternative has been set of rejecting one or
the other of the accounts in the matter of chronology. Conservative critics have favored the Johannine location (B.
Weiss). The liberals agree in rejecting the Fourth in favor
of the Synoptic account where Jesus' act in cleansing the temple seems to have been the one thing that so suddenly precip-
itated his death.

From our present point of view the difficulty is moral.
Here Jesus acts with a show of spirit that is exceptional for
him. Though the sources tell us nothing of the emotions that
stimulated or attended this act, nevertheless its execution could
not have been without strong emotional antecedents and attendants. In the course of the life-of-Jesus research the very
character of the act has led Jesus' biographers to speak of his
wrath or anger on this occasion. Some have been more careful and toneful in their choice of vocabulary and have spoken
of Jesus' *righteous indignation.*

The majority of critics, less psychological in their treatment and emphasis, have felt a certain incongruity between

this show of spirit, this aggressiveness of action, and Jesus'
own teaching and the type of conduct naturally expected of
him.

Some have solved the difficulty by declaring the whole
scene unhistorical. Volkmar regarded the cleansing of the
temple as morally nonsensical and physically inconceivable.
The whole account is purely symbolic. He laid all stress on
ἤρξατο. *He* (Jesus) *cleansed the temple universally* (S. 511ff).
For Neander the lifted whip of cords was never applied; it
was only a symbol. Besides, what could one lone man do
against so many? (S. 277).

Others declare themselves for the historicity of the incident and see Jesus here acting only in necessary accord with
his prophetic commission and consciousness. The success of
the act was due to his popular backing, or to the forcefulness
of the impression of his personality. Besides his act must have
met with tremendous popular approval. B. Weiss writes,
*Every pious Israelite must have approved in heart this bold
deed* (II 7). Bleek writes, *That those present obeyed his command and withdrew with their merchandise is primarily to be
conceived as the effect of the Lord's imposing person charged
as it was with a holy earnestness and a prophetic dignity,
rather than the effect of any kind of application of physical
force* (II 308).

Other critics, pronouncedly psychological in interest and
emphasis, have Jesus act under the impulse of all the stronger
emotions that would naturally accompany such a rigorous and
revolutionary step. Strauss found the act full of passion and
threw doubt upon the holiness of Jesus' wrath in its execution.
Keim saw Jesus in the temple as the revolutionary Messianic
zealot. It was his single step into the full possession of the
Messianic consciousness. Here he is a changed person and not
the real Jesus of the new Galilean religion. The expulsion
of the merchants is too rough and ready to fit into his gentler
nature and inclination. This act resulted in his being more
respected and feared than loved in Jerusalem, but it was the
greatest day of his life (III 95ff). O. Holtzmann cannot
conceive the cleansing of the temple as physically possible with-

out an intervention of force in which Jesus was supported by
his disciples.  It was doubtless a regular battle in which Jesus
captured the outer court of the temple and which he continued
to occupy (Mc 11,16) throughout the day (LJ, S. 326).   J.
Weiss, on the contrary, sees Jesus accomplish this feat alone,
not only unsupported but unaccompanied by his disciples.

Pathographically the incident has nothing to contribute.
The whip of cords belongs to the fourth evangelist.  Among
the Synoptics Mc's account is the most graphic and the fullest
of temper, yet less temperamental and more determined, for
verse 16 represents Jesus as policing the position he has taken.
(Spitta regards this notice of Mc as a later redaction; S. 309).
In the cleansing of the temple we see Jesus accepting and acting the role of the old prophet.   Had his act in any wise been
unjustifiable, his enemies would certainly never have failed to
arraign him for it at his trial where they seemed so embarrassed for tenable testimony.   The justifiability of the act,
combined with Jesus thus challenging the authority of the
chief priests, seems more than all else to have spurred his
enemies on to as speedy a revenge as possible.   Had this expulsion of the merchants been a real violation against the temple,
or unpopular, Jesus would not have been able to appear daily
preaching and teaching there.   The temple authorities do not
question the act itself, but only request credentials for such
authority as is clear from Mc 11,27ff (=Mt 21,23ff=Lc 20,
1ff) which is the logical continuation of Mc 11,18.

The only hope of finding pathographic matter in the
cleansing of the temple is in the mind and viewpoint of the
pathographer himself who sees in the prophetic consciousness,
and in all the pious pioneer souls of religion, only a morbid
psychological phenomenon.   Against this view of the prophetic
consciousness the writer would refer the reader to Dr. Dieckhoff's article, *Der Prophet Ezechiel*, in the *Zeitschrift fuer Religionspsychologie* (*Band I, Heft 5*, S. 193ff), in which he
insists that, from the medical point of view, it is permissible
to speak of some of the acts, words and experiences of the old
prophets as mistaken, but not as morbid.

Regarding the purely psychiatric judgment of conduct

and single acts it is well to cite the statements of two authorities. *It is well to observe that the conclusion of the existence of a psychic disorder cannot be drawn solely from conduct which is without motive and which cannot be sufficiently explained by psychological considerations; in each particular case it must be proven that m o r b i d l y impulsive actions are actually present which belong to definite psychoses clinically demonstrable* (Binswanger, S. 53). *No isolated act can be taken as an infallible index of the exact morbid condition* (Kraepelin, S. 95).

h)  Gethsemane Mt 26,36-46=Mc 14,32-42=Lc 22,39-46

Rasmussen sees in the Gethsemane scene a characteristic attack of epileptic *petit mal.* Jesus' fear on this occasion is morbid and is without parallel in the life of any healthy-minded person even when confronted with death itself. In Gethsemane Jesus falls to the ground, lies in agony, and vents himself in fervent prayer in a purely psychopathic manner. That his fear is morbid is clear from the fact that it as suddenly disappears as it appears; healthy fear continues till the danger is past (S. 138f). De Loosten finds that Jesus' agony in Gethsemane, though attended by visions, brings him down from his delirium to a fairly normal state of soul. It is only with his command to Peter to put up his sword (Mt 26,52-54) that Jesus' delirium breaks forth again with all of its old force; *with these words he came to himself again* (S. 82ff). Binet-Sanglé also finds Jesus' fear on this night morbid because of its intense physiological concomitants, its lack of sufficient reason, and its extreme persistency. In Gethsemane Jesus suffers a vaso-motoric attack attended by facial hematidrosia fundamentally due to diseased and disordered nerves and particularly occasioned by exposure to the chill and damp of the night air. The figure of the cup and the appearance of the

---

(In volume I, page 252f, Binet-Sanglé says that the agony of Jesus in Gethsemane presents all the characteristics of a morbid emotion; one of the three which he cites from Féré is that such an emotion is without sufficient reason or is entirely unfounded. In IV 355 he proceeds to contradict himself and seems to have forgotten what he wrote in volume I, for he says: *La cause occasionnelle de son attaque d'angoisse fut la crainte justifiée du supplice qui l'attendait).*

angel are visual hallucinations. The depressed and agitated state of consciousness in which Jesus found himself is morbid. The Gethsemane scene alone is sufficient to prove that the founder of the Christian religion was a mental degenerate (I 250-288).

In the history of Christian thought the scene in Gethsemane has been problematic for theological and christological rather than for historical and critical reasons. The theological solution began with the Fourth Gospel which does not report the scene; but that this solution by omission was not satisfactory is evident in the theological literature since, both the early and the late.

In view of the pathographic contention our interest in the scene is psychological and critical. Does Jesus here manifest morbid emotions? In order to be morbid, his fear on this occasion must be ungrounded or without sufficient objective reason. The ground for healthy fear must lie either in the immediate antecedents or in the anticipation of what is about to come; the greater the proximity of the antecedents or the anticipated fate the greater the impression upon the imagination and the more intense the fear. Jesus' fear in Gethsemane is fully justified in the antecedents and in the immediate consequences. The critical course of the Jerusalem contentions, the desperate bitterness of the religious authorities, and the desertion of a regular disciple would lead a man of any discernment whatever to know that the climax had been reached and that his hour had struck. Further, Jesus' fear is justified by what follows, for before he can leave the place of prayer he is arrested; his former disciple had served as guide. Had the arrest not taken place, and had Jesus enjoyed liberty for a considerable subsequent period, then one might begin to speak of his ungrounded fear in Gethsemane. But the acutest anticipations of Jesus' agonized soul during this last night realized themselves with the greatest possible speed, for before sundown of the following dawn he hung dead on the cross.

That Jesus foresaw his passion and death in all the details as the three prophecies, Mc 8,31 ; 9,31 ; 10,32, represent is very doubtful, for they are clearly modelled after the passion story itself. But that Jesus spoke of his end as a cup to be drunk or a baptism with which he was to be baptized (Mc 10,38f= Mt 20,22f=Lc 12,50a) is highly probable. But thus to speak with composure of his end which was yet far ahead in the future and while he was yet far from Jerusalem is quite a different thing from facing it as less than twenty-four hours away. There is nothing morbid in Jesus' emotions in Gethsemane; under the circumstances his state of soul is perfectly natural. The contrast of Jesus' conduct during his last night with that of Socrates has been drawn since the beginning of early Christian tradition, and to the disadvantage of Jesus. It is true that Jesus was not stoic in his view of suffering, neither in the case of others nor in his own case. But the normal and natural emotions of the healthy-minded person in an hour when death seems certain are those of Jesus and not those of Socrates. It was a no less distinguished thinker than Kant who pronounced stoic morality pathological because it set the springs of duty elsewhere than in the pure moral law of conscience (*Kritik der praktischen Vernunft, Reclam* 1111-1112, S. 104).

In Gethsemane we see Jesus taking serious things seriously. His emotions are not only normal and natural, but his assembly of volitional powers and his decisions are of such a high order and so unselfish that they are heroic in the noblest sense. Ch. H. Weisse made a pertinent point in this connection when he wrote: *It is a well established fact of psychology that just the uncertainty concerning external details in particular, even when a presentiment and inner certainty concerning the approach of a fateful hour is felt in general, can produce such an agony of soul in a character completely composed and sure of itself* (I 612).

The critical side of the Gethsemane scene has to do chiefly with Lc's account. Lc has very radically abbreviated the Marcan account, and doubtless for the reason, as Wernle suggests (SF, S. 33), that the early Christian community was beginning to take offense at this deep humiliation of Jesus. That there is tenable truth in this view is evident from the tendency of the fourth evangelist to strip all struggle from the life of Jesus; he leaves only the most ragged and hardly recognizable

remnant of the Gethsemane struggle in 12,27 and 18,11.
Spitta throws doubt upon the historicity of the whole Gethsemane scene because he fails to find in it traces of the original
Synoptic document (*Grundschrift*); our present Lc has borrowed the scene from Mc perhaps under the influence of Heb
5,7ff (S. 388ff).

The special point of interest in Lc's account for us here
is found in verses 43-44: *And there appeared unto him an
angel from heaven, strengthening him. And being in an agony
he prayed more earnestly; and his sweat became as it were great
drops of blood falling down upon the ground.* Attempts to
defend the literal historicity of these two verses have not been
unknown. Venturini has Mary play the role of the angel; *It
was Mary who, as an angel of God, appeared here in the bitter
struggle to comfort the magnificent martyr* (IV 96). Regarding the sweating of blood some have spoken of a physical indis-
position of Jesus on this particular night. Binet-Sanglé confirms this phenomenon from the medical point of view and cites
sixteen cases of hematidrosia among mystics (I 261-275). But
such naturalistic and medical methods are futile and unnecessary from the angle of textual criticism.

Regarding the appearance of the aiding angel it is to be
remembered that Lc is specially fond of these angelophanies
(See 1,11f; 1,26ff; 2,9-15; Acts 1,10; 5,19; 12,7; 16,9; 22,
17f; 23,11). Bruno Bauer found that Lc has the angel appear
at the wrong time for Jesus must pray still more earnestly
after this divine reinforcement (III 251). Paulus found the
sweating of blood merely a philological miracle (*bloss ein philo-
logisches Wunder;* EHB, IV 563).

No two verses of the canonical Gospels have a weaker literary and textual basis than Lc 22,43-44. They are not only
peculiar to the third Gospel, but they are not found in the
majority of its best texts. They are missing in Aleph[a] A B
N R T W 13-69-124-788-826-579 f sy[s] sa bo; they are found
in Aleph* D L Q X Θ  . .min lat sy[di c vg hl] arm aeth (Huck,
S. 197). Even B. Weiss regards them as so uncertain that
he neglects them entirely.

Further, no two verses of the canonical Gospels have been

more unanimously assigned by critics to legend, myth, or apocryphal addition, or dogmatic invention than these two verses.
Volkmar writes: *Luke's embellishment of his excerpt from
Mc had received such an apocryphal character that at a very
early date there was a desire to expunge* Lc 22,43-44 (S. 576).
On this apocryphal addition of Lc Réville remarks: *The first
notice possesses an aesthetic and symbolic value, the beauty of
which is incontestable, but the second is manifestly an exaggeration* (II 337).

The original author of Lc verse 44 sees Jesus' agony in
Gethsemane as an anticipation of his suffering on the cross;
the first drops of blood were not shed on the cross, but were
sweat in Gethsemane. The verse as a whole is written in the
light of the significance attached by the early Christian thought
to Jesus' suffering and shed blood. The whole of Lc's scene
in Gethsemane is simply a prelude to the great tragedy of the
cross.

In conclusion: Jesus' fear or agony in Gethsemane is not
morbid in a psychopathic, or any other sense; Lc's addition in
verses 43-44 is to be rejected as apocryphal. The pathographer
must seek elsewhere for his materials.

Of the biographical incidents as a whole that have figured in the contentions against Jesus' psychic health Weber says, *They are the strong yet
normal reactions of a psychically vigorous man to perturbing events important for his thought and life task* (Sp. 234).

# CHAPTER V

## The Personality of Jesus from the Pathographic
## Point of View

We now leave off the more detailed study of particular words of Jesus and incidents in his public career and turn to the study of his personality as a whole. Here, again, our study is not exhaustive in any sense of the word. We are interested only in those features of Jesus' personality that have figured in the pathographic contention. It is Rasmussen who, more than all others, though none neglect it entirely, has undertaken to show that Jesus was a psychopathic personality. For the convenience of approach to this problem we shall undertake to investigate in order Jesus' conduct, his character, and his consciousness as represented in the sources.

### 1) His Conduct

One important factor in determining the state of a man's mind as healthy or morbid is the understanding of the motives for his actions. Why does he do certain things that he does? If his conduct is usual and normal the question of his sanity never occurs to anyone. If his actions are unusual and striking, yet we can nevertheless see that the occasions are so unusual as to demand conduct of a striking character, no question of his psychic soundness arises. It is only when we see an incongruity between occasion and conduct, between cause and effect, that we must conclude that the real reason for a man's conduct lies elsewhere than in the occasion itself, that he is stimulated to such incongruous conduct by some sort of nervous disorder or psychic derangement. If his actions are without sufficient reason or wholly unmotived, we are then sure that he is the victim of some psychic malady.

The conduct of Jesus on three particular occasions, the

cleansing of the temple, the cursing of the fig tree and in Gethsemane, has already been discussed. Here we have to do with a more general characterization of Jesus' conduct as a whole. Rasmussen speaks of the vagabond restlessness of Jesus which causes him now to seek out the thoroughfares, again to retreat to the solitude of the mountains or the desert. For Binet-Sanglé the itinerary of Jesus is only the chronic vagabondage and the peregrinations of a paranoiac, the ambulomania of a theomegalomaniac (IV 79-188).

The chronology and geographical itinerary of Jesus' public career is one of the chief problems in the life of Jesus. Most scholars regard it as insoluble and declare that a life or biography of Jesus is an historical impossibility because the source material is inadequate to the task. The attempts at an historical reconstruction of the life of Jesus fall into three main classes: 1) those in which the Fourth Gospel is taken as the historical ground-work into which the Synoptic materials are fitted as represented by B. Weiss (most recently by Westphal and Lepsius) and by practically all of the lives of Jesus before Strauss; 2) those in which the Fourth Gospel is excluded as a reliable source and Mc is taken as the historical framework into which the non-Marcan matter of Mt and Lc is ingeniously inserted as represented by O. Holtzmann; 3) the eschatological reconstruction of A. Schweitzer in which all of Jesus' words and deeds are interpreted and resolved into eschatological addresses, acts, and sacraments. Over against all of these attempts stands the source-scepticism of Wrede and Wellhausen.

The hope of a reconstruction of the historical plan of the chronology and course of Jesus' public career on the basis of the Fourth Gospel is impossible in spite of the three volumes of B. Weiss. Binet-Sanglé's series of flights, campaigns about the sea of Tiberias, and attempts on Jerusalem (IV 124-179) are historical fiction. Mt and Lc are too composite and complicated in their arrangements of the sources which they employ to make the task much easier. Mc, because of his narrative character and the relative simplicity of his composition in so far as sources are concerned, furnishes us with materials that render possible only the most modest and tentative historical plan of Jesus' public career as a working hypothesis for the understanding of some otherwise inexplicable incidents in the life of Jesus, particularly with reference to the problem of his Messianic consciousness. Even from Mc about all that we can say with certainty regarding the chronology and course of Jesus' public career is that by far the greater half of Jesus' public ministry had its scene in Galilee and centered about the sea of Tiberias with headquarters in Capernaum; Jesus undertook two important journeys, one to the north (7,24) and the fatal journey to Jerusalem. There was only one chief shift of scene, from Galilee to Jerusalem, and the length of Jesus' activity in the capital was not more than a few days. The whole of Jesus' public career is to be reckoned, not in years, but in months, perhaps only in weeks.

So much for a general orientation concerning the chronology and course of Jesus' public career. We now turn to the sources, particularly to Mc, for the moral motivations back of the migrations of Jesus and the significant steps he takes. But it is just at this point of moral motivation for Jesus' acts that the Gospels leave us most consistently in the dark.

The evangelists seem to feel a greater obligation to tell us when, where, why, and to whom Jesus says certain things than they do to tell us why Jesus does certain things that he does or takes certain steps that he takes. Sometimes the Synoptists agree on the scene, setting, occasion and audience of certain of Jesus' discourses; more often they disagree in one or the other, or in all. This goes to show that scenes, settings, occasions and audiences are usually independently supplied or invented by the evangelists themselves. Mt and Lc feel at perfect literary liberty in these matters. Mt in particular seems anxious to give the scenes, setting, occasions and audience for certain of Jesus' words, for he breaks up his Q material and scatters it throughout the Marcan order attaching it wherever he believes he finds a suitable setting or connection. Lc is less concerned in this regard, for he inserts his Q material and special matter in two places in Mc's order, the lesser interpolation after Mc 3,19, the larger interpolation after Mc 9,50.

But independent of Mc's order Mt and Lc usually supply some
sort of scene or connection for most of Jesus' words.   Mt
groups his Lord's prayer topically in his Sermon on the Mount
(6,5-15) ; Lc does not include his Lord's prayer in his Sermon
on the Plain (6,17-49), but reports it in quite a different form
than Mt and supplies a specific occasion on which Jesus gives
the Lord's prayer in response to a request on the part of the
disciples (11,1ff).   This would all go to show, as Wernle
suggests, that the acts of Jesus were far less significant in the
religious life of the early Christian community than were his
words which seem to have had a catechetical importance.

This is at once clear when we turn to the acts and conduct
of Jesus.   Here we find that Jesus' moves and steps, particularly during his Galilean days, are unconnected, unprepared,
and unmotived both in what precedes and what follows.   Mc's
narration of events is graphic, but he gives us no connected
biography.   He supplies no motivations that help us from one
incident or step to the other.   Of Jesus' activity in Galilee we
have only a series of unrelated anecdotes, with the exception
of the famous day in Capernaum (Mc 1,21-38).   The account
is chaotic.   What leads Jesus from one place to another and
how long the intervening gap was we are not told.   A good
illustration of this is the section Mc 6,30-8,26 which J. Weiss
calls *a topographical jumble that is hardly to be untangled*
(AeE, S. 205).   Mc has the scene shift not less than thirty
times before Jesus reaches Jerusalem and not once does he tell
us why.

Still more serious is Mc's omission or neglect of moral
motivation for certain decisive steps taken by Jesus.   In 1,16-
20 Mc has Jesus call his first disciples without telling us of
any previous contact or personal acquaintance.   Such questions
as how Jesus knows that these two sets of brothers are just
the men he wants as his permanent companions, or what it is
that induces these fishermen to give up their occupation and
follow a total stranger, do not occur to Mc.   It is the second
question that is specially problematic for Lc who meets it by
having the calling of the first disciples follow the eventful day
in Capernaum and Simon's house and by modifying the whole

account of the calling as he does in 5,1-11 where Jesus preaches from Simon's boat, gives instruction for the miraculous catch of fishes, and then calls the first disciples. The fourth evangelist's representation of a previous personal contact between Jesus and his first disciples, perhaps occasioned by the preaching of the Baptist at the Jordan, has historical probability in its favor. But Lc's transposition and modification of Mc 1, 16-20 shows itself to be only his way of meeting a problem neglected by Mc and adds nothing to our historical information.

In 7,24 Mc has Jesus suddenly break camp and move rapidly to the north without telling us why Jesus goes, how long he is there, or what prompts him to return to Galilee again. The Fourth Gospel makes no mention of this journey and never has Jesus farther north than the sea of Galilee. This journey is a part of Lc's great omission of Marcan matter, 6,45-8,26; in the third Gospel Jesus never crosses the borders of native land and is never farther north than Caesarea Philippi.

This journey to the north marks one of the most important and significant steps in Jesus' public career. Whole lives of Jesus have been shaped and colored by the understanding of this one journey. In many lives of Jesus Mc 7,24 marks the second historical period in Jesus' public ministry. Mc gives us no answer to the question, Why did Jesus go north? The motives have therefore been supplied by the imagination of Jesus' biographers and the answers have been legion. 1) The old view was that Jesus went north in order to be alone with his disciples. It was a period in which Jesus gives up his public activity and devotes himself to the private training of the twelve. He instructs them in a purely spiritual view of the kingdom of God in order to prepare them for the tragic events soon to follow. 2) Loisy and others see here a forced flight of Jesus. The growing opposition of the religious authorities compel Jesus to surrender the early scene of his popular success. There had been a change in public sentiment as well since the return of the twelve. Jesus must wait in the north for the psychological moment (the Passover) in order to proceed to Jerusalem. 3) Spitta and Burkitt see here a flight before

Herod Antipas.  Jesus is a fugitive from justice; he flees in order to avoid the fate of his great forerunner, (Maurenbrecher combines 2 and 3).  4)  A. Schweitzer fits the northern journey into his eschatological scheme and sketch.  Ever since the return of the twelve Jesus had tried to get away from the people, and in his sojourn to the region of Tyre and Sidon he accomplishes the escape from the pressing popularity with the people which he had failed to accomplish by his crossings and recrossings of Tiberias.  Jesus goes north in order to remain unknown and to preserve his incognito; he thus prevents a premature betrayal of his identity.  5)  According to still another view Jesus goes north for no outward or external reason, but for purely internal reasons.  It is a period of rest and retirement from public activity during which Jesus passes through subjective struggles for clearness and certainty as to the role that he is to play personally in the coming kingdom; this period ends in the eventful confession at Caesarea Philippi.

In conclusion we can say that Mc furnishes us no motives or reasons for Jesus' journey to the north.  And any attempt at a reconstruction is a reading into the text and not a reading of the text; it is a conjecture supported only by the point of view of the biographer.  For some unknown reason, or reasons, Jesus suddenly breaks up his ministry in Galilee and proceeds to the north.  How long he remained there, what his activities, experiences and decisions were during this period we do not know.  But that it was eventful is clear from the fact that at its close Jesus strikes in on an entirely new course of action, his thought has developed out in a new direction, and a more serious tone has found its way into his words.

The motives or reasons for Jesus' decision to go to Jerusalem (Mc 10,1ff=Mt 19,1ff=Lc 9,51ff) are no better known to us than those for his northern journey.  However, we can better perhaps limit the extent of the reasons that determined Jesus upon this journey than upon that of Mc 7,24. In the journey to the north we are not at all sure whether the motives are objective or subjective.  But we are fairly safe in saying that the Jerusalem journey was the result of reasons and motives within the mind and consciousness of Jesus. It is difficult to assign any external motive for the journey to Jerusalem other than Jesus' desire to attend the Passover and intention to return to Galilee and continue his ministry. As Schweitzer has said (GdLJF, S. 437, Anm. 1) the lives of Jesus that have been written might be divided into two classes according as they have Jesus go to Jerusalem to continue his work there (Reimarus, Strauss, Brandt, Loisy) or to die (Weisse, A. Schweitzer, etc.).

But when we come to read the Synoptic sources we find that no reason is given for this journey of Jesus. The exact plan that Jesus had in mind in undertaking this move is not at all clear to us. We are not even certain that Jesus had any definite plan in mind. The prophecies of the passion make it clear that the Synoptists regard it as a journey to death, but that they actually represent the thoughts and motives of Jesus himself is a very different question. We can simply say that here as elsewhere Mc leaves us to guess and conjecture as to why Jesus makes certain important moves that he makes.

This lack of moral motivation in Mc is not peculiar to Jesus' conduct alone, but is generally true of the conduct of all the characters that figure in his narrative. The series of contentions, 2,1-3,6, is simply a topical grouping of Mc's own making, for there is no necessary chronological connection between these five incidents. The league of the Pharisees and the Herodians in 3,6 with the intent of destroying Jesus comes like a flash of lightning out of a clear sky. Mc 3,6 is not properly motived in anything that Jesus has said or done. Jesus' conduct is unconventional, but there is not the slightest ground for a determination upon his death. The same is true of Lc 4,28-30 where Lc has the people of Nazareth actually make an attempt upon Jesus' life at his very first public appearance, although he has said or done nothing in the synagogue (Lc 4,16-27) on this occasion that would justify such wrath and wickedness. Mc and Mt have Jesus in Nazareth much later in his Galilean career but there he encounters only unbelief (Mc 6,1-6=Mt 13,54-58). Besides Mc has Jesus open his public career in Capernaum (1,21-38), and Lc's shift of the scene to Nazareth is still evident in Lc's own account (4,23) where he has Jesus refer to the things he has done in Capernaum although Lc has not told us before that Jesus had been there. Lc's opening sermon in Nazareth is simply a transposition of the Marcan order and a modification of the Marcan account in favor of his dogmatic bias to the end of showing that Jesus was from the very outset rejected by his own people and must go to the Gentiles. The inaugural rejection in Nazareth is for Lc symbolic of Jesus' final rejection by his own nation.

The greatest moral mystery of the Gospels is the conduct of that disciple who betrayed Jesus into the hands of his enemies. After reading the name of Judas as the last in the catalogue of the twelve in Mc 3,19 (=Mt 10,4=Lc 6,16) we never hear of him again until 14,10f (=Mt 26,14ff=Lc 22,3ff) where he is in the very act of betraying Jesus. Judas' name never figures again in Mc or Lc except in the scene at the arrest (Mc 14,43ff=Mt 26,47ff=Lc 22,47ff). Mt 26,25 has Jesus definitely designate Judas as the traitor and tells us of his fate in 27,3-10 (Compare Acts 1,16-20). Mc makes no effort at all to prepare us for the shock that comes in 14,10f when one of Jesus' selected twelve turns against him and brings about his death.

The Judas-Jesus problem is as old and older than the Fourth Gospel in which the problem is clearly felt and no effort is spared to blacken the character of Judas and have Jesus know from the very beginning who should betray him (6,64 70-71; 12,4-6; 13,2; 13,10-11 18-19; 13,21-30; 17,12; 18,1ff). These two lines struck out by the fourth evangelist have been followed even down through the great modern lives of Jesus of the nineteenth century. Not one has left the two problems untouched, namely: Why did Judas betray Jesus? and, How did it happen that Jesus was so unfortunate as to select such a man as Judas as one of his intimate disciples? It is not the place here to review all the answers in their wide variety that have been given by Paulus, Hase, A. K. Emmerich, Noack, Renan, Brandt, etc. The most interesting turn of the problem is that given by A. Schweitzer (GdLJF, S. 441ff) who insists that it is not WHY Judas betrayed Jesus, but WHAT (1) he betrayed. But all suggested solutions of the Judas-Jesus problem are historical reconstructions that have no verified basis in the Synoptic sources. We must admit with Bruno Bauer that the sources offer us no means of solving the problem. Mc tells us nothing of the character of Judas, nothing of the circumstances of his calling, and gives not the slightest indication of the motives that led to his betrayal of Jesus.

Reviewing, then, this lack of moral motivation, not only for the conduct of Jesus at important junctures in his public career, but for the conduct of Jesus' contemporaries and the other characters of Mc's Gospel we can see clearly that it is due to the unconnected, chaotic, reminiscent and anecdotal character of Mc's Gospel where the whole interest centers in w h a t Jesus and others do, but not in w h y he or they do it. The second book of the New Testament is not a history or biography in the modern sense, for there is in it no modern interest in the logical relations and connections of events. Mc is a Gospel with a persuasive plan and purpose, and not a biography or life of Jesus.

This lack of moral motivation is not to be exploited in favor of the pathographic contention. Jesus' conduct can be explained by abundant historical reasons. His itinerary and peregrinations manifest nothing of the fretful restlessness and senseless vagabondage of those cases of morbid mentality who are forever dissatisfied and discontented with their present surroundings.

The other main feature in the general character of Jesus' conduct that has figured in the pathographic contention is his habit of retreat to solitude. Rasmussen sees in these retreats the pendulum swinging to that extreme of morbid fear which contrasts so strikingly with his unbalanced boldness on other occasions. Binet-Sanglé has Jesus retreat to solitude where in

---

(1) See Professor Bacon's identical formulation of the question in his article, *What Did Judas Betray?* Hibbert Journal, April 1921, XIX, 3, p. 476-493. Professor Bacon finds a very different *WHAT* (the anointing in Bethany) than does Schweitzer (the Messianic secret).

undisturbed seclusion he can give his imagination full and free play. While thus apart Jesus surrenders himself to his vesanic passion and delusion. *In the intimacy of his consciousness he played the part of king and God and abandoned himself to the contemplation of his work and the adoration of his own ego ...... No doubt many of these nocturnal seasons of prayer began in musings and ended in hallucinations* (III 114ff). More generally he remarks, *For such aliens retreat and prayer are pure pretexts; in reality they are a theater for a subjective cinematograph of a type of "contemplation" which in certain cases becomes hallucinatory* (III 71).

In the examination of the Synoptic sources we find that Jesus' retreats to solitude, with the exception of Gethsemane, are confined to Galilee. Mt recounts only one such retreat, Mc three, and Lc six. They are as follows:

| | | | |
|---|---|---|---|
| 1) ............. | Mc 1,35-38 (prayer) | Lc 4,42-43 | |
| 2) ............. | 1,45 | 5,16 | (prayer) |
| 3) ............. | ................ | 6,12ff | (prayer) |
| 4) Mt 14,23 (prayer) | 6,46 (prayer) | ................ | |
| 5) ............. | ................ | 9,18 | (prayer) |
| 6) ............. | ................ | 9,28-29 | (prayer) |
| 7) ............. | ................ | 11,1 | (prayer) |

This list shows that the motive and purpose of Jesus' retreats is not always given. In the initial retreat, Mc 1,35-38, Jesus' problem is pressingly personal and pointed; Lc in his parallel for some unknown reason eliminates the pressing personal element and in 4,42-43 he has Jesus simply withdrawing from Capernaum. Mc 1,45 has Jesus without in the desert places because his fame as a healer will no more allow him to openly enter a city; Lc's parallel in 5,16 gives a very different reason. That there is truth in Mc 1,45 to the effect that Jesus withdrew often to the desert places in order to escape the people and retire for rest and refreshment is clear from Mc 6,31 where Jesus invites the disciples to withdraw to a desert place for rest after their mission.

But, on the whole, the Synoptists regard prayer as the real purpose of Jesus' retreats to solitude. Mt's only retreat is for prayer; two of Mc's three are for prayer; and five of Lc's six are for prayer (Mc's parallel to Lc 4,42-43 is for prayer; Mc

6,46 is the second verse of Lc's great omission of Marcan matter).

Lc manifests the greatest interest in the devotional life of Jesus. Besides the five retreats for prayer listed above, he alone represents Jesus as praying at the baptism (3,21), as continuing all night in prayer to God before choosing the twelve (6,12-13) as praying at Caesarea Philippi (9,18) and at the transfiguration (9,28-29), and as having made special supplication for Simon in view of his denial (22,31-32). Lc alone reports the two priceless parables to the end that the disciples ought always to pray and pray persistently (18,1-14). For Lc the decisions and choices of Jesus at great moments and junctures in his public career are the result of prayer and petition.

These retreats for prayer seem, for the most part, to have been at night. Mc 1,35 Jesus rose up a great while before day; Lc 6,12 he spent all night in prayer; Lc 9,28(37) he is all night on the mountain with the three disciples, and Gethsemane is a nocturnal retreat. That there is nothing pathological in this habit of Jesus is clear from the fact that it accords with his instruction on the proper place for prayer as apart and secret (Mt 6,6).

Further, it is just in the satisfaction that these retreats afford Jesus that designates them as healthy. These retreats constitute what Dr. Moerchen would doubtless call a variety of genuine asceticism in which, over against pseudo-asceticism, he refuses to see anything pathological. He writes: *It is precisely in the actual satisfaction which it affords that we recognize the genuineness of a real asceticism over against a type of self-mortification that resembles it only in a most superficial way, such as we find in typical hysteria, particularly in the hysteric temperament* (PH, S. 23f).

Nothing pathological is to be found in Jesus' retreats to solitude except from the viewpoint of consequent *medical materialism*, which sees in all religious devotion and piety only a sign of mental malady or degeneration. Here Binet-Sanglé's words are characteristic and typical: *Piety is a mark of degeneracy to be observed only in emotional, sentimental and hyp-*

*ersuggestible characters incapable of observing, comparing, reasoning and thinking for themselves* (I 185).

In conclusion on Jesus' conduct as a whole we do best to quote the important psychiatric principle laid down by Dr. Moerchen: *In the judgment of thought and conduct w h a t a person says or does is not so important as w h y he says and does it* (PH, S. 32f). The sources furnish us no morbid w h y that would explain the conduct of Jesus.

## 2)   His Character

We cannot here attempt a delineation of the character of Jesus, nor even touch upon all of those traits in his character which have figured in the pathographic contention. Besides, character in general is a fruitless field for pathological psychanalysis. Some types of mental degeneracy and alienation often manifest and possess certain very amiable and even enviable traits of character. On the other hand, a perfectly healthy-minded person often manifests and possesses idiosyncrasies and eccentricities of character that are less common to the average run of men and are frequently paralleled in clinical cases. This state of the facts makes it forever impossible for certain single traits of character to serve as sure symptoms for a diagnosis of psychic health or malady. The diagnosis must go beyond and behind the character to its causes in order to be true. We here single out only two traits in Jesus' character that have been most consistently cited in the psychiatric discussion: Jesus' relations with his own family, and his attitude toward his enemies.

The question of Jesus' personal relations with his immediate family is to be kept distinctly separate from the more general question of his teaching regarding the family and marriage as social institutions. In this more general question such passages as Mc 10,2-12 (=Mt 19,3-9) and Mt 5,32 (=Lc 16,18) come into consideration. The relation of the family to the demands of discipleship is expressed in Mt 10,37 (Lc's parallel in 14,25f is still more exacting) and Mt 19,10-12. Mc 12,25 (=Mt 22,30=Lc 20,35f) excludes marriage relationships from the kingdom of God and furnishes A.

Schweitzer with the chief of his foundation pillars for the erection of a distinction between a permanent and probationary ethics in Jesus' teaching and preaching.

In the more special question of Jesus' relations with his immediate family two brief biographical incidents demand attention. The first is the scene described in Mc 3,31-35 (=Mt 12,46-50=Lc 8,19-21) in which Jesus' mother and brethren come from Nazareth and find Jesus in a Capernaum house to which they cannot gain entrance because of the crowd; they therefore have their request to see him communicated through the crowd that surrounds him. When the request reaches Jesus he does not reply to the real request at all, but asks, *Who is my mother and my brethren?* (Lc omits this rhetorical question.) *And looking round on them that sat round about him* (in Mt, *his disciples*) *he saith, Behold my mother and my brethren! For whosoever shall do the will of God, the same is my brother, and sister, and mother.* Lc's parallel is considerably abbreviated: 8,21b, *My mother and my brethren are these that hear the word of God, and do it.* Lc's form of Jesus' word here is practically identical with Jesus' reply to the woman in Lc 11,27-28 which is peculiar to Lc, and reads: *And it came to pass as he said these things, a certain woman out of the multitude lifted up her voice, and said unto him, Blessed is the womb that bare thee, and the breasts which thou didst suck. But he said, Yea rather, blessed are they that hear the word of God, and keep it.*

Not only Jesus' pathographers but his biographers have constituted a serious and real break and estrangement between Jesus and his family. Renan wrote, *Il prêcha hardiment la guerre à la nature, la totale rupture avec le sang.* O. Holtzmann writes of a definite break between Jesus and his family and supplies reasons for it (LJ, S. 193). Liberal criticism in recent years has found the Mary of Mc, as well as Jesus' brethren, to have been unsympathetic with Jesus' appearance in public, if not an avowed unbeliever. The Synoptics know nothing of the presence of Jesus' mother at the cross and his commission in her behalf to the beloved disciple; only the Fourth Gospel reports this, 19,25-27. During his lifetime we find

nothing that would lead us to think that any of Jesus' immediate family were identified with his following.

Rasmussen says that Jesus by word and example laid every
possible hindrance in the way of marriage; he raised new bar-
riers for the divorced by forbidding remarriage (S. 154). De
Loosten finds Jesus' lack of appreciation for the institution
of the family in general and his attitude toward his own family
in particular a sign of psychic degeneration *par excellence* (S.
59). *He had lost all natural human feelings . . . . . . Throughout his life he lived at enmity with his family, or at least without concern for it* (S. 51). In Mc 3,31ff he greets his own
mother with disrespect. Binet-Sanglé finds that Jesus never
returned the affection and love of his devoted mother, but relegated her to the shadows of inattention and indifference (I
114ff). However, he classes Mary as a believer, but divides the
brothers and sisters of Jesus into the *clan messianique* and the
*clan antimessianique* (I 122, 130).

We turn then to the two incidents, Mc 3,31-35 and Lc 11,
27-28. In regard to both we can say, as Strauss did of the
first, that they throw no light upon the actual state of relations
between Jesus and his immediate family. Strauss wrote in
his 1835 *Leben Jesu*, I 763: *No information concerning the
relation between Jesus and his family at this time is to be
gleaned from this notice, for it belongs rather to those exag-
gerations which Mark enjoys supplying, not only in his general delineations but in the introductions of particular incidents.* This statement of Strauss is true for two reasons. Mc's
representation of Jesus' seeming indifference toward his own
family's request upon this occasion belongs to his characteristic exaggeration of the lack of understanding for Jesus' mission and words, not only on the part of his disciples, but also
on the part of his own family. Still more important is the
fact that the Synoptists are interested in this scene, not in
and of itself, but only as it furnishes a setting for Jesus' word
regarding his true kinsmen among whom the Synoptists count
themselves and their confessing readers. The whole incident
has its climax in this word of Jesus. The Gospel writers never
seem to realize what an unfavorable light they throw upon their

hero and his relations to those whom he should naturally love best. *They* (Mt and Lc) *report only Jesus' sharp reply without thinking what an unfavorable light falls upon him when such an answer was not occasioned by very unbecoming conduct on the part of his mother and brethren* (P. W. Schmiedel, dVE, S. 19).

This scene belongs to those many uncompleted scenes in all four of the Gospels, for all four often leave scenes incomplete. Incidents are frequently developed to the point where they furnish an occasion for some word of Jesus and they are let drop because the evangelists have no further interest in them. This scene in Mc 3,31ff is one of them. Lc leaves the scene in 18,15-17 uncompleted; both Mt (19,15) and Mc (10, 16) complete it. Lc never tells us what becomes of the other nine lepers after he has the one Samaritan return to express his gratitude; we might think that only this one was cured (17,12-19). These unfinished incidents are specially frequent in the Fourth Gospel; the scene in 1,19f is not brought to an end, neither the Nicodemus scene in 3,1ff, nor the incident of the request of the Greeks in chapter 12.

In Mc 3,31ff we are not told whether Jesus responds to the request of his mother and brethren. We only know this, that if they came to Capernaum to bring him back to Nazareth they were unsuccessful (See O. Holtzmann, LJ, S. 194). Not one of the Synoptists feels obliged nor takes the trouble to complete the scene. We should have been very grateful to any one of them if he had done this, for we, with our modern code of ethics, should like to have more light on the relations of Jesus with his family. But the early Christian, whether writer or reader, had no such interest in this incident. He was interested above all in the fact that Jesus had proclaimed all who do God's will as his mother, his sister, and his brother.

Still more general considerations may be urged. For Jesus to have remained at home and in Nazareth would have made the fulfillment of his mission impossible. The very exigencies of his task forced him away from home and native city. As Renan said, this demand for a break with home and early surroundings was not easy for Jesus. He returned to Nazareth

at the very pinnacle of his Galilean success and popularity
(Mc 6,1-6=Mt 13,54-58) only to encounter an unbelief that
made a continued effort there impossible.   Jesus did not reject
Nazareth; Nazareth rejected him.   He did not even include
his native city among those upon which his woes fell (Mt 11,
20ff=Lc 10,12ff), yet it was there that he received his greatest rebuff.   As A. Harnack writes, *He who had not where to
lay his head does not speak as one who had broken with everything* (WC, S. 24).

The great men of history with great missions have often
followed exactly in the footsteps of Jesus in this regard.   Home
and family they have sacrificed in the interests of their larger
commissions and tasks which they could accomplish only by
recognizing and admitting no obstacles.   Dr. Moerchen writes
to the point:   *A thought, a passion, an aspiration can sway
them so completely that all the minor and major concerns of
daily life, even family and friends, in fact everything else appears to them so insignificant and unimportant that they cast
them aside and bear the eventual reactions of wounded affections with ease, even with an apparently paradoxical pleasure.
It is out of this metal that the h e r o e s , those of the state
as well as those of religion. . . . . . ., are moulded.   It is the recognizing of no obstacles that constitutes the hero* (PH, S. 12).
How many men, great and less great, have not found a great
cause or felt a great commission to be greater than the duties
of home and the ties of family!

The above remarks on Mc 3,31ff are pertinent to the scene
in Lc 11,37.   Schaefer gives a good comment on this incident:
*The really great men "who identify themselves completely with
their cause" not only find no gratification in such fickle flattery
but such is distasteful to them* (S. 73).

We now come to the second trait in Jesus' character which
has figured conspicuously in the pathographic position, namely, his attitude toward his enemies.   Here neither the Galilean
nor the Jerusalem contentions can come into consideration.
The Galilean contentions (Mc 2,1-3,6=Mt 9,1-17; 12,1-14=
Lc 5,17-6,11) (Mc 7,1-23=Mt 15,1-20) have as their main

issue the unconventional conduct of Jesus which accords perfectly with his preaching of the purer precepts of piety in Mt 6,1-18. The Jerusalem contentions (Mc 11,27-33=Mt 21,23-27=Lc 20,1-8) (Mc 12,13-17=Mt 22,15-22=Lc 20, 20-26) (Mc 12,18-27=Mt 22,23-33=Lc 20,27-38) (Mc 12, 35-37=Mt 22,41-46=Lc 20,41-44) only show how formidable a foe the Jerusalem authorities found in Jesus and how demolishing were the effects of his dialectic against them. The particular address that figures here is Jesus' scathing denunciation of the religion of the Pharisees and scribes in Mt 23,1-36=Mc 12,38-40=Lc 11,39-52; 20,45-47. Rasmussen writes, *Against his enemies he employed the coarse expressions of language* (S. 138). De Loosten finds Jesus incapable of brooking opposition, and against his contemporaries, as well as against his enemies, he hurls insult and slander in a truly degenerate fashion. Hirsch writes: *No one could have been more intolerant towards his opponents than he. Not only his "enemies," but everyone who does not believe in all his eccentricities should be punished by "eternal damnation," and, with a millstone about his neck, be thrown into the sea* (p. 133; Ger. S. 133).

That the Pharisees were not the renegade lot that we commonly suppose has been adequately shown by the research in the field of New Testament contemporary history on Jewish soil by men like E. Schuerer (1). But Jesus' address against them with its characterization of the false pity of the greater number of them stands as a true historical picture of their religion in his day. That Jesus had not broken with the Pharisees *en masse* is evident enough in the Gospel of Lc where Jesus, as in none other of the Gospels, is portrayed as a friend of the publicans, sinners, and social outcasts, yet in which Jesus often appears at the table of some Pharisee. Lc is especially fond of having Jesus at meat with some Pharisee: 7,36ff; 11,37ff; and the series of dinner addresses in 14,1-24.

(1)    (*Geschichte des juedischen Volkes im Zeitalter Jesu Christi;* Leipzig, 2. Auflage 1890, I. Teil 751 S., II. Teil 1886, 884 S.), W. Bousset (*Die Religion des Judentums im neutestamentlichen Zeitalter;* 2. Auflage Berlin 1906, 617 S.), and M. Friedlaender (*Die religioesen Bewegungen innerhalb des Judentums im Zeitalter Jesu;* Berlin 1905, 380 S.)

To return to the address of denunciation against the Pharisees, we can say that it is not the outburst of a frenzied fanatic but a true picture projected in a genuine prophetic tone. No less a distinguished scholar than Gottlieb Klein, Rabbi in Stockholm, lays this address as one of the foundation stones upon which Jesus stands as a real man of history. He finds Jesus' address in Mt 23,16ff so true to life and exact that he proclaims it an historical document of the very first order which *is comprehensible only in the light of history contemporary with Jesus. With each word Jesus hits the nail on the head* (S. 18).

Further, Jesus' enemies were not imaginary as are those of the alienated mind of the psychiatric clinic who sees a foe in his best friends and caretakers. Jesus' enemies were real; they had him nailed to the cross.

The Gospel writers never give us a delineation of the character of Jesus. We gain our impressions of his character only by the reactions of his contemporaries, both friends and foes. His first disciples follow him without a word (Mc 1,16-20), *prima vista* (Wellhausen, Einl., S. 38f). Why he calls them and why they follow him, we do not know. Never once do we read that he advises or consults with them. Just once, but never again, do they attempt to restrain him (Mc 8,32f). They fear him (Mc 4,41; 6,51; 9,6); when they do not understand him they dare ask him no questions (Mc 9,32; 10,32). Houses (Mc 1,29 33; 2,1; 3,19 31; 7,17 24; 9,28 33; 10,10; 14,3), boats (Mc 3,9; 4,1 36; 5,2 18 21; 6,32 51; 8,10 13; Lc 5,3), synagogues (Mc 1,21; 3,1; 6,2; Lc 4,15f), the temple (Mc 14,49; Lc 19,47), special rooms (Mc 14,14ff), tables (Mc 2,15; 14,3; 14,18; Lc 7,36; 11,37ff; 14,1ff; 19,5), and substance (Lc 8,3) are at his constant disposition. In all this not one word of thanks do we hear crossing his lips. His cures and words cause amazement and remarks; his fame spreads like wild-fire; he is thronged by the multitudes who hear him gladly (Mc 12,37; Lc 13,17) and bring their sick to be cured. He is touched by the faith of an afflicted woman (Mc 5,25ff) and he yields to a word well put (Mc 7,29).

The multitudes hang listening on his words for three days without having food (Mc 8,2). They anticipate him in reaching his landing points about the sea of Galilee where they await and welcome him (Lc 8,40). On some occasions the multitudes seek to stay him that he should not depart from them (Lc 4,42); other crowds fear and are anxious to be rid of him (Mc 5,17). He casts out demons with a word and cures as easily (Mt 8,16); afflicted bodies and members are restored to health and their normal functioning under the touch of his hand and at his rebuke a fever departs. Crowds throng him so that they cannot so much as eat bread (Mc 3,20), they tread upon one another (Lc 12,1), and the disciples fear that they will crush him (Lc 8,45). Because of his popularity he can no more openly enter into a city but must remain without in desert places (Mc 1,45), but the people stream unto him from every quarter. To escape the multitudes he withdraws from cities, crosses and recrosses the sea of Galilee, journeys to the north (Mc 7,24), travels incognito, but he cannot be hid. Great throngs accompany him to the passover and shout Hosannas as he enters the capital. He is arrested and condemned. For some unknown reason the people do not or cannot defend and save him. They follow him to the cross and go away smiting their breasts (Lc 23,48). A centurion confesses, *Truly this man was the Son of God* (Mc 15,39).

The only characterization of Jesus found in the Gospels is on the lips of his enemies, who say to him, *Teacher, we know that thou art true, and carest not for any one; for thou regardest not the person of men, but of a truth teachest the way of God* (Mc 12,14). How much of this is flattery we do not know. But Jesus' words and conduct early give rise to opposition. In his contentions with his enemies they are unsuccessful in their attempts to provoke him to ill-advised statements that would trap him. He silences them, puts questions that they cannot or dare not answer (Lc 14,6), he puts them to shame (Lc 13,17) and forces them to concede his points (Lc 20,39), and no one dares ask him any question (Mc 12,34). Herod is perplexed (Lc 9,7), would kill him (13,31), and sought long to see him (23,8).   Pilate is amazed at the eloquence of his silence (Mc 15,5).

The above outline is by no means an exhaustive list of the reactions that might serve in a more complete characterization of Jesus' personality, but it strikes upon the main points. We learn chiefly that he spoke as one having authority, that his congenial character readily won for him friends from all classes of his contemporaries, and that his unconventional conduct and teaching made for him many enemies among the religious leaders.   As a character Jesus appears to us in the Synoptics as congenial, yet commanding, as unconventional, yet uncompromising in the affairs pertaining to the kingdom of God.   None of these traits in Jesus' character necessitate or even suggest a psychopathic diagnosis.

### 3)   His Consciousness

The question of Jesus' consciousness, or better perhaps self-consciousness, has a very different bearing on the problem of his psychic health than does the question of his character. In fact, it is of paramount importance in the pathographic issue.   In certain serious forms of mental alienation, particularly in paranoia, it is the subject's estimate of his own ego that constitutes the surest symptom of his psychic derangement.   It is here that that deplorable divergence from reality, actuality, concrete condition and circumstance begins which is convincing in determining the subject's state as morbid.   The inmate of the institution for the insane imagines himself a president, a king, a general, a millionaire, a Messiah, or even a God, with all the pertaining pretentions, prerogatives, and plans.

It is Jesus' exalted self-consciousness, his assumption of a unique filial relationship with the Father, his acceptance of the Messianic role, and his identification of himself with the Son of man who was to appear on the clouds of heaven attended by angelic hosts, institute and conduct the great last assize and establish the new world order, that has been chiefly responsible for bringing on the charges against his psychic health.

It led Strauss to conclude that Jesus was a fanatic, and von Hartmann that he was a transcendental fanatic. In the 1905-form of the question it has directed and determined the diagnoses that have been made, particularly those of de Loosten, Binet-Sanglé and Hirsch who see in Jesus a typical clinical case of paranoia. They speak respectively of Jesus' excessively exalted self-consciousness that gradually developed into a veritable *Wahnsystem*, his delirium, *idée fixe*, vesanic pride, theomegalomania, and his delusions of grandeur. Rasmussen finds that Jesus possessed the characteristic prophetic *Groessenwahn*. Holtzmann contends that Jesus' self-consciousness began in, was based upon, and was bolstered up by experiences of ecstasy, for it goes out far beyond the common confines and compass of ordinary human consciousness. Even Schweitzer concedes that Jesus' exalted estimate of himself (*Selbsteinschaetzung*) admits of psychiatric discussion (PBJ, S. 44); also Dr. Moerchen (see above p. 125).

Beginning with the eighties of the last century Jesus' self-consciousness has become one of the most prominent and puzzling problems in the historical criticism of the New Testament. Increased investigation and research have led to new problems rather than to solutions. A whole series of subordinate questions have arisen. When and where did the full realization of his Messianic consciousness dawn upon Jesus, at the baptism, temptation, Caesarea Philippi, or the transfiguration? What was Jesus' attitude toward his Messianic mission? Did he feel it as a boon or a burden? What were the reasons for the careful reserve that he so long practiced? Were they political, pedagogical, or personal? In what sense did he understand and employ the expression *Son of man*, as Messiah, man, or simply a circumlocution in the third person for the first person pronoun "I"? Or did Jesus ever employ this expression, was it not linguistically impossible in the Aramaic? Was his understanding of the term *Son of God* theocratic or religio-ethical? (Compare H. J. Holtzmann, MBJ, S. 43). Into all of these rambling ramifications the writer cannot go, even if he were qualified. The two best single treatments of these questions are W. Baldensperger's

*Das Selbstbewusstsein Jesu* and H. J. Holtzmann's *Das messianische Bewusstsein Jesu.*

Our present interest confines our study to only those phases of Jesus' self-consciousness which have been presented as pathological in their bearing by Jesus' pathographers. These phases of the problem can best be formulated as follows: Was Jesus' self-consciousness morbid in its—1) rise; 2) reinforcement; 3) form; 4) content, control and confession? We proceed to deal with these phases in their designated order.

## A)   Its Rise

The birthplace or -hour of Jesus' self-consciousness is not at all clearly indicated in the Synoptic sources. In the course of the life-of-Jesus research its location and date have been left to the biographer's imagination, but all of Jesus' biographers have not imagined alike. This state of the sources has led not a few to regard any solution of the rise of Jesus' self-consciousness with suspicion. They regard it as Jesus' own secret how he came to this unusual consciousness and no psychology will ever succeed in unveiling it (thus A. Harnack, WC, S. 81). Others find a solution impossible because Jesus appears on the scene mature and finished in every respect. Here Weidel is representative: *Jesus appears on the scene a completed character like Pallas fully armed out of the head of Zeus* (S. 21). Harnack is of the same opinion: *It is very probable that at the time of his public appearance he was personally already fully developed and mature* (WC, S. 88). Still others find no change in Jesus' inner attitudes and orientations during his public career; they find only what Weizsaecker calls *an altered attitude toward the outside world* (S. 283). Here again Weidel writes: *There is nowhere the slightest trace of any kind of development in his person d u r i n g h i s p u b l i c c a r e e r. His views and ideas may change according to the particular occasions that call them forth, but at heart he remains the same* (S. 20). Several, with H. Wendt, make a distinction between Jesus' filial consciousness and his Messianic consciousness, the first forming the *sure groundwork* for his knowledge of the second (II 123ff). (Against this view of an earlier and later stage in Jesus' self-consciousness see W. Baldensperger, S. 160). Reorientations and readjustments on the part of Jesus in the matter of his consciousness are most frequent and pronounced in A. Schweitzer's consequent eschatology.

The majority of Jesus' biographers and critics have set his baptism at the Jordan as the birthplace and -hour of his Messianic consciousness. W. Beyschlag writes, *It was at this moment that Jesus experienced the full dawn of his Messianic consciousness and commission* (II 112). Of the voice at the Jordan W. Baldensperger writes, *It was the decisive and unequivocal declaration of Jesus' Messiahship* (S. 160). His view of the baptism is supernaturalistic: *The soil was ready and the divine omnipotence brought it about that Jesus went forth from his baptism unshakably certain of his Messiahship......* *He did not attain this consciousness for himself by any process of reasoning. One may regard the incident as one will, but it seems to be a thing of the purest impossibility that he by ever so profound a process of thought could have come to claim for himself the Messianic title...... It was rather a direct revelation made to him in the wonderful depths of his religious and spiritual life and by which, like an electric shock, his person was overwhelmingly and directly struck* (S. 163f). J. Weiss, from the more careful historical point of view, writes, *The experience at the baptism marks the birthplace of this* (Messianic) *consciousness* (JPvRG, S. 51).

If we turn to the Synoptic sources we find that the only thing that throws a Messianic light upon the baptism at the Jordan is the Messianic test that follows it immediately in Mt and Lc. Considering Mc alone there is no necessity for dating Jesus' Messianic consciousness with the baptism. For Mc the baptism is the moment of Jesus' special selection and election as the Son of God, the moment of his endowment and equipment with the Divine Spirit. It is the call to the career of the prophet similar to that of Amos (7,14-15) and Isaiah (6,1ff).

For Mt and Lc, however, the experience at the Jordan constitutes the Messianic call. From this moment on Jesus is the Messiah and feels himself as such. That this is the view of Mt and Lc relative to the revelation at the baptism is clear from the character of the temptation which immediately follows and which for both the first and third evangelists is a Messianic test. But that this test in the desert was really a Messianic test is quite another question. It becomes Messianic in Mt and Lc only due to the fact that they insert the three temptations from Q into Mc's order in connection with 1,12-13. Mc makes only a general mention of a temptation; of its character he tells us nothing. His mere reference to it would suggest that Mc attached no special significance or importance to this period of solitude in the desert. It is certainly not Messianic for Mc, for, as we have already pointed out above (page 157), the three Messianic temptations of Mt and Lc have their historical points of contact only in the later life of Jesus according to Mc. If Jesus' Messianic consciousness were given at the baptism, it would render the whole of Mc's Galilean account of Jesus unintelligible and contradictory. It would force a complete revision of the first day in Capernaum where Jesus' seems overtaken by surprise at the discovery that his word and touch can cure and heal. Up to this point in Mc's narrative Jesus' mission seems to consist, for himself at least, in message. The discovery of this new activity of which he is capable gives rise to a pressingly personal problem which drives him apart for prayer and petition a great while before day (Mc 1,35-38). The first day at Capernaum ended with Jesus feeling himself strangely endowed, yet strangely encumbered. The cures had thrown a new light upon his person. What was to be his mission, miracle or message?

Mt and Lc have altered and changed Mc's eventful day in Capernaum. Mt shatters it completely by reporting only the second and third of the four incidents that make it up; he omits the first and fourth, the most significant of the day, and reports the two which he does retain in a meaningless connection in the cycle of miracles (8,14-17). Lc follows the order of Mc and reports all four incidents (4,31-43), but the fourth he so tones down that the personal point to it entirely disappears. In Lc 4,42-43 Jesus is merely withdrawing from Capernaum.

The above consideration concerning the baptism, the temptation, and the first day in Capernaum go to show that the first two are not Messianic incidents in the life of Jesus; they have to do merely with Jesus' prophetic call to a public career and, perhaps, a period of general testing, similar in character, but briefer in extent, to Paul's retreat in Gal 1,17-18. The Messiahship was for Jesus not a general problem of calling and career, for he fulfils neither in the traditional Messianic sense, but a purely personal problem. Mc 1,35-38 shows us that Jesus' personal problems begin with that first and eventful day in Capernaum.

It is only as Jesus swings into the actual and active fulfillment of his mission that the possibilities of his person put in their appearance. His miracle-power and popularity force him to reckon with the possibilities, even with the probabilities, of the divine plan for his own person. The fact that all of Jesus' retreats to solitude for prayer, with the exception of Gethsemane, are confined to Galilee, and that all of them precede Caesarea Philippi, with the exception of Lc 9,28f, would seriously suggest that they stood in a real and essential relation to the appearance and development of his Messianic consciousness. At the close of the day in Capernaum Jesus' personal struggle begins. It is a struggle for clearness and certainty, not concerning his commission and career as a prophet and preacher of the kingdom of God, for concerning this point he is never in doubt, but regarding the personal role that he is to play in the final realization of this kingdom.

Von Delius makes a pertinent point in this connection: *In any case it seems to me certain that Jesus must have struggled long and hard regarding the foundation of his being. Ready, resplendent superiority is never the reward of anything but agonizing Cyclopean labor in the depths* (S. 118).

At what particular point Jesus' gains clearness and certainty regarding the personal role he is to play in the final realization of the kingdom of God we do not know. But we do know that this point, according to Mc at least, lies somewhere between the close of the day in Capernaum and Peter's confession in Mc 8,27ff. It is doubtful whether Jesus gained this clearness and certainty at any particular and special moment, or series of moments, but at Caesarea Philippi he knows himself to be or destined to be the Messiah. The first phase of his struggle is then over and the second begins. Henceforth it is a struggle of will and strength to fulfil the personal part that the divine plan has appointed him in the final consummation of the kingdom of God.

Jesus' Messianic consciousness was not a foreign self, a kind of extra-ego, that came to possess him, but was a personal development within his own consciousness as a called prophet and preacher of the kingdom of God. As H. J. Holtzmann writes: *Certain alone is it that Jesus at some time or other began to know that he was the Messiah, that he came to the point where he confessed and claimed such for himself, and that this step cost him his life because in the general opinion of his contemporaries he was evidently not the one he claimed to be* (MBJ, S. 49).

Jesus' Messianic consciousness forms an interesting and instructive contrast to Paul's apostolic consciousness. Paul's apostolic consciousness clearly dates from a single exceptional experience on the Damascus road. As Wrede writes: *Paul is one of that rare type of men whose lives are clearly cut into two halves by a single occurrence. He experienced a rupture that reached to the very depths, he became another and lived henceforth in the consciousness that he had become another and possessed as it were a new ego. This is, in and of itself, something astonishing. His whole psychic life was filled with an inextinguishable sense of contrast between once and now; it furnished the one great point of orientation for all his thought and feeling, and it thereby imparted to his personality a compactness and a conclusiveness that are inaccessible to the distracting existence of the crowd* (Paulus, S. 8).

Paul's experience on the Damascus road is revolutionary, not only in his career, but in his consciousness. From this experience everything dated as before and after. This high moment of his life related in Acts 9,1-9 he is represented as rehearsing twice again, 22,6-11 and 26,13-19. He reminisces upon it and refers to it in his epistles: I Cor 9,1; 15,8; II Cor 4,6; 12,1; Gal 1,16-17; Eph 3,3; Phil 3,12.

But the experience at the Jordan was in no such sense revolutionary in Jesus' self-consciousness. He never rehearses it, reminisces upon it, or refers to it. Jesus indulges in reminiscence but twice, Mc 8,19 and Lc 22,35. There is no pivotal or polar point in Jesus' experience about which everything turns, no drawn line before and after which all else dates, that corresponds at all to Paul's vision before Damascus. This single vision furnished to Paul the credentials for his Christian apostleship. But Jesus never refers to any single experience, or series of experiences, that lies in the past as constituting his Messianic call and credentials. *It is worthy of note that Jesus, even where he opposes the traditional or current methods of instruction as in the Sermon on the Mount, never referred like the prophets to special visitations, to any moment whatever when he had experienced a vision or received a revelation* (Werner, PGJ, S. 40).

The pathographers of Jesus, particularly those who diagnose paranoia, see in the baptism and the temptation important moments in the development of Jesus' psychosis and delusions of consciousness, but neither experience marks its rise. They mark rather the transition from the latent to the active phase of his pathological self-consciousness. Its origin lies back somewhere in his pre-public life, perhaps at the psychic crisis at puberty, and de Loosten and Binet-Sanglé trace it as far back as hereditary influence. In one thing Jesus' pathographers are right, namely, that Jesus' self-consciousness did not appear *ex abrupto* but organically. It was not the work of a single moment, or a single exceptional experience. The full answer to the question as to whether Jesus' self-consciousness was morbid in its rise can be given only in connection with the role that hallucinations played in his experience as discussed in the next paragraphs and the probability of hereditary burden as discussed in the following chapter.

## B)    Its Reinforcement

By the reinforcement of Jesus' self-consciousness we mean the role that hallucinations played in the support and encouragement of Jesus' understanding and estimate of himself. It is well then to cite a psychiatrist's definition of the psychic phenomenon known as the hallucination: *We designate as hallucinations those sensations which appear only in consequence of inner stimuli and without the excitation of the sense in question by an object of the outside world* (Binswanger, S. 5).

Psychologically the hallucination is clearly distinguished over against the illusion. Visions, however, are most frequently religious experiences, and because of their almost regular religious character and associations it is only reluctantly that popular thought, at least, has recognized in the vision only a species of hallucination. But the strictly scientific point of view has no such interest in the content and connections of psychic phenomena. Visions are, therefore, only a variety of hallucination. Properly speaking they figure in only one field of sense, the visual. In the more general understanding, however, they include auditory hallucinations. Thus the vision at the baptism would include hallucinations of both sight and hearing.

Even conservative New Testament critics speak of the occasional visions of Jesus, particularly at the baptism. Liberal scholars, fonder of psychological emphasis, speak more freely of Jesus' hallucinations, not numerous yet not confined to the baptism. Both allow these psychic experiences to influence Jesus in his decisions to some extent, but both protest against a pathological origin. Weidel writes: *Jesus had his experiences, subjective and objective, which influenced him and brought the potentialities of his person to development* (S. 20).

J. Weiss expresses his opinion thus: *The view that it is i n c o n c e i v a b l e that Jesus allowed himself to be guided by such experiences is definitely to be rejected. The directly religious and emotional life of the Oriental, particularly in times of agitations such as obtained in the days of Jesus and the Baptist, is much more liable to such states* (Lc 10,18) *than we are, and it is only an unhistorical confusion of time and place that designates such inspirations as "morbid"* (SdNT, I 446).

The hallucinations of Jesus have furnished abundant materials for his pathographers. Holtzmann speaks only of ecstatic visions of Jesus; however, he regards them as influential in Jesus' career and consciousness. Rasmussen says, *We do not know much about his hallucinations, but in any case no one is able to deny their presence in his experience* (S. 142). He mentions only the baptism and Lc 10,18. De Loosten finds it very probable that Jesus was very dependent upon such hallucinations as he had at the baptism for his decisions; therefore, they must have been frequent (S. 59). Hirsch knows that Jesus suffered with hallucinations: *that he "saw" and "heard" the creations of his own morbid imagination* (p. 112f; Ger. S. 109f). Binet-Sanglé makes the most exhaustive study of Jesus' hallucinations (II 346-394) and has the longest and most complete catalogue. He finds seven hallucinations in the sources as they now stand, but is sure that they must have been very numerous in the experience of Jesus going back as early as the age of twelve and appearing originally as the product of puberal auto-intoxication. He further finds that Jesus' hallucinations encouraged him in his delirium and in the pursuit of his vesanic passion.

The number of Jesus' hallucinations, as discovered by his pathographers, totals eight. The following catalogue is practically complete and summarizes the hallucinatory materials to be found in the sources:

| | | Mt | Mc | Lc | Field of sense |
|---|---|---|---|---|---|
| Baptism | 1) | 3,16-17 | 1,10-11 | 3,21-22 | visual and |
| Temptation | 2) | 4,3-4 | ...... | 4,3-4 | auditory |
| " | 3) | 5-6 | ...... | 9-12 | " " |
| " | 4) | 8-11 | ...... | 5-8 | " " |
| " | 5) | 11b | 13b 13c | .... | " |
| Transfiguration | 6) | 17,2-8 | 9,2b-8 | 9,29-36 | " " |
| Satan's fall | 7) | ...... | ...... | 10,18 | " |
| Gethsemane | 8) | ...... | ...... | 22,43 | " |

Binet-Sanglé ........1 2 3 4 5  7 8
de Loosten ..........  2 3 4  6 7
Hirsch ..............1 2 3 4  6
Rasmussen ..........1          7
Holtzmann ..........1 2 3 4    7 (ecstatic visions)

Hirsch finds that the very spirit that drove Jesus into the desert was the product of an hallucination (p. 112; Ger., S. 109); further he finds that Jn 8,26 28 38-40 refer to preceding hallucinations of sight and hearing. De Loosten adds Mc 3,21 22; 5,25-34; he regards the latter incident as a cutaneous hallucination (see page 75f) (1). Binet-Sanglé also speaks of kinaesthetic hallucinations (II 387ff). Binet-Sanglé, Hirsch and de Loosten speak of the illusions of Jesus; the first of his pseudo-hallucinations.

From the pathographers point of view the Gospel of Lc is richest in hallucinatory materials since 7 and 8 are peculiar to the third Gospel. Lc omits the ministering angels in the temptation scene (5) and the appearance of the wild beasts which is peculiar to Mc (13b of 5). Mc 1,13b, however, has nothing to do with hallucinations or any sort of psychic experience. It is simply one of Mc's characteristic narrative details added to make the picture of solitude more graphic. Our previous study of the biographical incidents from the pathographic point of view eliminates 2, 3, 4, 5, 6, and 8 as usable pathographic matter. As to 1 there is no need of doubting or denying that Jesus experienced a vision at the baptism. 7 alone requires discussion here.

Lc 10,18 reads: *And he said unto them, I beheld Satan fallen as lightning from heaven.* On this word of Jesus peculiar to Lc Holtzmann writes: *Jesus answers the jubilant report of the returning disciples by referring to a vision he had experienced...... Such is ecstatic for it transcends the compass of human conceptions. To this is attached an ecstatic promise...... Both utterances transcend the measure of man* (WJE, S. 15, Anm. 1) (2). Rasmussen (S. 142) and de Loosten (S. 61) class Lc 10,18 as an hallucination; Binet-Sanglé describes it as *une hallucination haute et lumineuse* (II 382ff).

---

(1)   Against de Loosten on this particular point (Mc 5,25-34) Schweitzer writes: *In reality Jesus only verified the fact that someone had touched his garment.   That he did this because he had felt power go out from him is a naïve conjecture of the evangelist* (PBJ, S. 8, Anm. 4).

(2)   Two years before Holtzmann found an historical explanation sufficient: *In a picture of Jewish apocalyptic known to him from youth up Jesus declares to them:......(Lc 10,18).   It is an allusion to a bit of primitive mythology well known to Semitics and Indo-Europeans, according to which the enemy of the gods scales his way up to their very mountain only from there to be hurled again ignominiously into the abyss.   It is with this picture that Jesus described the success of the disciples' preaching of repentance* (LJ, S. 219).

Wellhausen regards Lc 10,18 as apocryphal: *The "seeing" of the incident could be conceived as a vision of Jesus and explained in the light of Isa.* 14,12 *(Rev.* 12,9). *But for this the saying is too dull and incomplete; besides, everything visionary (though not every emotion) is otherwise kept at a distance from Jesus...... In any case, I regard this isolated word as wholly apocryphal* (Lucae, S. 50f). H. J. Holtzmann finds here a vision of Jesus analogous to Mc 1,10 (HC, I 359); J. Weiss also speaks of a vision of Jesus (SdNT, I 446).

But this word of Jesus is rather to be understood in the light of its connections. It merely expresses in a figurative fashion his elation over the success of the seventy. The address of Jesus to the twelve on sending them out stood in both Mc and Q, but in a quite different form. Mc and Mt know of only one mission of the disciples and consequently have only one address. Mc's brief address is found in 6,7-12. Mt, however, combines the Marcan and Q addresses into one long address delivered to the twelve in 10,1-11,1. Lc keeps the two forms of the address separate and consequently has two missions; he has the Marcan address delivered to the twelve in 9,1-6, and the Q address to the seventy in 10,1-16. Two of the Synoptists tell us of the return of the twelve and the success of their mission; two of them report but a single reminiscence, Mc 9,38=Lc 9,49. Lc, however, tells of the jubilant return and report of the seventy in 10,17, and this supplies abundant occasion for the figurative word of Jesus in 10,18 without resorting to either normal or abnormal psychology for an explanation.

In fact, Jesus' word in Lc 10,18 is closely analogous to the three temptations of Mt and Lc. It furnishes the best key to the understanding of the three temptations as going back originally to figurative words of Jesus to his disciples concerning victorious contests with Satan. There he tells the disciples that he has triumphed over Satan; here he tells them that they have done the same by their preaching and healing tour.

Returning, then, to the role that hallucinations or visions played in the reinforcement and encouragement of Jesus' self-consciousness we find again an interesting contrast in the case of Paul. Not to refer to his experience on the Damascus road, we know that Paul, if we are to believe the book of Acts, had his visions, trances, and dreams at important junctures in his career and that he acted according to their indications (Acts 16,9; [=II Cor 2,12-13]; 18,9-10; 22,17-21; 23,11; 27,23; Gal 2,2). Weinel writes: *We know that at decisive hours in his life Paul had visions and that at certain important moments he was guided by dreams* (Paulus, S. 52); A. Deissman, *Dreams become for him divine suggestions* (S. 57); W. Wrede, *His own reflections were converted into revelations, or the revelations in turn roused him to decisions* (Paulus, S. 16).

Jesus' self-consciousness did not originate in visions or hallucinations, nor was it supported, reinforced, bolstered up, or regulated by them. Jesus may have had his visions and inner experiences, such as that at the baptism, but they never had a regulative or reassuring influence either in his conduct or consciousness. He never shows himself morbidly dependent upon them at important junctures in his public career.

In concluding our study of Jesus' visions or hallucinations it is well to cite the statement of three medical experts concerning this psychic phenomenon, when occasional and isolated, as a symptom of a pathological psychic constitution. Of the church's saints, whose biographies and confessions are infinitely richer in visions, etc., than are our records of Jesus, Dr. Moerchen writes: *We must guard ourselves against drawing too extreme conclusions from the analogies between saintliness and morbid depressions* (PH, S. 20). In defense of the psychic soundness of the old prophets in general and of Ezekiel in particular, Dr. Dieckhoff says: *It would be overhasty and incorrect to conclude at once the existence of some psychic malady simply because of the presence of these illusions of sense. It is true that we find such usually as the symptoms of psychic disorders, but they are also to be met in psychically sound persons, precisely in the psychically élite* (S. 200). Exactly to our present point Dr. Binswanger urges: *In recent times the effort is in vogue to stamp the heroes of religious history, in particular Mohammed, the Apostle Paul, Martin Luther, and even Jesus*

*(E. Rasmussen), as psychopaths, hysterics and epileptics be-
cause they occasionally experienced more or less reliably attested hallucinations.. To this point let it be remarked that
the occurrence of isolated hallucinations or illusions is by no
means a proof of the existence of a psychic disorder, or even
of a psychopathic constitution.    Under the influence of long
continued physical privation (fasting), psychic over-exertion,
especially in states of strongly roused emotions (religio-ecsta-
tic moods) hallucinations can appear in psychically sound persons (S. 8).*

As a psychosensorial process the hallucination is abnormal;
it is due to a disturbed psychic function under abnormal conditions (Krafft-Ebing, p. 104).    When taken seriously and held
as true, hallucinations falsify both the objective and subjective
consciousness (p. 95).    When chronic they lead to mental im-
poverishment and result in a complete clouding of consciousness.
The judgment is overpowered (Kraepelin, p. 9) and the ordinary psychic correctives exercised upon the elements of experience are swept aside.    Hallucinations are of paramount importance in the formation of delusions to which they give certain
definite forms and appropriate expression (Binswanger, S.
34f).    They render the patient incapable of withdrawing from
their influence and regulate his conduct, if aggressive they spur
him on to action according to their indications.

Krafft-Ebing says that the French view which regards hallucinations as signs of insanity is without justification; *for, in
the first place, an hallucination, even when it is regarded as an
actual fact, is only an elementary phenomenon that reveals nothing concerning the general state of the individual, and nothing concerning the condition of the brain; and, in the second
place, experience offers us examples of many persons who have
believed in the reality of their hallucinations but who could not
be regarded as insane (Mohammed, Napoleon, Socrates, Pascal,
Jean d'Arc, Luther).    The explanation of this is not difficult,
when it is remembered that such hallucinated persons controlled
by the delusions and superstitions of their time, or by the tendency to the belief in wonders and mysticism, were not disposed
to correct these creations of their imagination........But*

*nevertheless we must hold fast to the fact that hallucinations
that are held to be true are manifestations that endanger the integrity of relations to the actual world* (p. 109f).

*Hallucinations......are not in themselves decisive as to the
existence of insanity. The most that they can prove is the existence of an abnormal cerebral condition. Their significance
as one of the symptoms of a psychosis depends upon the demonstration of the existence of a psychosis. Hallucinations appear
in their true light only when they stand in relation to the other
elementary disturbances (depression, attacks of anxiety, etc.),
and in the disturbed state of consciousness are no longer corrected and exercise influence on action* (Krafft-Ebing, p. 238).

## C) Its Form

Jesus' acceptance of the Messianic title gives rise to a serious psychological problem. Loofs has stated this problem well:
*To say the least, the Messianic consciousness comprises within
itself of necessity an extraordinary enhancement of self-consciousness. Indeed it makes us almost dizzy when we realize how
much it meant for Jesus to regard himself as the Messiah* (S.
151). Werner states the problem from the psychopathic angle:
*This s e l f - c o n s c i o u s n e s s transcends everything that a
psychically sound person, even though he be one of the greatest,
can think of himself* (PGJ, S. 11). Such an exalted estimate
of his own ego as is implied in Jesus' Messianic consciousness
involves certain striking features which transcend and cannot
be compelled within the confines and compass of common human
consciousness and which demand an explanation.

Jesus' pathographers have not been slow in finding this explanation; they speak of his megalomania, delirium, and delusions of grandeur. In Jesus' Messianic consciousness they
find evidences of his psychic degeneration *par excellence*. But
before going over to the psychopathic phase of the question,
and this is the extent of our present interest in Jesus' Messianic
consciousness, it might be well to note how various camps of
theologians have met the problem.

The conservative camp is represented by Loofs who sees no

hope of an historical solution of Jesus' Messianic consciousness. He takes the purely confessional and christological position. *If an understanding of the historical person of Jesus is to be reached at all, this possibility can be realized by faith alone* (S. 172). *What the historian as such cannot do, faith can. Faith can compose o n e picture which historical research is not in a position to assemble* (S. 222). *This formulary can in reality do justice to both, namely, the real humanity of Jesus and his self-consciousness which completely transcends the limits of the finite: it fits the faith that Jesus was, on the one hand, the most perfect revelation of God and, on the other hand, at the same time the originator of a new humanity* (S. 244).

A second position regarding Jesus' Messianic consciousness is that of source-scepticism as represented by Wrede and Wellhausen. Wrede maintains that Jesus never held himself to be, nor gave himself out to be the Messiah. His Messiahship is the work of primitive Christian faith as the result of the resurrection experiences. *It is only with the resurrection that Jesus becomes the Messiah* (MGE, S. 213). The Messianic consciousness and confessions of Jesus in Mc are unhistorical; they are simply read back into Mc in view of the earliest Christian Easter experiences and faith. Wellhausen allows it as possible that Jesus confessed his Messiahship before the high priest, but his Messianic consciousness played little or no role in what Jesus considered his mission and message. The sources, even Mc, are too strongly christianized to enable us to get anything like an historical picture of Jesus. Jesus never spoke to his disciples of his passion, resurrection, or parousia (1).

The large group of liberal theologians sees in Jesus first and last the great preacher and prophet of the kingdom of God. He is not consumed in the personal role that he is to play in the realization of this kingdom, but in the kingdom itself and its coming. They recognize an eschatological element in Jesus' teaching, but with few exceptions find it of no essential importance in the understanding of Jesus' person and career.

---

(1)   *Als sicher kann gelten, dass, wenn Jesus seine Juenger nicht einmal zum voraus ueber sein Leiden und Auferstehn belehrt hat, so erst recht nicht ueber seine Parusie* (Einl., S. 96).

They allow freely his Messianic consciousness as confessed at Caesarea Philippi and during his trial. This consciousness, however, is to be construed and conceived within the compass of common human consciousness. Its form is *zeitgeschichtlich* comprehensible. The charges of Loofs and Werner against this purely human and historical interpretation of Jesus' self-consciousness was presented above, p. 39ff. Against the liberals Werner further writes: *Ever so high titles may be ascribed to him, but it is and remains an unparalleled fanaticism, the counterpart of which is to be found only in institutions for the insane, when he makes himself the future judge of the whole human race and presents the prospect of his imminent triumphant return on the clouds of heaven* (PGJ, S. 44). *If he had no right to do this (forgive sins, etc.), then the chief testimony is given for the indictment against his psychic health. Such an immeasurable self-exaltation, of which he is thereby guilty, is unquestionably of morbid origin. This conclusion is unavoidable. Over the whole psychic life of Jesus the measure is broken. Jesus was a thoroughly morbid mind* (PGJ, S. 11).

Conservative and consequent eschatology is respectively represented by J. Weiss and A. Schweitzer. The latter finds the eschatological element in Jesus' words and deeds to be exclusively essential to the understanding of him. Eschatology alone explains his self-consciousness, conduct, and career; all are directly dominated by his eschatological conception of the kingdom of God and his own person. As we have pointed out above, both conservatives and liberals charge Schweitzer with surrendering, or at least imperiling the psychic health of Jesus (see above p. 119f). To these charges may be added that of Loofs, who writes of Schweitzer's Jesus of eschatology, *Jesus is for him a man of our history, a man who with mistaken thoughts allowed himself to be filled with the Messianic hope and who with his Messianic hope came to shipwreck* (S. 29). *Thus construed the self-consciousness of Jesus strongly resembles that of an abnormal person. Even if this abnormality does not fit into any p s y c h i a t r i c scheme, Jesus nevertheless belongs in the fanatics' corner whither the historian must banish many men and women whose psychic health (in the psychiatric sense) and moral integrity he does not in the least call in question* (S. 127).

Turning to the Synoptic sources themselves we find that eschatology constituted an essential element in the discourses and words of Jesus. The following is not an exhaustive list, but it does include the principal passages: Mt 10,23b; Mt 16,27-28=Mc 8,38b-9,1=Lc 9,26b-27; Mt 19,28=Lc 22,28-30; Mt 22,30=Mc 12,25=Lc 20,35; Mt 24,30-36=Mc 13, 26,32=Lc 21,27-33; Mt 24,37-41=Lc 17,26-27 34-35; Mt 26-29=Mc 14,25=Lc 22,18; Mt 26,64=Mc 14,62=Lc 22,69. The parables in Mt 24,42-44=Lc 12,39-40; Mt 24,45-51= Lc 12,42-46; Mt 25,1-13 31-46 are eschatological in thought but have acquired a decidedly early Christian character.

Whether or not one agrees with the extreme eschatological emphasis of Schweitzer, or accepts his long list of eschatological words, acts and sacraments, or his *Intermsethik* (GdLJF, S. 390-443), the abundance of the references in the preceding paragraph shows that eschatology was an essential element in Jesus' thought and teaching.

But our problem is not to be solved by citing references, for we do not know just what type of eschatology was current and how widely it obtained in Jesus' day. Even Schweitzer himself states that we have no sources to assure us whether the popular eschatological hopes of Jesus' contemporaries were prophetic, apocalyptic in the later Judaic sense, or Christian. He candidly admits that his own sketch is only an attempt at a reconstruction and is largely conjecture. H. J. Holtzmann sums the matter up well: *It is very doubtful whether the conception of the Messiah at the time of Jesus existed in the form of a regularly stamped coin of universally recognized currency* (MBJ, S. 15, Anm. 1).

Although we are not sure as to the exact character and extent of the eschatological hopes of Jesus' day, we do know that his eschatology, his picture of the future, was not a picture peculiar to himself, but was a picture painted before him as early as Dan. 7,13 and that it was not shared by Jesus alone, but by many of his own people of his own day (1). That Jesus' view was a common view is clear from the fact that he no more finds it necessary to explain or define it than he does the notion of the kingdom of God. He simply refers to it, perhaps in somewhat more glowing terms, as a well-known element in the religious acumen and atmosphere of his day and people. How widely this view obtained, or was entertained by Jesus' national contemporaries cannot be determined; the sources are too inadequate. But they do attest that when Jesus spoke of the future in such glowing terms his teaching was not new and strange, but well enough understood to dispense with definition. It was a picture so vividly visualized by Jesus' disciples that they even engaged in a dispute as to their respective roles in the future and requested reservations for prominent places (Mc 10,35ff). They had but two questions to ask: Where? (Lc 13,39), and When? (Mc 13,4).

This fantastic view of the future in Jesus' day, though very foreign to us, cannot be looked upon as a psychopathic product of the popular mind. Dr. Dieckhoff gives a significant statement on this point: *The greatest of errors have at times been accepted as incontestably correct, also by the wisest and the most intelligent. One needs only to recall the belief in witches: the men of the sixteenth century were just as psychically sound as we, and yet they entertained ideas and prejudices so absurd and inhuman that they are quite inconceivable to us* (S. 201).

Even if we knew more about the popular eschatological conceptions of Jesus' day, we would still not be sure of exactly what they meant for him. As Schweitzer says: *We possess no psychology of the Messiah* (GdLJF, S. 9). We still less possess a psychology of Jesus. But that his view of the future was not paranoiac is clear from the fact that not he alone but many of

---

(1) *In making an estimate of a man from the psychological and psychopathological point of view it is of greatest importance to know what are the circumstances of life, the cultural and moral views of the time as well as of the immediate environment in which he lives* (Weber, Sp. 232).

his contemporaries held it.   In order that a view be psychopathic, in this instance paranoiac, it must exhibit such eccentric
peculiarities that it departs from the common view to the degree
of abnormality.   Such cannot be proven, in fact the exact opposite is evident, as regards Jesus' view of the future.

There is no reason why Jesus should not share the views of
his contemporaries on this point.   His very historicity and our
own historical judgment demand it.   The offense is not old, but
modern.   As Schweitzer says, modern Christianity fears the *all-
too-historical* Jesus, for he registers a condemnation unpleasant to the comfortable modern view of Christianity.   It makes
Jesus too enthusiastic and too confident for modern Christianity to feel at ease and still profess discipleship.   It reminds
modern Christianity of its losses and relapses from the *religion
of Jesus*.   It is much more comfortable to confess to a *religion
about Jesus* than it is to strive to live the *religion of Jesus* after
him.   The apostles' creed is easily repeated, but to believe what
Jesus believed and to believe as he believed is a very different
task.   To believe that there actually is a kingdom of God, that
it is of and from God, that it can and will come, and that soon,
and to devote one's life to the preparing of one's self and others
for its coming to the extent of exhausting one's life in its service, that is the religion and faith *of* Jesus.

One of Jesus' chief gifts to his followers was the gift of
imagination.   Jesus visualized the future, not as we would visu-
alize it to be sure, but in such a way as appealed to the popular
imagination of his day.   He, further, visualized the future so
vividly that it gave him no minute of rest, it drove him apart
for prayer, and was a constant spur to his present.   As Renan
said, *Jesus is the man who believed most energetically of all in
the reality of the ideal* (S. 185).   Jesus' habit of living in the
future and in the terms of the future is not a symptom of paranoia, or any other psychosis, but is his gift of imagination, a
gift by which the world is not only inspired but led to progress.
Modern Christianity has not inherited Jesus' gift of imagination.

Jesus' view of the future as God's and as of vital concern
in matters of present conduct and coming destiny for each in-

dividual is not the peculiarity of a paranoiac, but the very essence of Christianity.  In this respect Rothenburg is more consistent in discarding both Christianity and Jesus than are Schweitzer's critics who will remain Christian yet discard eschatology as degenerating Jesus and who will leave him to be the teacher of a set of morals and ethics reactionary in his own day but pleasant to the modern conscience.  The eschatology of Jesus' ethics is as reactionary as ever and Jesus' true disciple today can never feel at ease as long as social and individual evils are never out of his sight.  To eliminate the eschatological element from Jesus' teaching and person is to strip him of his power and influence.  To be sure, our picture of the future will differ as widely from his as the first from the twentieth century.  But we must share his view that there is a future, that God has great and good things in store for it, and that this future demands service and sacrifice in the present.  Most of all, we must share his zeal and passion in working toward it if we are to remain his disciples.

Eschatology with reservations has its evident elements of strength: 1) it is conservative in its use of the sources; 2) it leaves Jesus to live seriously and genuinely in his own day and time; 3) it also offers what Strauss called in his 1835 *Leben Jesu* "*true and splendid elements*" (I 554) which are not to be underestimated; 4) it pays a tremendous tribute to Jesus himself in that it shows that primitive, and essential, Christianity was not committed to the formal fulfillment of any one particular word of Jesus, but to his Person and cause.

### D)   Its Content, Control, and Confession

It is in this connection that Binet-Sanglé and Hirsch commit the gravest of their historical errors.  They represent Jesus as believing in his own divinity, and the winning of others over to this vesanic conviction as the sole content of his message and the intent of his mission.  This view they, of course, gather from the Fourth Gospel where the whole content of Jesus' message is his own person and its prerogatives, and where he is represented as confessing his divine dignity in an indiscriminate and uncontrolled manner before both friend and foe.

But the problem of Jesus' self-consciousness in the Synoptic Gospels is a very different one.   The fact that Jesus has so little to say about himself in the Synoptic sources creates one of the most hopeless problems of New Testament criticism, namely, What did Jesus think of himself?   The answers to this question can be at best not more than tentative historical reconstructions.   These answers do not concern us seriously here.   Our question is, Is Jesus' self-consciousness as represented in the Synoptic sources pathological in its content, control, and confession or claims?

The content of Jesus' self-consciousness in the first three Gospels is not his own person, its prerogatives, and pretentions. Jesus is not consumed in his own ego, but in the great cause of the kingdom of God which he champions even to the cross.   The kingdom of God is the theme of his preaching and teaching, of his every prophecy, parable, and prayer.   His own ego he relegates so completely to the background that it is a hopeless task to try to ascertain what and how he esteemed himself. From the beginning to the end the kingdom of God, of which he is the preacher and the prophet, remains in the foreground of his mission and message.   As H. J. Holtzmann writes: *The Messianic question was neither distinctive for the personal piety of Jesus nor of central significance in his message* (MBJ, S. 76).

Our previous discussion of the egocentric words of Jesus made it clear that Jesus never set confessional conditions for entrance into or participation in the kingdom of God.   His requirements were the rigid requirements of moral and ethical

| Mt 7,21-23 | Lc 6,46 |
|---|---|
| *Not everyone that saith unto me, Lord, Lord shall enter into the kingdom of heaven; but he that doeth the will of my Father who is in heaven.          Many will say to me in that day, Lord, Lord, did we not prophecy by thy name, and by thy name cast out demons, and by thy name do many mighty works? And then will I prophecy unto them, I never knew you;        depart from me, ye   that work iniquity.* | *Why call ye me, Lord, Lord,* <br><br> *and do not the things which I say?   13,26-27 Then shall ye begin to say,* <br><br> *we did eat and drink in thy presence, and thou didst teach us in our streets And he shall say, I tell you, I know not whence ye are; depart from me, all ye workers of iniquity.* |

conduct as is evinced by numerous passages in the Synoptics, of which the passage on the preceding page is a striking example.

Here we see clearly what Jesus regards as the essence of religion. It is not c o n f e s s i o n to his person, or the person of any other, but moral and ethical c o n d u c t. In Lc 6,46 Jesus says that it is absurd to call him Lord, Lord, and do not the things which he says. In Mt. 7,21 it is impossible to enter into the kingdom of God unless one performs the will of the Father who is in heaven. In Mt the pretendants base their claims upon the efficient way in which they have used the name of Jesus; in Lc upon their personal associations with him. Here Jesus ascribes a very subordinate role to his person in deciding the issues of the kingdom of God. Jesus even warns against confession to his person as a dangerous self-delusion.

Jesus' Messianic consciousness was his own private and personal problem. Its solution and issue never seriously altered the content of his message, although it greatly increased the demands upon his mission. The prominence of the part that he was to play in the final realization of the kingdom of God never caused him to parade his person and neglect his cause and calling as a preacher and prophet of that kingdom. It rather led him to warn against too exclusive attachment to his person and to insist more emphatically than ever upon rigorous religious conduct. His self-consciousness brought him to a still more serious conception of his calling, for a more serious and earnest tone enters into his words as he strikes in upon a new course of action after the confession at Caesarea Philippi.

Jesus, in clear contradiction to the paranoiac character, was not consumed with the claims of his own consciousness but with the chief cause which he championed, the kingdom of God. He did not advertise his person, nor did he force himself upon others in the matter of his dignity. He challenged his hearers to believe *with* him rather than *on* or *in* him. It was only most rarely, reluctantly, and reservedly that he spoke of himself. Even the highest pretentions regarding the personal role that was destined for him in the future were subjected and subordinated to the divine will.

Whatever may have been its content Jesus subjected his self-

consciousness to the most consciousness c o n t r o l.  He seems
to have felt restricted and restrained rather than refreshed and
rejuvenated by it.  It pressed him apart to prayer and petition rather than encouraged him to elusive enterprises and augmented aggressiveness.  He did not rush ruthlessly ahead, but
moved reluctantly seeking clearness and certainty, awaiting the
divine direction.  *We have seen the Messianic ministry of Jesus
and the Messianic attestation, which he gives for himself, conditioned and controlled by a deep and unique religious disposition* (Baldensperger S. 155).  *His appearance as the Messiah
was not usurpation but obedience, not free choice but inexorable
divine necessity* (S. 191).  H. J. Holtzmann writes to the point:
*Although the Messianic consciousness marks the greatest ven-
ture of finite consciousness, a fully sufficient guarantee against
autocratic superhumanism is given at least in the unconditional
subordination of the Messianic thought to the thought
of God which towers over all* (MBJ, S. 82).  P. W. Schmiedel writes: *I n  a n y  c a s e  it  was  not  o u t  o f  p r e -
s u m p t i o n  that  Jesus  regarded  himself  a s  t h e  M e s -
s i a h  but  only  after  severe  struggle* (PJSMG, S. 16) (1).

The self-consciousness of the paranoiac never becomes seriously problematic for himself.  He accepts his deliriant dignity
as the merest matter of course.  He may sink into sulky sullen-
ness when his emotional exaltations ebb, but when he is in the
full swing of his delirium the thought of moral responsibilities
and obligations never occurs to him.  If its full realization lies
yet in the future, he either lies in wait for the appropriate opportunity or attempts to force the ways that will lead him to
his coveted end.  He feels that he naturally enjoys exceptional
exterritoriality in all the affairs and fields of conduct.  He may
do whatsoever he will whenever and wherever he will.  Whether
he feels it or not, he acts as though he were exempt even from
the precepts and proprieties of right and wrong.  He does not
see the foolishness and futility of his harmless enterprises; he
can commit a wrong, or even a crime, with clear and undis-

---

(1)  *We may observe exalted self-consciousness and belief in a definite
mission that verges on to delusional ideas in great men who possess none
of the features characteristic of psychic disorders* (Weber, Sp. 234).

turbed conscience, and even later retrospection and reflection sometimes fail to bring him to regret and remorse.

Regular reserve and reticence such as Jesus practiced regarding his identity is thoroughly uncharacteristic of the paranoiac. In fact he has exactly the opposite inclination. The whole world must know who he is and recognize him as such. He must make it clear to all that he is really not the one he seems or is commonly supposed to be; he is another, someone really great. He may have his periods of sullen silence brought on by his lack of success in convincing others, but soon the old delusion breaks forth afresh and he is again at his old task of trying to convince others of his unsuspected dignity. The confirmed paranoiac seldom has a great cause for which his person is sacrificed and which he serves; if he has any cause at all, it figures only as it contributes to the high claims which he makes for himself.

Jesus' self-consciousness appears less in the form of a claim and more in the form of a concession to the divine will which he first confesses privately to his most intimate disciples and later publicly before the high priest. Jesus' acceptance of the Messianic title with such modifications and reservations as he forced upon it amounted practically to an annulment and negation of it. Paul designated it as a stumbling-block to the Jew and as foolishness to the Greek.

In closing our study of the self-consciousness of Jesus from the pathographic point of view it is well to cite a word of Shirley Jackson Case, which is one of the most significant utterances regarding the understanding of the problem of Jesus' self-consciousness in recent times: *The messianic thought did not master him; he was its conqueror, not its victim, and he attained this position by placing more stress upon his choice of God than upon God's choice of him* (P. 289).

In all the features of his self-consciousness Jesus forms the clearest sort of contrast to all those types of insanity in which self-estimation is most extremely exalted and falsely exaggerated.

# EXCURSUS
## The Affliction of Paul

It is not at all surprising that Jesus' pathographers also come upon the question of Paul's psychic health. Frenssen, hardly a pathographer of Jesus, writes of Paul: *He was a morbid man through and through. And according to what he writes in many passages in his letters to his friends, his malady was something as follows: he was racked by severe nervous and psychic disturbances which made natural life appear to him as misery, nausea and death; from time to time this condition was aggravated to epileptic attacks during which, in a state of unconsciousness, he beheld visions of wondrous heavenly splendor and magnificence* (S. 90). Of Paul's experience on the Damascus road Baumann says: *Today we would doubtless regard the incident narrated as an hysterico-epileptic attack; in II Cor 12,10 Paul manifests a constitution similar to that of Jesus* (S. 64). Rasmussen naturally finds Paul an epileptic: *That he, in spite of his greatness, was an epileptic psychopath was announced long ago by specialists in psychic diseases and is incontrovertably clear in the sources......in his own letters* (S. 79f).

Hirsch devotes considerable space to Paul (p. 174-207; Ger. S. 179-216); of course, Paul was a paranoiac. *There cannot be the slightest doubt that in Paul we have a typical case of paranoia. In the meagre accounts which we have of him, all the symptoms which go to make up the clinical picture of paranoia are characteristically described. His psychical efficacy was dominated by delusions and hallucinations, and all his actions were governed by these psychopathic processes* (p. 203). *Like Jesus Christ, Paul was a paranoiac, whose thoughts and acts all rested on delusions and hallucinations. His writings which were handed down to us, and which laid the foundation stone of the Christian religion, are in every way characteristic of the insanity at the bottom of them* (p. 207).

Before the pathographers of Jesus had put in their appearance the Pauline research in the field of New Testament criticism came upon the question of Paul's affliction, particularly in connection with the nature of his conversion on the Damascus road and his confession of a *thorn in the flesh* in II Cor 12,7ff.

Some students of Paul find in his II Cor 12 confession only a physical affliction that greatly hampered and hindered the apostle in his missionary activity and as having no connection with his conversion or any of his unusual experiences. Dr. E. Preuschen (Article entitled *Paulus als Antichrist* in the *Zeitschrift fuer die N. T. liche Wissenschaft; Giessen,* 1901) argues that Paul was afflicted with leprosy as evinced by his seven days' purification and sin-offering (Acts 21,26) by which he hoped to be cured (see Conybeare, p. 363). H. Weinel sees in Paul's experience before Damascus only the culmination of a series of severe inner struggles that condensed themselves at this point in a vision which was devoid of all connections with any physiologic or psychic ailment (Paulus, S. 53).

A. Diessmann is sceptical about any definite diagnosis in Paul's case because of the scantiness of the materials in the sources. Of II Cor 12,7ff he writes: *We cannot determine to what special malady these symptoms point. Various conjectures have been attempted often, but without sufficient certainty: the meagre hints which Paul himself gives admonish caution* (S. 43). However, he connects Paul's Damascus experience directly with his strong inclination toward exceptional ecstatic moments: *The Damascus incident is not to be isolated but must be regarded as the fundamental mystic experience of the religious genius who in his later life knew that he was honored with definite extraordinary ecstatic visitations* (S. 83).

Otto Pfleiderer sees in both II Cor 12,1ff and in the conversion of Paul typical states of ecstasy, toward which the apostle was strongly predisposed by his excessively nervous and excitable physical and psychic constitution. *Specially significant in this connection is the passage* II Cor 12,1ff *where the ecstatic state of consciousness during the visions, whose objectivity was for Paul beyond all question of doubt, reveals itself in the notice: he does not know whether he is in the body or out of the body while he is caught away into the third heaven. But when in the same connection peculiar bodily sufferings and exhaustions, which were connected with the exalted visions, are spoken of, such points unmistakably to states of nervous convulsion which usually attend the ecstatic consciousness, or furnish it a physiological basis.  Hence we may conclude with certainty that the physiologic-psychic organism of Paul was in general favorably disposed to such experiences...... The psychic conditions which lay at the base of the Damascus incident are to be clearly recognized thus far: a nervous irritable constitution which was by nature predisposed to visionary states, a soul terribly shaken and torn by painful doubting because it had become uncertain regarding the rightness of its fanatical conduct* (S. 62ff).

Not a few New Testament critics agree with the diagnosis of Rasmussen that Paul was an epileptic and that his numerous visions and special revelations are to be accounted for in the light of his affliction; however, they disagree with Rasmussen in designating Paul as a psychopath.

A. Juelicher: *It has been concluded with great plausibility from II Cor 12,7-9 that he* (Paul) *as a Christian convert..... and indeed not without connection with the intense religious excitement which manifested itself in him in numerous "visions and revelations"......became an epileptic* (Einl. S. 34).

F. C. Conybeare also is of the opinion that Paul was an epileptic.  He speaks of Paul's *hallucinations and transcendental fancies* (p. 9).  *Paul was pre-eminently a man of visions and dreams, prizing what in moments of ecstasy he beheld more highly than waking realities* (p. 3).  *He was, like many a later saint, of a temperament naturally ecstatic and perpetually saw Christ, and conversed with him in visions; his words and actions, even his missionary movements, as he is careful to inform us, were inspired and directed not by reflection but by revelation* (p. 4).  On II Cor 12,1ff Conybeare remarks: *The affliction in question was undoubtedly the epilepsy which often attends such temperaments* (p. 4).  *Partial or even complete blindness is a frequent concomitant of epilepsy, and if Paul had suffered therefrom it would explain another passage* (the first passage being Gal 4,14) *at the end of the epistle to the Galatians, 6,11: "See with what large letters I have written to you with my own hand." It was certainly an effort to him to use his own hand in writing, and when he did so he had to write a large hand. Elsewhere he refers to the use of amanuenses. These passages point to a partial blindness. His visitation on the way to Damascus was accompanied by temporary blind- ness* (p. 363).

Hans Lietzmann finds that the materials for a diagnosis of Paul's affliction in II Cor 12,7 are inadequate for a definite diagnosis. Judged on the basis of two passages, one in Euse- bius and one in Hieronymous, the buffeting at the hands of Satan's messenger is hardly epilepsy, rather night-mare. There is no necessary connection between the affliction referred to in II Cor 12,7 and the abundance of Paul's ecstatic visions. Lietz- mann finds only two surely attested hallucinations of Paul in a period of twenty-two years. Gal 4,14f would seem to indi- cate some sort of eye-trouble as the apostle's affliction. Tem- porary blindness and weak eyes are common in cases of epil- epsy; epilepsy in the case of Paul is not necessarily excluded, but nowhere required. II Cor 12,7 seems to fit hysteria best (III, 218ff).

In the first edition of his work, *Die hellenistisch-roemische Kultur in ihren Beziehungen zu Judentum und Christentum,* P. Wendland determined upon epilepsy as the malady of Paul on the basis of II Cor 12,7. But in the second-third edition of his work he regards the epilepsy hypothesis as uncertain in view of expert medical opinion to the effect that the materials in the sources are too meagre for any definite diagnosis (S. 218, Anm. 1).

This modification of Wendland's opinion was occasioned by the pamphlet, *War Paulus Epileptiker?* (Leipzig, J. C. Heinrichs, 1910, 82 S.) (1) by Dr. Adolf Seeligmueller, noted nerve specialist in Halle. Dr. Seeligmueller op- poses the assumption that Paul was an epileptic for the following reasons: Paul manifests none of the intellec- tual, affective or volitional symptoms of epilepsy; the his- torical data, such as the *thorn in the flesh,* the visions and the supposed eye-trouble, cannot be regarded as stigmata of that

---

(1) Dr. Seeligmueller's conclusions were accessible to the writer only in Dr. Weber's review in the *Theologische Literaturzeitung,* 1911, Nr. 8, Sp. 235-36.

disease in the light of present-day scientific psychiatry; that
any of Paul's unusual psychic experiences were epileptic attacks is excluded by the apostle's ability to recall them as incidents and relate their contents.   Dr. Seeligmueller favors attacks of megrim or malaria as the probable affliction of Paul.

Dr. Weber himself remarks: *That Paul was seriously afflicted with epilepsy is not to be concluded from the materials
at our disposition.   What the nature  of his affliction was, if
he was afflicted at all, is not to be determined with incontestable certainty* (Sp. 236).

A. Hausrath: *It is not to be doubted that the visions of Paul
were connected with his morbid nervous constitution.   Whether
he had similar experiences before his Damascus vision he has not
told us, but this vision seems to be associated with an epileptic
attack* (I 275).

G. Hollmann's statement to the effect that Paul was an epileptic has been cited above (see p. 40f).

Of II Cor 12,7ff W. Wrede writes: *Here a definite pathological picture is presented: Paul, like other great men of history
(Caesar and Napoleon), suffered with epileptic attacks.   This
is more than mere conjecture, for the description of the apostle
is verified by the fact that visions are to be observed frequently
in epileptic victims.   The blissful state of beholding sublime
scenes, the disappearance of bodily consciousness, the attack
with its convulsions......all this is a single pathological process.   Was such also the case on the way to Damascus?   We
have no reason to think so.   In any case a quite special light is
thrown upon the rise of this first vision* (Paulus, S. 17).   However, Wrede adds: *The impression of health is nevertheless predominant in the case of Paul* (S. 18).

W. Bousset finds that Paul's struggle with his handicap is
one of the finest traits in his character.   To the passage II Cor
12,5-10 he gives the title, *Die Krankheit des Paulus.*   He regards this malady of the apostle as chronic and as expressing
itself in single, but severe attacks.   It was probably epilepsy,
or some sort of painful affliction of a rheumatic, neuralgic, or
hysteric nature.   *We may conclude that the whole visionary,
ecstatic peculiarity of Paul, such as is manifest here and in*

*other passages, had its ground-work for the most part in a certain pathological organization. Indeed we may perhaps assume that the visions and revelations of Paul stood in a manifold direct relation with such morbid attacks...... We have no right to be startled at these conclusions. What we admire in Paul is precisely how he with heroic energy compelled into service again and again the body that failed him often, the manner in which he raised himself above the distress and pain of his physical existence in unbroken trust in the power of God working through him and in submissive self-denial......Experience has taught repeatedly that psychically highly gifted persons, instead of submitting to a malicious and stubborn sickness or other physical ailment, develop their splendid steel-like energy in struggle and resistance* (SdNT, II 217ff).

Turning to the sources themselves, we find that in II Cor 12,7-9 Paul confesses to some sort of affliction which he regards as a great handicap: *And by reason of the exceeding greatness of the revelations, that I should not be exalted overmuch, there was given to me a thorn in the flesh, a messenger of Satan to buffet me, that I should not be exalted overmuch. Concerning this thing I besought the Lord thrice, that it might depart from me. And he hath said unto me, My grace is sufficient for thee: for my power is made perfect in weakness.* Paul here seems afflicted with some ailment which was chronic and which had been the theme of repeated prayer and petition for relief. Not only Paul himself is aware of it, but also the readers of his letters; he writes in Gal 4,13-14, *But ye know that because of an infirmity of the flesh I preached the Gospel unto you the first time, and that which was a temptation to you in my flesh ye despised not, nor rejected; but ye received me as an angel of God, even as Christ Jesus.*

We see that Paul speaks regularly of his infirmity as *in the flesh,* but that by no means would indicate it as purely physiological and devoid of psychic connections. That his affliction did have its psychic side is clear from the fact that he speaks of it directly in connection with the abundance of his visions and revelations in II Cor 12, 1 of which he cites two particular instances in the three following verses: *I know a man in*

*Christ, fourteen years ago (whether in the body, I know not; or whether out of the body, I know not; God knoweth), such a one caught up even to the third heaven. And I know such a man (whether in the body, or out of the body, I know not; God knoweth), how that he was caught up into Paradise, and heard unspeakable words, which it is not lawful for a man to utter.* Here we have doubtless to deal with experiences of a highly ecstatic character attended by hallucinations in both the visual and auditory fields of sense and with the complete loss of bodily consciousness.

Beyond the character, the frequency of Paul's elated and extraordinary experiences would show that they were organically connected with what he calls his infirmity (Acts 9,1-10; 16,9 [=II Cor 2,12-13]; 18,9-10; 22,17-21; 23,11; 27,23; Gal 2,2). Moreover, Paul ascribes great importance to these experiences and acts according to them at important junctures in his career. His experience on the Damascus road includes both visual and auditory hallucinations, and it is absolutely revolutionary in his conduct and consciousness henceforth as a called apostle of Christ. He rehearses this experience, reminisces upon it and refers to it (Acts 22,6-11; 26,12-19; I Cor 9,1; 15,8; II Cor 4,6; 12,1; Gal 1,16-17; Eph 3,3; Phil 3,12). It constitutes the credentials of his apostleship.

Further, the indwelling Christ of Christian experience was for Paul a kind of second self, or extra-ego. It would be unjust and unhistorical to overlook the mystical character of Paul's thought and language in such expressions, and to regard them from the purely psychanalytic viewpoint. Nevertheless, Paul regards his call to Christ as a dissolution of his old ego which is replaced by a new ego which he identifies with Christ himself.

The severe moral test, amounting almost to depreciation, to which Paul subjected certain unusual psychic, supposed manifestations of the Spirit in the early Christian community would seem to suggest that he was sceptical regarding their supernatural origin, perhaps on the basis of what he knew to be the pathological origin of certain of his own inner experiences.

It is not permissible to save the psychic health of Jesus at the expense of Paul, but any observant reader of the Synoptic Gospels, Acts, and the Pauline epistles will find that the New Testament records concerning Paul are much richer and more abundant in pathographic materials than are those concerning Jesus. But in spite of his dreams, trances, visions, and states of ecstasy the impression that we get of Paul as we read of him in the New Testament is that he was a man of healthy heart and mind.

# CHAPTER VI

## The Pathography of Jesus

### 1)   The Possibility of a Diagnosis in the Case of Jesus

No medical scientist is franker in recognizing and admitting the difficulties, limitations, even provisionalities, of any diagnosis he may make than the schooled and experienced specialist in mental diseases.   Here Krafft-Ebing is representative: *Even in the domain of physical disease, where exact physical means for diagnosis are at hand, it is often difficult to decide where health changes to disease.   How much more difficult must it be, then, in the psychic domain, where a standard of mental health can only be thought of as ideal; where no individual is exactly like another, and emotions, passions, and variations of feeling, of thought, and of will from the majority of mankind, even errors of the understanding and illusions of sense, are possible within the limits of physiologic life, and as elementary mental disturbances, are absolutely compatible with the existence of mental clearness and free will* (p. 231f).

The most necessary factor in making a diagnosis of any kind of disease, physical or psychic, is, of course, personal observation and examination.   This observation and examination must, further, be long, painstaking and carefully continued.   Even then the physiologic and psychic symptoms may be so complicated and complex that the diagnostician is not only not clear as to what special type of mental alienation he has before him, but often is not sure whether his subject is healthy or diseased.   The healthy or diseased state is to be determined only by a careful analysis of the sensory stimuli to which the subject is exposed, his response to them, and the issues in motor expression that ensue in words and acts.   *In absentia* and *post mortem* examinations lack the most important and necessary means for a diagnosis.   A pathographic study, then, must of necessity dispense with this fundamental principle of observation. It is just for this reason of precluded observation that psychiatrists in general accord little or no recognition to comparative psychopathology and pathography. In fact, pathographers have fallen into great discredit with skilled specialists in mental disease.

Turning to Jesus, we find that the possibility of observation, the indispensable prerequisite of all scientific judgment, is hopelessly out of the question in the case of an historical personage who died on the cross nineteen centuries ago. We shall never see Jesus act or hear him speak again as a man of history. What he did and said, how he acted and spoke is transmitted to us only in the meagre records containing the recollections and reminiscences of a handful of his disciples and followers.

The next important factor in the diagnosis of a psychosis is the knowledge and careful tracing of the course of its development. The course of a psychosis Krafft-Ebing considers next in importance to the symptoms themselves (p. 199). Binswanger writes: *The diagnosis of a psychic disorder cannot be made with certainty from the determination of a typical state, but only from the most exact knowledge of the process of its development and entire course* (S. 80). No single symptom will suffice, and as large a portion of the subject's life as possible must be brought under consideration. The diagnosis involves the determination of the time of the inception, the causes back of the inception, the delineation of the progress of the disease through the latent stages, its transition to and its course through the active phase. As to the duration of a psychosis, it may last for months, even years; acuter types may reach the acme and termination within a few weeks.

Here too pathological psychanalysis is embarrassed in the case of Jesus. The sources furnish us no materials which make it possible to trace the rise and development of any psychic phenomena peculiar to Jesus. Keim was the first to attempt to trace the development of Jesus' self-consciousness, but scholars since have become increasingly sceptical on this point. The first thirty years of Jesus' life are shrouded in darkness.

He is a mature man when he appears at the Jordan, and the Gospels furnish us no clues for the confirmation of any changes or transitions in his self-consciousness from one psychic type to another. Further, his public career is too short; as stated before, it is to be reckoned in months, some even in weeks (Burkitt—400 days), and not in years. It is only by the employment of the Fourth Gospel, where Jesus' public ministry extends well into the third year, that the pathographers can trace a developmental psychosis. Then the Fourth Gospel becomes *the biography of the decline* (Binet-Sanglé). The very brevity of Jesus' public career forces his pathographers (de Loosten, Hirsch, Binet-Sanglé) to locate the transition from the latent to the active stage at the Jordan or in the desert as the promoting cause of his public appearance in Galilee. During his public career, of which alone we have record, we find that Jesus is and remains one and the same character and person.

The necessary steps to be taken in the diagnosis of a psychosis are to be found elaborately outlined in any textbook on insanity (see Binswanger, S. 78f; Kraepelin, p. 97ff; Krafft-Ebing, p. 240ff). They are most succinctly summarized by Kraepelin as follows: a) anamnesis of family, b) personal history previous to disease, c) anamnesis of the disease, d) status praesens. This bare outline suffices to show that the available materials for a diagnosis in the case of Jesus are so meagre as to make a diagnosis next to impossible, unless the most pronounced and characteristic pathological symptoms are discovered in the sources. We therefore proceed to look into the heredity of Jesus and to sift the sources for any somatic or psychic symptoms.

## 2)   Heredity

Since 60-70% (Binswanger) of the inmates of institutions for the insane suffer under some hereditary burden, it is not at all surprising that Jesus' pathographers have endeavored to exploit this fertile field (1). Soury was the first; he

---

(1) *By far the most important cause of insanity is the transmissibility of psychopathic dispositions or cerebral infirmities by way of heredity;* Krafft-Ebing, p. 157. Clinical observation also finds that in point of nationality insanity is most frequent among the Jews.

accounted for the cerebral paralysis with which Jesus suffered
by the assumption of an hereditary burden which manifested
itself in another member of Jesus' family, his brother James
(see above p. 21f). De Loosten found evidences of a
collateral and direct hereditary influence through the maternal side of the family; John the Baptist was a psychopath, perhaps also James, the brother of Jesus. Binet-
Sanglé reckons with a converging and cumulative hereditary
burden which, coming chiefly from the paternal side of the family, resulted in the extinction of Joseph's family within four
generations.

On turning to the New Testament sources in search of
materials concerning the health history of Jesus' family, we
find that Jesus' father never figures personally in Jesus' public career. Joseph is referred to by name in Lc 4,22 (3,23),
by occupation in Mt 13,55, but by neither in Mc. (Mc 6,3
reads ὁ τοῦ τέκτονος υἱὸς in 13 69 33 597 . . . . a b c e i aur aeth;
Huck, S. 83.) The general supposition is that Joseph died
long before Jesus' public appearance, for Mary seems to be
known in Nazareth as a widow (Mc 3,31=Mt 12,46=Lc 8,19).
Joseph figures personally only in the narratives of the nativity
in the first and third Gospels; in Lc he plays a purely minor
role, but in Mt's birth stories he is very prominent. Here he
appears more after the manner of an Old Testament patriarch
to whom God reveals himself by angels in dreams (1,20ff;
2,13ff; 2,19; 2,22).

Jesus' mother, however, does appear personally in the
course of his public career in Mc 3,31 and she is mentioned by
name in 6,3. In Lc's narrative of the nativity she plays the
leading role and is the recipient of a special revelation in a
state of waking in 1,26ff. In the Synoptics Jesus' mother and
brethren are not represented as at all sympathetic with his
appearance in public (Mc 3,21). Binet-Sanglé's picture of
Mary is taken from the Fourth Gospel, especially from the
Cana incident and the scene at the cross.

If we turn to the rest of the family of Joseph and Mary,
we find a list of four brothers named in Mc 6,3 (=Mt 13,55f)
and unnamed sisters. From among these four brothers of Jesus

James has been singled out as the other psychopath of the family, doubtless for the reason that we hear of him more frequently in the New Testament. We know that he joined the early Christian community in Jerusalem at an early date in consequence of a resurrection vision, I Cor 15,7. He was known to Paul and the author of Acts as one of the leading figures in the primitive Christian community at Jerusalem (Gal 1,19; 2,9 12; Acts 15,13ff; 21,18). According to these authors James seems to have been a conservative character yet capable of considerable liberality as is clear from his address in Acts 15,13-21 and the letter of the Jerusalem apostles and elders to the Gentile converts of Paul and Barnabas which seems to have been the work of James (Acts 15,23-29). The New Testament furnishes us no reasons for concluding that James, the brother of Jesus, was a psychopath.

Concerning the Baptist, whom ecclesiastical tradition has regarded as a first cousin of Jesus, we are much more fully informed. For our New Testament information concerning the Baptist we are chiefly indebted to the document Q. As it is preserved in Mt and Lc we learn considerable about the sinister character of the Baptist's message as well as its content (Mt 3,7-10)=Lc 3,7-9, his impression upon his contemporaries and Jesus' own high estimate and appreciation of him (Mt 11,7-19; 21,32—Lc 7,24-35). Adding to Q Mc and Acts, as well as special notices of Lc in his Gospel, we learn more of the Baptist's ascetic and eccentric habits of life, (Mt 3,4 —Mc 1,6), the organized and specially instructed character of his following (Mc 2,18; Lc 11,1; Acts 18,25; 19,3), and Herod's fear of him and the Baptist's death at his hands (Mc 6,14ff; Mt 14,1ff; Lc 9,7ff). (Compare Josephus' account of the Baptist's death in his *Antiquities,* XVIII, 5, 2).

The Baptist figured prominently in Jesus' public career; he announced the Messiah, baptized Jesus, sent a deputation to him, and his message fits organically into that of Jesus. Mt 4,17 represents Jesus as repeating verbatim the message of John in 3,2 and in 10,7 he recommends it word for word to his disciples as they go out on their mission. In the eyes of the public John was a prophet, but like Jesus he must hear from the religious authorities the charge of insanity; in his address on the Baptist Jesus cites a contemporary judgment upon the Baptist to the effect that *he hath a demon* (Mt 11,18 =Lc 7,33).

We know too little of the Baptist to make a discussion of his psychic soundness worth while. That the religious leaders should pronounce him insane is only natural in view of the Baptist's attitude toward them. But that their judgment was correct is not at all to be demonstrated. The picture that we gather of him, especially from Q, is that the Baptist was a decidedly capable character, an impressive and forceful personality, and a great prophet and preacher with a message and mission of his own. The picture of the Baptist in Mc, where he is merely the forerunner or advance agent of the Messiah, and in the Fourth Gospel, where he is deliberately subordinated and reduced to a mere foil of Jesus, is purely the early Christian view of the Baptist and the function of his person and appearance, and does him great historical injustice. In this respect Jesus' own view of the Baptist is less Christian than that of Mc and Jn.

The Baptist's ascetic and eccentric habits of life do not in the least compromise his psychic soundness. His demands upon the various classes of his contemporaries who respond to his message are serious, sane, and very practical (Lc 3,10-14). The very restrictions and reservations which he sets upon his own person and work are not only rare in cases of mental morbidity, but show us that we have a really great man before us.

That Jesus and John were related by blood is based solely upon Lc 1,36 where the angel in his announcement to Mary refers to Elizabeth, the mother of John, as her *kinswoman* (συγγενίς). From the point of view of heredity it is very important to know the degree of the kinship. The term συγγενίς does not tell us whether this relationship was immediate or distant family relationship, or merely tribal (1). Even granting an immediate blood kinship, collateral hereditary influence is still more improbable than probable.

---

(1) Werner assumes that it was a remote family relationship on the basis of Jn 1,31.

Summing up the New Testament evidence on the health history of Jesus' family, we can say that there are no collateral, direct, or converging lines that would lead to the assumption of an hereditary burden. The only possible materials to be gleaned are psychanalytically worthless. They are, for the most part, (the psychic experiences of Joseph and Mary and the latter's kinship with the mother of the Baptist) historically unreliable and legendary.

A word concerning the role that heredity plays in the transmission of a nervous constitution fertile to the appearance of a psychosis, or insanity itself, as expressed by expert medical opinion may be added. Binswanger reminds his readers that the significance of heredity, in spite of its importance, has been greatly overestimated (S. 55). *Insanity in the mother is more dangerous to descendants than insanity in the father; if only the father or the mother is tainted, then the question depends essentially upon which parent the individual psychically resembles* (Krafft-Ebing, p. 228f). *In families which are burdened by heredity either on the paternal or maternal side, the majority of the descendants, reckoned through several generations, are psychically sound. However, in heavily burdened families, particularly where the hereditary burden is converging and cumulative, the number of the psychically and nervously morbid individuals later on is notably larger* (Binswanger, S. 55). *Hereditary burden gains a decisive influence in the formation of a psychosis only when it is degenerative in character...... Hereditary degeneration does not create its own peculiar forms of psychic morbidity, but gives to those forms already present a special stamp by the alteration of the process of development, by the grouping of symptoms and by the termination* (S. 59). *We may add the further limitation that from the proof of an hereditary burden it may by no means be concluded that the individual in question m u s t sooner or later fall psychically ill* (S. 61).

*One is not justified in assuming a degeneration even as probable solely from hereditary burden; for this is demanded the demonstration of signs of psychic degeneration in the individual himself* (Weber, Sp. 234).

### 3)  Somatic Symptoms

A thorough physical examination is indispensable in the case of both physiologic and psychic diagnosis. Somatic symptoms and deviating physiological details and formations are of great importance.

In no single item do the Gospels furnish us less information about Jesus than in physiological details and descriptions. Of Jesus' outward appearance we know nothing. Whether he was tall, short, or of medium stature we cannot say. That he was short of stature because Zacchaeus had to climb a tree in order to see him, or because he rode into Jerusalem on the colt of an ass is a conclusion drawn from the biographer's imagination. Jesus' mien, mannerisms, postures, carriage, facial expression, etc., the Gospel writers left unfortunately to the artist's imagination (see G. S. Hall, I. Chapter I). His habit of association with the social outcasts, the publicans and sinners, was unconventional for the religious leaders; otherwise his habits of life and dress were not so striking and eccentric as to attract special attention and come down to written record as did those of the Baptist.

The physiological details in the Gospels are limited to the following indications: *He stretched forth his hand* (Mc 1,41); *laid his hands on the children* or *took them in his arms* (Mc 10,16); put his fingers in the deaf man's ear and touched his speechless tongue (Mt 7,33); *he opened his mouth* (Mt 5,2) or *lifted up his eyes* (Lc 6,20); *his face did shine as the sun* (Mt 17,2=Lc 9,29); *he fell asleep* (Mc 4,38); *he hungered* (Mc 11,12); etc. *In the tomb of silence was laid the body of Jesus, and only the angel of imagination can roll away the stone that shut from mortal sight the image of the man* (Washburn, p. 7).

The Gospel writers, further, tell us nothing of the physical health of Jesus; whether he was strong and well, or of a more delicate constitution as traditional art was fond of portraying him, we do not know. Binet-Sanglé speaks of Jesus' inability to carry his own cross as a sign of his bodily weakness. But the Gospels tell us nothing of an inability of Jesus to carry

his own cross (Mc 15,21=Mt 27,32=Lc 23,26); that Simon
the Cyrene was pressed into service seems rather a wanton cap-
rice of the Roman soldiers who seem to have found a considerable amount of jest in the trial and execution of a Jewish peasant king.    Jesus' surprisingly quick death on the cross can
furnish no medical material, as de Loosten imagines.    The
spear thrust and the issue of water and blood, of which Binet-
Sanglé makes so much, has only a Johannine literary basis,
and is rather to be regarded as a later Christian legend typify-
ing the two great Christian symbols.    The Synoptics would
hardly have been unanimous in neglecting such an incident in
the crucifixion scene.    If historical, it is medically worthless.

### 4)  Psychic Symptoms

The Synoptic sources are rich in psychic phenomena as
compared with their complete lack of somatic details and descriptions.    The emotions that attended a word or act of Jesus
are not infrequently referred to; we have his words and teaching by which we can gauge to a considerable extent his intellectual capacity and capabilities; his acts and decisions furnish us a fair clue to the soundness of his volitional powers.
But before going into a study of the psychic phenomena that
are to be sifted from the sources, it is necessary to say a word
regarding standards of psychic normality.

The standard of psychic normality naturally varies with
the stage of civilization and culture, nationality, milieu, age,
sex, profession or occupation, degree of education, etc.    With
variance of these items, what is normal for one may be abnormal for the other.    In this connection Moses writes: *We consider normal what was considered such by the race and age
which gave it birth, so long as their beliefs did not lead to
practices detrimental to the physical and psychical health of
the people who entertained them.    It is unfair and unscientific
to arbitrarily assume any age or religion as a standard by
which to measure all other ages and religions* (p. 177).

Coming down to the individual, we find that no two are physically or psychically exactly alike.    The world is not popu-

lated and inhabited by types, but by individuals, each with h i s
o w n physical and psychical features and peculiarities which
constitute him as an i n d i v i d u a l over against his fellow
members of the human race. Types are intellectual abstrac-
tions and ideal creations from which each concrete individual
varies in some or in several respects. None of us are free from
certain deviations from the type. Within the limits of physical
and psychic health these deviations are called features of identity, personal peculiarities and eccentricities; outside of these
limits they constitute our infirmities, and it is highly doubtful
if any person is entirely free from some of them.

Ribot writes: *Leaving apart characters that are perfectly
consistent, (in the rigorous sense of the word they do not exist),
there are in every one of us tendencies of all sorts, all kinds
of possible contradictions, all kinds of intermediate shades, and
among these tendencies all possible combinations* (DP, p. 68);
...... *The ego of all of us is made up of contradictory tendencies: virtues and vices, modesty and pride, avarice and prodigality, desire for rest and craving for action, and of a host
of others* (p. 60). In normal persons these opposite tendencies
are balanced and counterpoised; in abnormal persons there is
no possibility of equilibrium.

Binet-Sanglé's understanding of normality is too indefinite
and loose: *The normal constitution, the constitution that is
healthy and rational, is the physiologic and mental condition
of the greatest number of men. Vices of constitution, disease
and insanity, are deviations from this normal type* (IV 334).

Dr. Moerchen's distinction and definition of normal, abnormal, and morbid states of soul is sufficiently scientific. He
writes: *The psychic individuality comprises n o r m a l l y
the totality of the elementary psychic functions at every instant, and we can first of all theoretically accept as normal that
state of soul in which the various elements of the psychic processes subsist in a mediating relationship to and with one another. A b n o r m a l states appear when the individual elementary functions have suffered either a qualitative or a quan-
titative modification, specially the latter, when they come into*

*such a relationship one to the other that one elementary func-*
*tion predominates in a striking way to the disadvantage of the*
*others. But even then in and of itself the substance of the no-*
*tion of the m o r b i d is not yet realized. With this there*
*appears in the psychic processes something new, a modification*
*not of a relative but of an absolute, positive kind* (PH, S. 10 (1).

*Empiric psychology recognizes mind only as a unit in which*
*the various faculties present only aspects of psychic activity*
*which are specially prominent* (Krafft-Ebing, p. 48). Although
the older faculty-psychology has been surrendered, we nevertheless, for the sake of convenience of treatment as is still usual
in textbooks on both normal and abnormal psychology, proceed to study the emotions, the intellect, and the will of Jesus.

### A)  The Emotions of Jesus

In cases of mental alienation, almost without exception, it
is the emotions that are attacked first and affected. The first
psychic symptoms take on the form of *affective disturbances,*
*anomalous feelings and states of altered emotional excitability*
(Krafft-Ebing, p. 200).

Emotions may be morbid in their nature, or form, or in
both. Differentiation of normal from abnormal emotions is
often very difficult. Even in health personal emotional peculiarities often closely resemble anomalous affective states. The
normally depressed person may have the same feelings as the
chronic melancholiac.

Psychanalysis looks first to the causes of emotions and the
conditions of affective impressionability. Emotions are ano-
molous and morbid when adequate external causes are wanting.
Emotional impressionability may rise high above or fall far below the normal level. The threshold of excitability may lie
deeper than is usual in health; this state is called hyperesthesia.
Here the *emotional reaction occurs with abnormal ease* (Krafft-
Ebing, p. 51). The subject's emotions become the prey of
momentary conditions. The slightest excitation results in vio-

---

(1)   For Dr. Moerchen's elaboration of his own definition see his article
listed "MKP" in the attached bibliography, S. 424f.

lent emotional outbreaks with a strong inclination to motor discharge. These emotional states are highly unstable, shallow, and superficial. Silly things are taken seriously, and serious things are not able to claim the attention. The subject is peevish and capricious. He may be morbidly frivolous (hyperthymia), or morbidly depressed (dysthemia), *if a crass disparity exists between the affective impulses and the gravity, that is, the duration of the affective depression* (Binswanger, S. 45). If the threshold of emotional excitability is set abnormally high, we have the condition designated as anesthesia which is characterized by *a complete lack of emotional reaction or its diminution in the presence of adequate impressions* (Krafft-Ebing, p. 53). The subject is in a state of apathy in which the usual, even the strongest, stimulations call forth no emotional response.

The emotions may present anomalies in intensity and persistence and *require an unusually long time in subsiding......* *An emotional state seems abnormally intense when the affected individual loses consciousness and his motor acts lose the characteristics of voluntary acts* (Krafft-Ebing, p. 212). Such affects defy all attempts at control. Moral checks are often absent. The subject loses *all feeling for the higher claims of propriety, morality and religion* (Kraepelin, p. 63). The higher ethic and esthetic sentiments are displaced by the lower sensuous feelings. The subject is selfish, overestimates himself, and is unsympathetic for the welfare and feelings of others. Here we have a complete perversion of the emotions.

Turning to the sources of our knowledge concerning Jesus we find that many of the above questions in which psychanalysis is interested cannot be answered. However, the emotions which attended certain of Jesus' words and acts are not infrequently given. Other words and acts of Jesus by their very nature and character necessarily indicate the tone in which they were spoken and the emotional state in which they were done.

| | Mt | Mc | Lc |
|---|---|---|---|
| 1) | .............. | 1,25 *rebuked* | 4,35 *rebuked* |
| 2) | (8,3 omits) | 1,41 *compassion* (D a ff² r syd i read ὀργισθείς — anger) | (5,13 omits) |
| 3) | (8,3-4 omits) | 1,43 *sternly charged* ἐμβρισησάμενος | 5,14 *charged* παρήγγειλεν |
| 4) | 8,10 *marvelled* | ................ | 7,9 *marvelled* |
| 5) | .............. | ................ | 7,13 *compassion* |
| 6) | 9,30 *strictly charged* ἐνεβριμήθη | ................ | ................ |
| 7) | 9,36 *compassion* | (6,34) *compassion* | ................ |
| 8) | 11,20 *upbraid* | ................ | (10,13 omits) |
| 9) | (12,12-13 omits) | 3,5 *anger and grieved* | ( 6,10 omits) |
| 10) | 12,16 *charged* | 3,12 *charged much* | 4,41 *rebuked* |
| 11) | (13,58 omits) | 6,6 *marvelled* | ................ |
| 12) | 14,14 *compassion* | 6,34 *compassion* | 9,11 *welcomed* |
| 13) | .............. | 7,34 *sighed* | ................ |
| 14) | 15,32 *compassion* | 8,2 *compassion* | ................ |
| 15) | (16,2 omits) | 8,12 *sighed deeply* | (11,29; 12,54 omit) |
| 16) | (16,23 omits) | 8,33 *rebuke* | ................ |
| 17) | 17,17 (impatience) | 9,19 (impatience) | 9,41 (impatience) |
| 18) | (18,2 omits) | 9,36 (affection) | (9,47 omits) |
| 19) | .............. | ................ | 9,55 *rebuke* |
| 20) | (11,25 omits) | ................ | 10,21 *rejoiced* |
| 21) | (19,14 omits) | 10,14 *indignation* | (18,16 omits) |
| 22) | (19,14-15 omits) | 10,16 (affection) | (18,17 omits) |
| 23) | (19,20-21 omits) | 10,21 *loved him* | (18,22 omits) |
| 24) | 20,34 *compassion* | (10,52 omits) | (18,42 omits) |
| 25) | 23,37-39 (disappointment) | ................ | 13,34b (disappointment) |
| 26) | .............. | ................ | 22,15 *desire* |
| 27) | 26,37-38 *sorrowful, sore troubled, exceeding sorrowful.* | 14,33-34 *greatly amazed, sore troubled, exceeding sorrowful.* | (22,40 o ) ( m ) ( i ) ( t ) ( s ) |
| 28) | .............. | ................ | 23,34 43 (compassion) |
| 29) | 27,46 (distress) | 15,34 (distress) | ................ |

The above catalogue, which is not wholly exhaustive yet thoroughly representative, makes it clear that Mc is the Synoptic psychologist, for he shows the greatest interest in the emotional attendants of Jesus' words and actions. He allows Jesus to act and speak in the greatest variety of natural emotions. Many of these temperamental details, in which Mc is richest, Mt and Lc agree in suppressing or modifying (3). They are specially careful to eliminate those features of Mc which represent Jesus as speaking and acting under the impulse of the sterner and stronger (3, 9, 21) as well as the too affectionate (18, 22, 23) emotions. Lc is more radical in his eliminations and modifications than Mt (6); he even strips the emotions from Jesus' states of soul in Gethsemane (27), and displaces the words of distress on the cross with words of compassion, forgiveness, and love (28, 29). This suppression of temperamental affects by Mt and Lc in their reproduction of Mc belongs to the theology of the Gospels (compare Wellhausen, Einl., S. 51f; Carpenter, p. 212ff; Sir John Hawkins, p. 117ff).

The Synoptists tell us that Jesus went, went about, up, up to, up into, on, through; journeyed; came, came down, into, nigh; drew near; entered into a city, village, boat, house, synagogue, the temple; left, departed, withdrew; walked by, upon, on, in; passed by, along; stood, stood still, over, by; sat, sat down, by, thereon, at meat; arose, turned, turned about; brought out, let go, took with; gave thanks, blessed, brake, gave; opened, read, closed; lodged, dwelt; fell asleep, awoke; taught, preached, healed; showed; called, called unto, welcomed; sent, sent out, away, forth; appointed, gave authority; suffered, suffered not, put forth; said, told, spoke in parables, asked, was told, answered, finished, ended (sayings); held his peace, put to silence; charged, charged strictly, sternly, constrained, commanded; rebuked, upbraided, cursed (fig tree); cast out, overthrew; was tempted, fell on his face, kneeled down, prayed, wept; looked up, around, about, saw, beheld; heard; perceived, knew; touched, took hold, raised up; fasted, ate, hungered, tasted, drank; cried with a loud voice and yielded up the spirit.

Such is the extent and simplicity of the vocabulary of the Synoptists in their narrations of Jesus' words and deeds. The tone of his words and the manner of his actions with the attending emotions are only meagrely given to us. We know that he felt compassion and love for his people and for the afflicted who presented themselves to him for cure, that he welcomed the multitudes on one occasion, rejoiced at the return and report of his disciples, and felt affection for little children and loved the rich young ruler. We know that he marvelled, sighed deeply, was angry, grieved, impatient, indignant and disappointed; that he desired with great desire, was exceedingly sorrowful, greatly amazed, sore troubled, in distress and despair. Weidel writes in his characteristic way: *The variety of his moods is astonishing: he could tell a story vividly, stirringly rouse, pulverizingly punish, gently comfort, shame with biting scorn, bitterly rebuke, be violently angry, and enthusiastically rejoice* (S. 72).

There is nothing pathological in the nature of Jesus' emotions. Every healthy person has felt all the emotions which the Synoptics ascribe to him. Nor is there anything morbid in the causes or occasions of Jesus' emotions; all are adequately and sufficiently motived.

This much can be said with certainty concerning the emotions of Jesus, namely, that he was never their victim. His soul was raised to the highest heights of exaltation and expectancy. His emotions often ran high, but never to the clouding of a clear consciousness nor to the impairment of controlled conscience. He had his times of depression and he must seek and struggle for clearness regarding the divine will. But whether exalted or depressed in soul, the issue in his conduct is always the same. He always ranges himself within the dictates of the divine decision. Moments of elation do not destroy the compass and scope of his reflection, nor deflect him from the rigid regime of righteousness. Depression does not develop into despondency and despair. In his darkest hour he does not desert God, but asks why God has deserted him.

Professor Law does well when he speaks of the joy, and not of joys, of Jesus (p. 5). We never see Jesus completely surrendering himself to, or exhausting himself in a single sentiment. His affective life and impulses are regularly held within the most healthy bounds by those inhibitive and controlling checks which govern and belong to the highest order of personal and individual self-discipline and control.

### B)   The Intellect of Jesus

Among his pathographers de Loosten alone recognizes the

exceptional intellectual ability and capabilities of Jesus. For Binet-Sanglé Jesus' words and teaching are merely the pitiable products of a mind that had completely collapsed.

It is only later in the course of a psychosis that the mind is affected and intellectual disturbances begin to appear. The psychopath never escapes intellectual deterioration and degeneration, except in certain peculiar types of paranoia where the intellect can remain intact for a considerable period, or revive itself to intense activity during periods of lucidity. Intellectual disturbances may be formal, affecting the processes of perception and the most elementary thought formations, or logical, affecting the content of thought.

Anomalies of perception and association are to be observed when these processes are abnormally slow or rapid. When the process of perception and association is abnormally slow there results an intellectual stagnation and mental monotony due to a lack of variety in thought. The associative process does not reach its goal; in more serious cases of mental alienation even the simplest associations of judgment are rendered impossible. If the process of perception and association of ideas is abnormally accelerated, the result is a chain of disconnected ideas illogically, incoherently, even unintelligibly expressed. The very flood of ideas causes a complete confusion of thought and psychic exhaustion. This wealth of ideas renders the course of thought irresolute, unstable, and infinitely distractible. *The train of thought will not proceed systematically to a definite aim, but constantly falls into new pathways which are immediately abandoned again* (Kraepelin, p. 37). Krafft-Ebing speaks of other formal disturbances: disturbances of association in so far as certain kinds of associations predominate; anomalies in which a certain limited number of ideas occupy consciousness with abnormal intensity and duration; disturbances of apperception, memory and imagination.

Disturbances in the content of thought express themselves in delusions which dominate the thought, experience, feeling and conduct of the subject due to an inadequate functioning of reason and judgment. *It does not follow because some one has expressed a delusional idea that he is insane...... Even the circumstance that a man acts in accordance with the delusion he expresses can be no criterion* (Krafft-Ebing, p. 71). The delusion of a sane person is corrected sooner or later by argument or experience; the morbidly deluded person is accessible to neither of these corrective factors. *The delusion needs no other support than the absolute conviction of the deluded......* *At the height of the disease they are as firmly established as reason herself* (Kraepelin, p. 49). Insane delusions stand in closest relations to the ego of the patient; they lead to a falsified consciousness and an erroneously exalted or depreciative estimate of the self and its relation to the outside world.

We would be in a sorry plight if we were solely dependent upon the Fourth Gospel for a demonstration of the intellectual resourcefulness of Jesus and his freedom from delusions. There we find no short pregnant utterances, no rich gnomic and impressive sententious words, no sharp, telling, pointed answers (except 8,2-11, which must be genuine because it is so thoroughly characteristic of Jesus and in spite of the weak literary basis and the lateness of its incorporation in the canonical text), and no parables which in the Synoptics are so remarkable in the variety and richness of their thought that Jesus stands alone in history as the unrivalled master of this form of address and instruction. In the Synoptics Jesus is not forever discoursing upon himself and his dignity in the monotonous repetitious way that he does in the Fourth Gospel, but neglects his own person entirely in his preaching and teaching the kingdom of God, and in a way that causes even modern pedagogy to marvel at its simplicity and effectiveness.

Jesus' faculties of observation as reflected in his parables are of the highest order. The materials of his perfect perception he reworks and reproduces in such discourse as is intelligible to the most ordinary mind, and yet stimulates the élite of intellect to repeated reflection. The characters that figure in his parables are not always moral models of conduct (the unrighteous steward in Lc 16,1-13; the unjust judge in Lc 18,1-8), but they are always true to life and are drawn from the real world and not from fable and fancy.

It is worth while to review the persons and things that fur-

nished the suggestions and materials for his parables.  They
are something as follows: a slave serving his master; servants,
wicked, faithful and unfaithful; an unrighteous steward; children playing in the market place, where a man is hiring labor-
ers throughout the day and a merchantman is buying goodly
pearls; a son requesting his father; a pupil and his teacher;
a thief in the night; a master returning late to his house; a
bridal party or procession; a man building a tower; a king
going to war; a man and his adversary on the way to the
judge; guests choosing preferred places at a feast; a friend
disturbed by a neighbor in the night; a widow persistently
pleading her cause before an unjust judge; a lender and his
debtors; a shepherd seeking for his lost sheep; a woman sweeping her house in search of a lost coin; an anxious father running to greet a wayward son; a father and his two unlike
sons; dishonest husbandmen; a sower sowing seed; a woman
mixing dough; a man digging in a field; the discovery of a
hidden treasure; a waylaid traveller aided by an unknown
friend; a strong man protecting his house; a rich man enlarg-
ing his barns, or sitting at a sumptuous table while a beggar
starves at his gate; a barren or budding fig tree; a sturdy mus-
tard plant in the garden; a city on a hill; a candle on a candle-
stick; a new patch on an old garment; an old skin bursted by
new wine; seed sprouting from the earth; tares in the growing
grain; eagles circling about a carcase; a dragnet cast into the
sea; a sheep in a pit; money set at interest; salt; light; etc.
(As figures: the foxes in their dens; the birds of the air; the
flowers of the field; wolves among the sheep; harmless doves;
shrewd serpents; etc.)

Whenever did a case of delusional insanity find the time
and inclination to notice such prosaic pursuits and facts of life
and experience, or find in them such rich suggestions, or employ them as universally intelligible vehicles for the conveyance
and presentation of truths that survive over generations and
centuries? Delusional insanity is usually characterized, not *by
great wealth of ideas*, such as we see in Jesus' parables, but *by
a conspicuous poverty of thought* (Kraepelin, p. 38). As Dr.
Moerchen says, psychically and nervously mediocre minds pro-

duce for the most part fruits that represent no positive values by which either society or the individual would experience any enrichment or advance (PH, S. 46).

Apart from his parables are the short sententious sayings and the paradoxical, yet pregnant utterances of Jesus, which are not the products of an intermittent lucidity but of an intellect constantly intact and always at its best (Mc 4,22 25; 8,35; 9,35; Lc 6,39; 11,9f; 13,30; 14,11; 17,33).

Concerning the more distinctly logical faculties of Jesus we have abundant evidences of their capabilities in the collection of Galilean contentions in Mc 2,1-3,6 where Jesus' telling answers, aided by his command of his people's Scriptures and traditions, prove him more than a match for his crafty opponents and establish the outposts of real religion. The resourcefulness and play of Jesus' intellectual faculties in his encounters with his Jerusalem enemies (Mc 11,27-33; 12,13-17 18-27 28-34 35-37; Jn 8,2-11), as de Loosten himself states, still await their parallels in history. Here Jesus meets his enemies on their own ground and defeats them with their own weapons. When he goes over from defense to offense they no longer dare to ask him any questions.

To conclude this section by applying statements of Ribot on the delusional diseases of personality we can say: in Jesus we find no change in *mental habitude*, no *shift in the center of gravity of his consciousness*, no *alteration of personality* or *arrest of development*, no *fixed or erroneous state of consciousness*. We do not see that Jesus' personality was *drained for the profit of a single idea* (DP, p. 119). Jesus was not a case of *false personality reducible to a fixed idea, to a dominant idea, toward which a whole group of concordant ideas converges, all others being eliminated, practically annihilated* (p. 81). No single issue, not even the kingdom of God, no single idea, his conviction of his commission, so completely engrossed and engaged the mind of Jesus that it resulted either in the entire or partial suppression of the other natural and normal elements of his consciousness.

### C)   The Will of Jesus

*Insanity removes the possibility of free will. This fact is recognized by the laws of all civilized nations* (Krafft-Ebing, p. 95). The motor expressions by which a patient realizes his ideas, feelings and impulses are very important in the diagnosis of a morbid psychic constitution. The morbid disturbances of volition are as follows: diminution of volitional impulse which is marked by a complete suspension or paralysis of will and in which the strongest moral and personal incentives are unable to influence the patient (abulia); unlimited increase of volitional impulse characterized by a disproportion between the intensity of excitation and the importance of motives (hyperbulia); impeded release of volition in which special exertion is necessary in every act of will, one impulse is suppressed by a counter impulse and the flood and balance of counter impulses results in a blocking of the will; facilitated release of volition in which there is an uncontrolled and unrestricted discharge of impulses; deviated direction of will by external and internal influences as in hypersuggestibility (where the patient is a prey to every influence even the most accidental), distractibility (where sudden resolutions are half executed only to give way to new ones), and stereotypy of will; the suppression of normal will by morbid impulses; and the conversion of natural impulses into morbid ones (Kraepelin, p. 77ff).

In cases of impaired or diseased volition *the will so little resembles a faculty reigning as mistress that it depends at each instant upon the most trivial and hidden causes; it is at their mercy* (Ribot, DW, p. 41). The patient has no definite reasons for the execution of his acts; they occur without forethought; he has no other motive than that he must do this or that without knowing why or to what end. Rational motives neither stimulate nor restrain. He does not appreciate the futility or the inefficacy of the methods he employs. He is irresistibly driven to acts which he later recognizes as foolish, or even reprobates (see Ribot, DW, p. 54ff). The patient's will expresses itself *in violent, purposeless running about, or impul-*

*sive acts that are hardly conscious, and which find a motive
only in a dim consciousness of the need of a change of psychic
situation at any cost; or they may lead finally to blind ravings,
true psychic convulsions, comparable to those unconscious,
violent motor explosions that characterize an epileptic attack*
(Krafft-Ebing, p. 129).

We have already spoken of the high character of Jesus'
will in our discussion of the temptation and we shall refer to
it again in the section on fanaticism. There are three other
Synoptic incidents that throw a clear light upon the will of
Jesus: the close of the inaugural day in Capernaum where Jesus
decides upon message rather than miracle as the essence of his
mission, feels his popularity as a serious moral problem to which
he refuses to yield, and finds the possibility of a degeneration
into a professional healer repulsive (Mc 1,35-38) ; his refusal
to respond to the demand for a sign and his renewed emphasis
upon message and not miracle (Mc 8,11-12=Mt 16,1-4=Lc
11,29; 12,54-56) ; and the Gethsemane scene where he sub-
missively bows to a will of a still higher order at the price of
the greatest personal sacrifice. Besides these specific instances
are those fine features which characterize his conduct throughout his career: the careful conscientiousness with which he devoted himself to the fulfillment of his commission and which
always distinguished the course of his conduct, his refusal to
deviate from the appointed path of duty in lieu of selfish interests and personal preservation, his search and struggle for
orientation, his quest for and openness to new illuminations,
and his calmness and composure in the most exacting hours
when personal demands were heaviest upon him.

In Jesus we see no *morbid perplexity of intellect, no endless precautions,* no venting of self *with reckless prodigality
in speeches, projects, enterprises, and incessant fruitless journeys* (Ribot, DP, p. 56), no *dissolution of the ego* either by
excess or defect of volitional impulse, no *infractions of perfect
co-ordination* (DW, p. 129), no *two contrary or different tendencies that dominate in turn,* no *two alternate centers of gravity, two points of convergence for successively preponderating*

*but partial co-ordinations,* no pathology of will where the equilibrium is broken and where the intense impulses are *no longer an accident but a habit, no longer one side of the character but the character itself* (p. 129f).

Jesus belongs to that higher order of wills where the co-ordination is perfect and is characterized by *unity, stability and power* (p. 128). He belongs to that class of great men whose end remains the same because they remain the same. *Their fundamental element is a mighty, inextinguishable passion which enlists their ideas in its service...... They present a type of life always in harmony with itself, because in them everything conspires together, converges, and consents* (p. 128f). We see in Jesus *the will of the rational man* (which) *is an extremely complex and unstable co-ordination fragile by its very superiority,* because it is *the highest force which nature has developed—the last consummate blossom of all her marvelous works* (Maudsley as cited by Ribot, p. 134).

The wholesome character of Jesus' choices and decisions abundantly attests the health and virtuous vigor of his will.

### 5)   Was Jesus an Epileptic?

*By epilepsy we mean a pronounced chronic disorder of the central nervous system which is characterized by frequently recurring attacks of cramps attended by loss of consciousness, or by the partial appearances of these attacks, or by the psychopathic attendant or subsequent states of these attacks; only one point is to be emphasized, namely, that the various disturbances appear independent of objective occasions.*[1]

---

(1)  *Man versteht unter Epilepsie eine ausgesprochen chronische Erkrankung des Zentralnervensystems, die durch oefter wiederkehrende Krampfanfaelle mit Bewusstlosigkeit oder durch Teilerscheinungen dieser Anfaelle oder durch psychopathologische Begleit- und Folgezustaende dieser Anfaelle gekennzeichnet ist; hervorzuheben ist nur, dass die verschiedenen Stoerungen unabhaengig von aeusseren Gruenden auftreten* (E. Schultze, S. 323; for special studies of epilepsy see Schultze's chapter in Binswanger's textbook, S. 322-346; Kraepelin, p. 434-456; Krafft-Ebing, p. 472-492).

The chief symptom of epilepsy is the classic epileptic attack (*haut ou grand mal*). In this attack the victim suffers a complete loss of consciousness and undergoes the most violent somatic convulsions; his face turns pale, he falls to the ground with rigid body and muscles, head drawn to one side with eyes fixed at an angle and protruded tongue. Presently the rigid somatic state is broken; the eyes begin to roll; the head hammers up and down; foam gushes from the mouth; respiration comes by fits and starts, and the muscles convulse violently. Such an attack usually leaves the victim exhausted, with aching head and muscles, agitated, and in a confused state of mind. It is frequently attended by horrible hallucinations.

Epilepsy in its serious form leads sooner or later to alterations of the emotions, intellect, consciousness, and character. There is a complete loss of memory for the period of the attack; a general aggravation and retardation of all psychic processes for the immediate or remoter future; attention, comprehension, and logical judgment are disturbed or even lost; aphasia often results for a shorter or longer period; there is a marked poverty of thought and adequate expression; address is no longer coherent and connected, but abrupt and jerky; the result is stupor or dementia. The victim has not the will to think, will, or work. Chronic convulsions render him incapable of the higher grades of mental and physical accomplishment. The affective life is not only disturbed but often perverted. Delirious states of consciousness come to constitute the character; the deliriums may take the form of religious expansive ideas, or of moria.

Chronic epilepsy usually results in a change of the character; of all clinical characters the epileptic is the least consistent. This change is usually in the direction of moral and ethical degeneration due to the loss of such judgments. The epileptic is depressed, pessimistic, distrustful, fearful, terrorized; he is capricious, peevish, ill-humored, impatient, irritable, fault-finding, obstinate, morose, unruly, tyrannical, quarrelsome, wrathful, threatening, combative, ruthless [1], violent,

_____

(1) *Ruecksichtslos gegen andere verlangt der Epileptiker fuer sich die groesste Ruecksichtsnahme;* Schultze, S. 334.

brutal, dangerous, criminal; he is egoistic, contemptuous, uncompromising, bigoted, and hypocritical. Over against this he
may be a foolishly frivolous character. Of those who turn
toward religion Samt writes: *Poor epileptics, who with a
prayer-book in the pocket and a word of God on the tongue,
have the most extreme wickedness in the heart* (quoted by
Krafft-Ebing, p. 474).

In *petit mal* are to be observed befogged states of consciousness, also cloudy, dreamy and twilight states; only partial losses or brief interruptions of consciousness completely
without or only slight somatic convulsions, as in dizziness or
fainting; absentia, loss of orientation restored by heavy and
slow reflection.

We recall that Rasmussen finds in the public career of Jesus
instances of both types of epileptic attack, *petit mal* in Gethsemane, and *grand mal* at the cleansing of the temple. But
when psychiatrists today admit great difficulties in diagnosing
epilepsy in a living person under careful and continued observation, we can see how little worth attaches to Rasmussen's
pathographic diagnosis. (Krafft-Ebing writes, *A single
symptom is not sufficient to establish the diagnosis of epilepsy
nor is a single epileptic attack;* p. 473). Our study of the
biographical incidents showed us that pathographic materials
are to be exploited neither from the Gethsemane incident nor
from the cleansing of the temple. Nowhere in the Gospels do
we find an experience or incident in the life of Jesus comparable
to either *petit* or *grand mal.*

The Synoptists were not unacquainted with psychic abnormalities and their symptoms; they often do not neglect to describe them, Mc 1,26=Lc 4,35; Mc 5,2-5 15=Mt 8,28=Lc
8,27 29. Mt 4,24 tells us that epileptics, σεληνιαζομένους,
were among the classes of afflicted cured by Jesus. One cure
of Jesus reported by all three Synoptists is so clear in its
description that the paragraph Mc 9,14-27 (=Mt 17,14-18
—Lc 9,37-42) bears the title, "The Epileptic Boy." Mt alone
speaks of the boy as epileptic, σεληνιάζεται.

My son...... is epi-
leptic, and suffereth
grievously

My son...hath a dumb
spirit;
    and whenever
it    taketh him

and behold
a spirit taketh him,
and he suddenly crieth
out; and it teareth
him that he foameth,
and it hardly departeth
from him, bruising him
sorely.

    it dasheth him
down; and he foameth,
and grindeth his
teeth, and pineth

for oft-times
he falleth
into the fire, and oft-
times into the water.

away: and oft-times
it hath cast him both
into the fire and
    into the waters
to destroy him; the
spirit

the
demon dashed him
down
tare him grievously.

tare him grievously;
and he fell to the
ground, and wallowed
foaming.... How long
time is it since this
hath come upon him?..
From a child... And
having cried out and
torn him much, he came
out;    and the boy
became as one dead;
insomuch that the more
part said He is dead.

the demon went
out of him.

In reading Mc here we can almost imagine ourselves reading an account of a clinical case of epileptic *grand mal* attack
in a textbook on psychiatry. If Jesus had suffered with epilepsy it is impossible that the observer whose report lies at the
base of Mc's account could have been mistaken as to the nature
of his malady. Rasmussen must resort to the idea that Jesus'
biographers purposely left out what they knew, but he thus
leaves us unclear as to how they could ever have been impressed
by a morbid man or inspired to recount not only his public
words and deeds but believe in him as the Messiah. Rasmussen encounters here the same order of moral and historical difficulty in accounting for the origin and rise of the early Christian faith and community as Reimarus did when he explained
the resurrection by the disciples' theft of the dead body of
Jesus from the tomb.

Our previous study of the psychic side of Jesus' life, in so
far as it is accessible to our study, shows us that his person

and character manifest none of those degenerations commonly subsequent in cases of chronic epilepsy.

### 6)   Was Jesus a Paranoiac?

Our reviews of the positions of de Loosten, Hirsch, and Binet-Sanglé made it clear to us what these pathographers mean by the religious paranoia of Jesus. We can, therefore, dispense with a full presentation of this disease-picture, except in its briefest and most characteristic outlines. (For brief psychiatric studies of paranoia see E. Siemerling's chapter in Binswanger's textbook; S. 160-191; Kraepelin, p. 423-433; Krafft-Ebing, p. 368-413.)

Kraepelin thus defines this disease: *Paranoia is a chronic progressive psychosis occurring most in early adult life, characterized by a gradual development of a stable, progressive system of delusions, without marked mental deterioration, clouding of consciousness, or disorder of thought, will, or conduct* (p. 423). E. Siemerling takes exception to this definition of Kraepelin because he finds it too narrow and such cases too rare; he includes under paranoia those delusional psychoses which involve minor, or even major, intellectual, affective and motor disturbances and deteriorations. But Kraepelin in another connection (p. 53) speaks of paranoia as almost always involving *a decided weakness of judgment*. In religious paranoia the delusions have regular religious content and character *and terminate in states of mental weakness* (Krafft-Ebing, p. 406).

Krafft-Ebing in the observation of one thousand cases of paranoia never found one free from hereditary taint; others admit that the percent is exceedingly high. The onset of the disease is gradual, often unobserved, and its course is protracted. At its acme the whole realm of the subject's experience is changed. Perception is falsified and real experiences are misinterpreted. He not only has a false apprehension of self, but of his environment. The whole world of persons and things secretly plots against his welfare (delusions of persecution), or publicly and privately does him homage (delusions of grandeur).

These delusions, single or combined, occupy the citadel of consciousness; they characterize and control the whole disease-picture. They are held with great persistency. Hallucinations contribute to the rise, reinforcement, character, content and claims of the delusions. The subject is frequently unreservedly dominated by his hallucinations and he abandons himself to them in an unrestrained way. *In reality the patient's attitude toward his illusions and hallucinations is not the same as his attitude toward his actual perceptions. No healthy individual would refer to himself such words as "That is the President," and then immediately believe that he must be the president. But when these words form the keystone of a long chain of secret misgivings, an hallucination of that sort makes the most profound impression, and immediately there arises a firm conviction, not only that the words were really spoken, but that they express the truth* (Kraepelin, p. 10).

The delusions usually become methodically systematized and coherently combined into a formal delusional structure. When thus systematized these delusions result in a complete metamorphosis of the entire personality. The ego constitutes a nucleus or keystone about which all the falsified items of experience logically gather contributing to and supporting the delusional structure. The subject is borne along by an extremely exalted sense of self and an exaggerated feeling of his own importance. The emotional attitudes usually correspond to the character of the delusions. The intellect often remains relatively well intact. The paranoiac is often capable of remarkable reasoning, however from false premises, and one is often struck by his logic and clearness. But his critical and corrective powers are usually seriously impaired or entirely lost. A correction of his delusion is practically excluded. Considerations learned by experience, possibility, probability, logic, instruction, and even moral and ethical considerations of conscience are of no avail. Even the much remarked periods of lucidity are of ephemeral duration (Krafft-Ebing).

The contrast of Jesus' character to that of the paranoiac we have already pointed out in the discussion of his self-consciousness. The main difficulty in a diagnosis of paranoia in the case of Jesus is the demonstration of delusions with which he suffered, and which falsified his experience and completed a change and transformation of his personality. Jesus' thought, as we saw in our study of the egocentric words ascribed to him, does not center upon himself but upon the kingdom of God. The sources furnish us no hallucinatory materials that kindled and fired him to delirious delusions about his own dignity. Never once does he present, nor even refer to any credentials of authority for his commission. What and how Jesus thought of himself is insolubly problematic. On this point the paranoiac never leaves those whom he encounters long in doubt. Jesus never seems concerned about convincing others of any exalted dignity, or present or future identity that he possesses or that awaits him. Here we cannot but think of the pitiable attempts of the paranoiac who packs about with him the most meaningless scraps of paper in which he deliriously discovers the official documents confirming his delusion and with which he would convince others that he is right and that they are wrong unless they concede his claims. Jesus never made claims in his own behalf, except as a called preacher and prophet of the kingdom of God for which he demanded serious, yet sane, moral and ethical preparation. He was never guilty of lapses or breaches in the critical correctives that are naturally furnished by healthy mentality and experience.

### 7) Was Jesus an Ecstatic? (1)

Ecstasy belongs to those unusual psychic phenomena which lie on the borderland between mental health and malady. It is unquestionably an abnormal disturbance of consciousness, but it is not a signal symptom of mental alienation. Ecstatic states may appear and frequently do appear within the limits of psychic health; however, they are often the products of a diseased nervous system and are psychopathic in their origin (2).

(1) *Ekstatiker ist ueberhaupt kein klinisch scharf zu umschreibender Begriff* (Weber, Sp. 234).
(2) On ecstasy see Ribot, DW, p. 94-103; Cutten, chapter IV.

Ribot classes ecstasy among the diseases of the will; *the mental state of ecstasy is a complete infraction of the laws of the normal mechanism of consciousness* (DW, p. 101); it marks the extinction of volition; it is *the annihilation of the will in its highest form* (p. 103). Ribot, however, is not passing these judgments from the strictly psychiatric point of view.

The ecstatic state does not involve the loss of consciousness; it is rather the highly intense focalization of consciousness within the most compact compass. The whole of consciousness is absorbed in just one item and such collateral matter as may contribute to it; all else is excluded. As general psychic characteristics of the ecstatic state Ribot lists: exhaustive focusing of the attention upon one idea, usually abstract; loss of normal self-control; extinction of general sensibility; intense emotional excitement; subsequent memory and reproduction of the elements of the experience. The ecstatic state is usually of an agreeable, lulling, rapturous nature and the subject deplores its departure and his return to the real world; this often leads to intemperate indulgence.

*When this state is attained, the ecstatic presents certain physical characteristics: sometimes motionless and mute; sometimes expressing the vision that possesses him by words, songs, and attitudes. He rarely moves from his position. His physiognomy is expressive; but his eyes, even though open, do not see. Sounds no longer affect him; save, in some cases, the voice of a particular person. General sensibility is extinct; no contact is felt; no pricking nor burning causes pain* (Ribot, DW, p. 95f).

Habitual ecstatics flee society and seek out seclusion and solitude in order to give themselves in an undisturbed way to their visions and hallucinations. Ecstasy is usually the natural and spontaneous expression of the ecstatic constitution; however, it may be produced by artificial means as the biographies and autobiographies of various religious mystics abundantly attest (1). For the habitual ecstatic his experiences of

---

(1) Saint Teresa is the most interesting and instructive ecstatic character in the ecclesiastical calendar; see Ribot's extracts from her autobiography, (DW, p. 96ff).

ecstasy become so rare in the rapture they afford, so deliciously delightful, that they become goals of conscious effort, ends in themselves instead of means of inspiration and vehicles of revelation.  His joy and exaltation during such times are so completely intoxicating that he not only decidedly desires, but deliberately devises their return and reproduction.

Of all the canonical Scriptures the book of Ezekiel is richest and most elaborate in visions; among Biblical ecstatics Ezekiel occupies the chief seat.  In his inaugural vision and prophetic call (chapters 1-3) he sees all sorts of fantastic figures and he swallows a written roll presented to him for consumption by a mysterious hand; in chapter 4 he receives the symbols portraying the siege of the holy city; in chapters 8-11 he sees cherubim, fiery coals carried in the naked hand, and celestial chariots with whirling wheels; his vision of the temple in chapters 40-48 constitutes a marvel of memory.  His striking experiences are not purely psychic, but are attended by unusual somatic symptoms.  He is overwhelmed for seven days (anesthesia) in 3,15f; he is struck dumb (aphasia) in 3,25f and he regains his speech in 24,25ff or in 33,21f; in 4,4-8 he lies 390 days on his left side and then 40 days on his right side (hemiplegia) as respectively symbolic of the fates of Israel and Judah.

These somatic symptoms have led even liberal theologians to regard Ezekiel as a cataleptic.  Bernhard Duhm writes: *It is possible, even probable, that he from time to time fell into dreamy c a t a l e p t i c  s t a t e s and that during such moments, or rather hours and days, he beheld a host of pictures, forms and dramatic transactions pass before him, to which he ascribed an objective reality when in fact they were but the product and continuation of the study and reflection pursued by him during clear consciousness* (S. 231) (1). Dr. Dieckhoff protests against the liberal theological view of Ezekiel as a psychopath (he has Orelli specially in mind).  In spite of all the autobiographic materials found in the book of Ezekiel he finds that it is not at all necessary to

---

(1)  On this point see Dr. A. C. Knudson's *The Beacon Lights of Prophecy*, (p. 216ff).

think of Ezekiel as a psychosis.   He concludes his article on
this great prophet by stating that his study is *an attempt to
show that that in the prophet Ezekiel which is regarded by
positive theology as miracle, by many as invention with a purpose, by others to some extent the product of a psychic disorder, that all that according to our modern views and knowledge
can be described without affectation as the ideas and acts of a
highly gifted and psychically sound man* (S. 206).

When Dr. Dieckhoff from the medical viewpoint so stoutly
defends the psychic health of Ezekiel, whose prophecies are so
abundant in pathographic materials in comparison with the
Gospel account of Jesus, the demonstration of an ecstatic constitution in the case of Jesus is hopeless.   In the Gospels we
find not the slightest trace of Jesus' entrance into or emergence
from a state of ecstasy; however, we do have an account of
the emergence of the disciples from a state of vision on the
mount of transfiguration in Mc 9,6-8=Mt 17,5-8=Lc 9,34-36.
The only possible usable material is the vision at the baptism,
but this account is so expressive of Mc's theology and christology and the repetition of the same words by the voice at the
transfiguration (Mc 9,7=Mt 17,5=Lc 9,35) and in the mouth
of the centurion at the foot of the cross (Mc 15,39=Mt 27,
54) makes the exact location of this revelation uncertain, or
it may even be regarded as expressing an early Christian conviction rather than a moment of special exaltation in the experience of Jesus.   No such special moments stand out as mile-
stones in his experience.   He never once refers to such in public or in private.   He never recounts his call as coming, or his
message as imparted, at some special time or place in some
striking psychic manner.   Jesus' consciousness of his call and
his conviction concerning his commission rested upon something far deeper and more fundamental than the work of a
single moment or series of states of ecstatic exaltation.

Throughout his book Holtzmann must so modify and explain the peculiar variations of Jesus' case of ecstasy from
the ordinary type as it is commonly known that when he has
finished with his modifications and explanations we wonder if
we have anything of regularly recognized ecstasy left in Jesus.

He must concede that the ecstatic element in Jesus was only
one element, that it did not stir him to restlessness, as is usually
the case, but imparted composure (S. 42), that Jesus as an
ecstatic calmed contagion rather than spread it (S. 95), and
that his own non-ecstatic features are so prominent that one
easily overlooks the ecstatic element in his character (S. 123).

### 8)    Was Jesus a Fanatic?

From the strictly scientific point of view fanaticism is a
meaningless and useless term for psychiatry, although there
always attaches to fanaticism something of the delusional.
Hirsch writes: *The intensity of one's actions, even if it approaches fanaticism, is not necessarily a symptom of disease.
This psychic faculty is not infrequently found in great men
who have made a discovery or an invention in the acceptance
of which they have met with the strong opposition of their
contemporaries. Ingenious artists, who have branched out into
new paths of art, are often forced by obstacles and opposition
to a perfect fanaticism without which they would never have
reached their goal. On the other hand, it is a well-known fact
that actions that are the result of delusions, are most intense,
and not seldom bear the character of fanaticism, so that persistent fanatics arouse at least the suspicion of being psychical
anomalies* (p. 180; Ger. S. 185).

From the standpoint of the religion of healthy-mindedness
Moses writes: *The very word fanaticism suggests immediately
psychical abnormality, or frenzy, and excessive religious activity, and this is in general what it really is...... The very
fact that men devote their whole lives to religion and hold all
other human interests and activities in contempt is sufficient
proof of their physical unbalance* (p. 215f). Professor James
found that religious fanaticism is *only loyalty carried to a
convulsive extreme* (p. 340); the fanatic is a *theopath of narrow mind and active will*, characterized by a *despotic intellect
and temperament*, engrossingly preoccupied and driven by a
feverish fervor. Dr. Moerchen agrees that fanaticism is
*founded in a concurrence of limited or one-*

*s i d e d   i n t e l l e c t u a l   capacity and unbridled will* (PH,
S. 38) (1).

From Reinhard (1781) down to Wernle (1916) not one
great life or character study of Jesus has left the question of
his fanaticism entirely untouched.    As no other theologian
Reinhard took pains to defend Jesus against the suspicion of
fanaticism.    In his *Plan* he presents Jesus as the founder of
the universal religion of reason.    Jesus' plan was not a chim-
era, an impossible dream, the foolish project of a fanatic, for
his plan contained nothing impossible.    He writes:  *He* (Jesus)
*sustained opposition gladly and condescended to answer the
most absurd objections and the most malicious charges with an
incredible patience.    And in doing so he never broke out in
heated condemnation; he always justified himself with calm
earnestness and noble moderation although he as frankly at
times announced the fateful consequences which must necessarily
follow upon the unprecedented stubbornness of many of his
enemies.    He never forced the truth upon anyone* (S. 214f).
*Fanatics forget their actual relationships, overlook that which
lies at hand and often in daily life violate the commonest rules
of prudence as soon as they begin to act.    Here also the mind
of Jesus distinguishes itself in a most favorable fashion.    With
all the zeal with which he embraced his great plan and kept it
always before him, he never lost out of sight the position in
which he found himself with his people and devoted himself to
the trivial concerns that were brought to him there with such
a perfect wisdom, with such a practiced sagacity and deliberation, that it might seem that he had nothing else to think
of but them* (S. 414ff).    *One cannot come upon the suspicion
of fanaticism.    How were this possible in a mind that thought
more correctly, clearly, strongly and profoundly than any
human mind has ever thought?    Fanaticism and clarified reason—who can conceive of these two things united in a mind, if
he knows human nature?    Further, one does not perceive in the
founder of the Christian religion that comfort in death and
that rigid unnatural insensitiveness which distinguish the fan-*

---

(1)  On fanaticism see James, p. 338ff; on moral fanaticism, Kant,
*Kritik der praktischen Vernunft,* (Reklam, S. 87ff).

*atic so strikingly* (S. 432). *He, the greatest of all reformers, was a man of gentlest habits in whose disposition and conduct no trace of hot-tempered excitement, frantic impetuosity and apathetic harshness is discernible* (S. 440). *One must not know what fanaticism is if one should be able even to divine it here. The one observation that the predominant tone of his soul was not enthusiasm, not untamed zeal and tempestuous passion, but a calm rational composure which was not disturbed and interrupted by passing fits of ecstasy and fanatical fury; this single observation destroys all suspicion of fanaticism* (S. 482) (1).

In his *Jesus* Wernle devotes considerable attention to the question of Jesus' fanaticism (see p. 243-271). In reference to Jesus' hope of the imminent kingdom of God he writes: *It is quite clear that we are now at the point where fanaticism and earnest expectation border close on each other, and we involuntarily look about for a reliable criterion of the saneness of this expectation. First and foremost, two points are involved: the e f f e c t of this exalted hope on Jesus and his hearers, the connection between hope and demand, and the c o n s t a n c y of this hope in Jesus himself. We shall have to designate a hope as fanaticism which shifts the moral center of piety and which falls in danger of losing its stability in default of the fulfillment of the hope* (S. 243). In reply Wernle writes: *We must confidently say: although the particulars of this hope were not fulfilled and the deep longing fluttered restlessly farther and farther out toward the wondrous future, the thing that remains and substantiates itself is this fundamentally serious and honest self-command, this pure concentration upon the simple and central duties, the refined conscience, the unadorned humility and the new exalted earnestness. From these fundamental energies the new religion will live and through them will find a way to survive all disappointments. The charge of fanaticism against Jesus collapses in the*

---

(1) Upon all this A. Schweitzer remarks, *How fortunate that Reinhard did not surmise how enthusiastic Jesus was and how he trampled reason under his feet* (GdLJF, S. 34).

*face of his elementary principle: Whoever doeth the will of God shall enter into the kingdom of God* (S. 251) (2).

We see in Jesus a range of reflection, a reverence and regard for the traditional precepts of piety, and yet an independence over against them that marks a distinct advance, a moral code and control of conduct, a fearlessness that is not blinded to the futility of undertaking certain courses of action, a rejection of the principle that the end justifies the means, an antipathy for acquiring unfair advantage, a sensitiveness to suggestions from within, without and above, a wealth of will unwasted in volcanic vomitings, a depth of genuine emotion devoid of stoicism and devoted to the works of sympathy, pity and compassion, a consideration for contemporaries, a determinedness of devotion to duty as divinely dictated, a careful, even cautious conscientiousness of commission, an insight into the worth as well as the weakness of existing institutions, an appreciation of the plainer provisions of Providence in the beauties of nature and the boon of life itself, and a willingness to walk and work along the more placid yet more painful paths of moral progress; of all of which the confirmed fanatic is incapable.

From our modern point of view Jesus' picture of the future, and that of many of his contemporaries, was fantastic and fanciful, but it was not fanatical. It was not the one bright point that glowed and glared, and upon which his whole attention was centered and toward which his acts aggressed to the ruthless rejection of all else. The future, what and who was to figure in it, was God's and not his.

## 9)  Pathography

Pathography, even when modestly and carefully undertaken, has its serious limitations. A diagnosis based upon archives alone, even when the records are of recent date, is always dubious and still more so when they date from antiquity. From the scientific point of view pathography is readily ex-

---

(2)  See P. W. Schmiedel's fine paragraph on the fanaticism of Jesus in his PJSMG, S. 17.

posed to very definite dangers, the chief of which Dr. Moerchen designates as follows: *We do not fail to realize the danger that one, whose intention is to proceed pathographically, easily falls victim to an a priori procedure, that is, he is too strongly inclined as a matter of course to regard all states of soul that deviate from the norm as pathological, an error from which some authors at least have not held themselves guiltless* (PH, S. 8).

In investigating the biographies and autobiographies of prominent persons for morbid psychic manifestations, pathographers have fallen into great discredit with professional psychiatrists. Dr. Schaefer writes: *Pathography is at a very low rate of value, even in the estimate of its psychiatric colleagues; many still reckon it among the unprofitable occupations* (S. 10). *Modern pathographies do not represent the best in our clinical research...... Pathography as scientific method has its very precarious phases..... Historical research can furnish us incontestably only detached pathological features of historical personalities; never with equal certainty can it transmit to us the total psychic picture* (Weber, Sp. 233). This is because the pathographers have played fast and loose with the scientific principles of psychiatry. The more one reads the works of Rasmussen, de Loosten, Hirsch, and Binet-Sanglé the less one is impressed with them. After reading and rereading the works of Jesus' pathographers and then the works of recognized psychiatrists one cannot but see that Jesus' pathographers have presented only the sunnier aspects of mental alienation which might find parallels in the experience of any normal and healthy person, but which are not at all specially characteristic of psychic degeneracy, and have left out those graver psychic phenomena which really characterize the insane. Krafft-Ebing reminds his medical readers, *There is no functional disturbance that occurs in the insane which is not occasionally observed within the limits of health* (p. 234).

From the viewpoint of the historico-critical study of the New Testament those who pathographically diagnose the case of Jesus, with the exception perhaps of Rasmussen (Holtzmann does not belong, we again repeat, to the pathographers of

Jesus), are unacquainted with even the more general course and conclusions of the New Testament criticism. They take the Scriptures with a gullible literality that would make even the most uncritical of orthodox souls marvel at their credulity concerning the word of God. They confirm the exact historical reliability of the sources of our knowledge concerning Jesus even down to the last letter; they are sure that Jesus spoke and did just as his biographers tell us and always in the deepest sort of sincerity and in the most genuine conviction. But all of this at the expense of Jesus' psychic health. They isolate words and incidents from their connections and context in the Gospels and treat them pathographically without seeking any insight into an historical plan of the course of Jesus' public career, and neglect entirely any underlying historical motives that might explain the special character of any unusual word or incident in the public life of Jesus.

A pathography of Jesus is possible only upon the basis of a lack of acquaintance with the course and conclusions of New Testament criticism and an amateur application of the principles of the science of psychiatry.

Further, the pathographers of Jesus have not played fair with the popular mind which still entertains horrible superstitions about insanity and its symptoms and has not yet been educated and accustomed to look upon pathological states of mind as diseases, demanding compassion, if possible cure, and adequate care in exactly the same way as do the diseases of the body.

Last of all, the pathographers of Jesus have toyed wantonly and wilfully with the one figure in history to which are attached the sincerest sentiments and the dearest affections of the occidental religious world; and without sufficient reason or justification.

\*    \*    \*    \*    \*

We have reached the end of our study of the psychic health of Jesus. In conclusion the writer attempts no delineation of the character and personality of Jesus. Scores have been projected in the course of the life-of-Jesus research, a very few impressive and forceful, some helpful, more ordinary, many inferior and mediocre, and again not a few worthless, ridiculous and absurd. Every attempt to picture Jesus in a modern way and language to the thought of a modern world seems to lack something vital and organic. We read them and we lay them down again with the feeling that, though we have not heard the last loud cry on the cross, the life has gone out of him. He lives best in the New Testament. There he seems most at home. There he does and speaks as man never yet did or spoke. To those who would see and know him as he really was and is, the writer would recommend that they take up the first three books of the New Testament and read them with a will, and feel again the warm unartificial and natural impression that radiates from the currents, cross-currents, and counter-currents of the life of him who is their theme.

Jesus is great and grand enough as he stands in the New Testament and history. No matter how striking the style, no matter how careful the command and choice of language, we cannot by taking either thought or pen add a single cubit to his stature.

# BIBLIOGRAPHY

Baldensperger, W.
*Das Selbstbewusstsein Jesu im Lichte der messianischen Hoffnungen seiner Zeit.* Heitz, Strassburg, 1888; 192 S.

Barth, F.
*Die Hauptprobleme des Lebens Jesu.* Bertelsmann, Guetersloh; 4. Auflage, 1911, 333 S.

Bauer, Bruno
*Kritik der evangelischen Geschichte der Synoptiker.* Wigand, Leipzig; 2. Auflage, 1846, 3 Baende, 1149 S.

Bauer, Walter
*Das Leben Jesu im Zeitalter der neutestamentlichen Apokryphen.* Mohr, Tuebingen; 1909, 568 S.

Baumann, Julius
*Die Gemuetsart Jesu. Nach jetziger wissenschaftlicher, insbesondere jetziger psychologischer Methode erkennbar gemacht.* Kroener, Leipzig; 1908, 80 S.

van den Bergh van Eysinga, G. A.
*Indische Einfluesse auf evangelische Erzaehlungen.* Vandenhoeck & Ruprecht, Goettingen; 2. Auflage, 1909, 118 S.

Beyschlag, W.
*Das Leben Jesu.* Strien, Gross-Salze; I. Teil, 4. Auflage, 1902, 481 S.; II. Teil, 5. Auflage, 1912, 508 S.

Binet-Sanglé, C.
*La Folie de Jésus.* Maloine, Paris; Tome I, 3. édition, 1911; 372 p.; Tome II, 5. mille, 1910, 516 p.; Tome III, 2. mille, 1912, 537 p.; Tome IV, chez l'auteur, Alger, 1915; 489 p.

Binswanger, O., u. a.
*Lehrbuch der Psychiatrie.* Fischer, Jena; 5. Auflage, 1920, 458 S.

Bleek, F.
*Synoptische Erklaerung der drei ersten Evangelien.*
Herausgegeben von H. J. Holtzmann. Engelmann, Leipzig; 1862, 2 Baende, 1064 S.

Bollinger, Adolf
*Markus; der Bearbeiter des Matthaeus-Evangeliums.* Reinhardt, Basel; 1902, 100 S.

Bousset, W.
*Jesus.* Mohr, Tuebingen; Religionsgeschichtliche Volksbuecher, 1. Reihe 2/3 Heft, 3. Auflage, 1907, 100 S.
*Der erste Brief an die Korinther.* Schriften des Neuen Testaments II. Band (Siehe J. Weiss).

Burkitt, F. C.
*The Gospel History and its Transmission.* Clark, Edinburgh, 3. edition, 1911, 366 p.

Carpenter, J. E.
*The First Three Gospels.* Lindsey Press, London; 4. edition, 1906, 401 p.

Case, S. J.
*The Historicity of Jesus.* University of Chicago Press, Chicago; 1912, 352 p.

Castor, G. A.
*Matthew's Sayings of Jesus.* University of Chicago Press, Chicago; 1918; 250 p.

Conybeare, F. C.
*Myth, Magic and Morals.* Beacon Press, Boston; Second Edition, 1910, 282 p.

Cutten, G. B.
*The Psychological Phenomena of Christianity.* Scribner's, New York; 1912, 497 p.

Deissmann, A.
*Paulus. Eine Kultur- und religionsgeschichtliche Skizze.* Mohr, Tuebingen; 1911, 202 S.

von Delius, R.
*Jesus. Sein Kampf, seine Persoenlichkeit und seine Legende.* Langen, Muenchen; 1909, 182 S.

Dieckhoff, Dr.
  *Der Prophet Ezechiel.* (Siehe A. Dorner; S. 193-206).
Dorner, A.
  *Ueber die Begrenzung der psychologischen Methode der Religionsforschung.* Zeitschrift fuer Religionspsychologie, Marhold, Halle a. S.; Band I, Heft 5, 1907, S. 185-193.
Duhm, B.
  *Israels Propheten.* Lebensfragen. Mohr, Tuebingen; 1916, 483 S.
Emmet, C. W.
  *The Eschatological Element in the Gospels.* Clark, Edinburgh; 1911, 239 p.
Frenssen, G.
  *Das Leben des Heilands.* (Auszug von seinem Roman *Hilligenlei*); Grote, Berlin; 1907, 109 S.
Hall, G. S.
  *Jesus, the Christ, in the Light of Psychology.* Doubleday, Page & Co., New York; 1917, 2 volumes, 733 p.
Harnack, A.
  WC. *Das Wesen des Christentums.* Hinrichs, Leipzig; Ausgabe fuers Feld, 63. Tausend, 1915, 2 Hefte, 189 S.
  SuRJ. *Sprueche und Reden Jesu.* Hinrichs, Leipzig; 1907, 219 S.
  *Die Apostelgeschichte.* Hinrichs, Leipzig; 1908, 225 S.
von Hartmann, E.
  *Das Christentum des Neuen Testaments.* Haacke, Sashsa im Harz; 1905, 316 S.
von Hase, K.
  *Geschichte Jesu.* Breitkopf & Haertel, Leipzig; 1891, 774 S.
Hausrath, A.
  *Jesus und die neutestamentlichen Schriftsteller.* Grote, Berlin; I. Band, 1908, 700 S.; II. Band, 1909, 516 S.
Hawkins, Sir John C.
  *Horae Synopticae.* Clarendon Press, Oxford: 2. edition, 1909, 223 p.

Heitmueller, W.
*Jesus.* Mohr, Leipzig; 1913, 184 S.

Hennig, R.
*Das Wesen der Inspiration.* Schriften der Gesellschaft fuer psychologische Forschung; IV. Sammlung, Heft 17; Barth, Leipzig; 1912, S. 89-160.

Hirsch, W.
*Religion und Civilisation vom Standpunkte des Psychiaters.* Bonsels & Co., Muenchen, 1910, 652 S.—*Religion and Civilization: the Conclusions of a Psychiatrist.* Truth Seeker, New York; 1912, 610 p.

Hoffman, R. A.
*Das Markusevangelium und seine Quellen.* Thomas & Oppermann, Koenigsberg, i. Pr.; 1904, 644 S.

Hollman, G.
*Leben und Lehre Jesu II.* Theologische Rundschau. Mohr, Tuebingen; 9. Jahrgang, 7. Heft, Juli, 1906, S. 270-275.

Holtzmann, H. J.
MBJ. *Das messianische Bewusstsein Jesu: Ein Beitrag zur Leben-Jesu-Forschung.* Mohr, Tuebingen; 1907, 100 S.
SE. *Die synoptischen Evangelien: Ihr Ursprung und geschichtlicher Charakter.* Engelmann, Leipzig; 1863, 514 S.
HC. *Hand-Commentar zum Neuen Testament.* Mohr, Tuebingen; I. Band, 3. Auflage, 1901, 428 S.

Holtzmann, O.
LJ. *Leben Jesu.* Mohr, Tuebingen und Leipzig, 1901, 428 S.
WJE. *War Jesus Ekstatiker?* Mohr, Leipzig; 1903, 143 S.

Huck, A.
*Synopse der drei ersten Evangelien* (griechisch). Mohr, Tuebingen, 5. Auflage, 1916, 222 S.

Jackson, L.
*The Problem of the Fourth Gospel.* Cambridge University Press, Cambridge; 1918, 170 p.

James, William
  *The Varieties of Religious Experience.* Longmans, Green
  & Co., New York; 22. impression, 1912, 534 p.

Jordan, Hermann
  JMJB. *Jesus und die modernen Jesusbilder.* Biblische
  Zeit- und Streitfragen; herausgegeben von F. Kropatscheck;
  Verlag v. E. Runge in Gr. Lichterfelde, Berlin; V. Serie,
  5/6 Heft, 1909, 115 S.
  *Jesus im Kampfe der Parteien der Gegenwart.* Zeitfragen
  des christlichen Volkslebens; Belser, Stuttgart; Band
  XXXII. Heft 1, 1907, 53 S.

Juelicher, A.
  GRJ. *Die Gleichnisreden Jesu.* Mohr, Tuebingen; 2.
  Auflage, 1910, 2 Teile, 971 S.
  Einl. *Einleitung in das Neue Testament.* Mohr, Tuebin-
  gen; 5. u. 6. Auflage, 1913, 581 S.
  *Neue Linien in der Kritik der evangelischen Ueberlieferung.*
  Toepelmann, Giessen; 1906, 76 S.

Keim, Theodor
  *Geschichte Jesu von Nazara.* Orell, Fuessli und Comp.,
  Zuerich; 1867, 3 Baende, 1935 S.

Klein, Gottlieb
  *Ist Jesus eine historische Persoenlichkeit?* Mohr, Tuebingen; 1910, 46 S.

Kneib, Philipp
  *Moderne Leben-Jesu-Forschung unter dem Einflusse der
  Psychiatrie. Eine kritische Darstellung fuer Gebildete aller
  Staende.* Kirchheim & Co., Mainz; 1908, 76 S.

Knudson, Albert C.
  *The Beacon Lights of Prophecy.* Eaton & Mains, New
  York; 1914, 281 p.

Koegel, Julius
  *Probleme der Geschichte Jesu und die moderne Kritik.*
  Tempelverlag, Gross-Lichterfelde; 1906, 98 S.

Kraepelin
  *Clinical Psychiatry.* Abstracted and translated from the
  seventh German edition of *Lehrbuch der Psychiatrie* by A.

R. Diefendorf.   MacMillan, New York; 1918, 562 p.

von Krafft-Ebing, R.
>   *Text-book of Insanity.*   Translated by C. G. Chaddock.
>   Davis, Philadelphia; 1905, 638 p.

Law, Robert
>   *The Emotions of Jesus.*   Scribner's, New York; 1915,
>   155 p.

Leipoldt, Johannes
>   *Vom Jesusbilde der Gegenwart.*   Doerffling & Franke, Leip-
>   zeig, 1913, 445 S.

Lepsius, J.
>   *Das Leben Jesu.*   Tempelverlag, Potsdam; Band I, 1917,
>   381 S.   Band II, 1918, 397 S.

Lietzmann, Hans
>   *II. Korinther Brief*—Handbuch zum Neuen Testament
>   herausgegeben von Lietzmann u. a., III. Band, J. C. B.
>   Mohr, Tuebingen, 1913.

Lombroso, C.
>   *Genie und Irrsinn in ihren Beziehungen zum Gesetz, zur*
>   *Kritik und zur Geschichte.*   Nach der 4.  Auflage des
>   italienischen Originaltextes uebersetzt von A. Courth.
>   Reclam, Leipzig, 1887, 434 S.

Loofs, Friedrich
>   *Wer War Jesus Christus?.  Fuer Theologen und den*
>   *weiteren Kreis gebildeter Christen eroertert.*   (German
>   revision of *What Is the Truth About Jesus Christ?*  Scrib-
>   ner's, New York; 1913).   Niemeyer, Halle a. d. S.; 1916,
>   255 S.

de Loosten (George Lomer)
>   *Jesus Christus von Standpunkte des Psychiaters.*   Handels-
>   Druckerei, Bamberg; 1905, 104 S.

Moerchen, F.
>   PH.  *Die Psychologie der Heiligkeit.  Eine religionswissen-*
>   *schaftliche Studie.*   Marhold, Halle a. S.; 1908, 47 S.
>   MKP.  *Zur psychiatrischen Betrachtung des ueberlieferten*
>   *Christusbildes* (Monatsschrift fuer die kirchliche Praxis,

Oktober, 1906, 10. Heft, S. 422-26).

Moses, Josiah
*Pathological Aspects of Religions.* Clark University Press, Worcester; 1906, 264 p.

Naumann, Johannes
*Jesus Christus vom Standpunkte des Psychiaters.* Die Christliche Welt, Marburg; Nr. 12, 22. Maerz 1906, S. 266-271.

Neander, August
*Das Leben Jesu Christi in seinem geschichtlichen Zusammenhang und seiner geschichtlichen Entwicklung.* Perthes, Hamburg; 5. Auflage, 1852, 803 S.

Nestle, Eberhard
*The Greek Testament.* Revell; 3. issue, 1906.

Niebergall, Fr.
Review of Rasmussen's book in the *Zeitschrift fuer Religionspsychologie;* Band I, Heft 5, 1907, S. 223-226.

Ninck, Joh.
*Jesus als Charakter.* Hinrichs, Leipzig; 2. Auflage, 1910, 396 S.

Nietzsche, Friedrich
*Also Sprach Zarathustra.* Kroener, Leipzig; 167.-168. Tausend, 1918, 502 S.

Otto, Rudolph
*Leben und Wirken Jesu nach historisch-kritischer Auffassung.* Vandenhoeck & Ruprecht, Goettingen; 1902, 76 S.

Paulus, H. E. G.
EHB. *Exegetisches Handbuch ueber die drei ersten Evangelien.* Heidelberg; 4 Baende, 1830-1833, 2402 S.
LJ. *Das Leben Jesu.* Winter, Heidelberg; 1828, 2 Baende, 1194 S.

Pfannmueller, Gustav
*Jesus im Urteil der Jahrhunderte.* Teubner, Leipzig u. Berlin; 1908, 578 S.

Pfleiderer, Otto
*Das Christentum: seine Schriften und Lehren in geschicht-*

*lichem Zusammenhang.* Reimer, Berlin; I. Band, 2. Auflage, 1902, 696 S.

Rasmussen, Emil
*Jesus: Eine vergleichende psychopathologische Studie.* Aus dem Daenischen uebertragen und herausgegeben von Arthur Rothenberg. Zeitler, Leipzig; 1905, 167 S.

Reinhard, Franz V.
*Versuch ueber den Plan, welchen der Stifter der christlichen Religion zum Besten der Menschen entwarf.* Frankfurt und Leipzig; 4. Auflage, 1802, 488 S.

Renan, Ernest
*La Vie de Jésus.* Nelson, Paris; première édition 1863, 282 p.

Resch, Alfred
*Aussercanonische Paralleltexte.* Hinrichs, Leipzig; 3 Teile, 5 Hefte, 1893-97, 2023 S.

Réville, Albert
*Jésus de Nazareth. Études critiques sur les antécédents de l'histoire évangélique et la vie de Jésus.* Fischbacher, Paris; 2. édition, 1906, 2 Tomes, 930 p.

Ribot, Th.
DP. *Diseases of Personality.* Open Court, Chicago; 4. edition, 1906, 163 p.
DW. *Diseases of the Will.* Open Court, Chicago; 4. edition, 1915, 137 p.

Sanday, William
*Christologies: Ancient and Modern.* Oxford University Press, American Branch, New York; 1910, 244 p.

Schaefer, H.
*Jesus in psychiatrischer Beleuchtung.* Hoffmann & Co., Berlin; 1910, 178 S.

Schmiedel, Otto
*Die Hauptprobleme der Leben-Jesu-Forschung.* Mohr, Tuebingen; 1906, 124 S.

Schmiedel, P. W.
dVE. *Das vierte Evangelium gegenueber den drei ersten.*

Religionsgeschichtliche Volksbuecher; Mohr, Tuebingen;
I. Reihe, 8/10 Heft, 1906, 131 S.

PJSMG. *Die Person Jesu im Streite der Meinungen der
Gegenwart.* Heinsius Nachfolger, Leipzig; 1906, 31 S.

Schultze, E.
*Epilepsie.* (Siehe Binswanger).

Schuster, H.
*Jesus.* Vier Vortraege von Bornemann, W. Veit, H.
Schuster und E. Foerster. Diesterweg, Frankfort am
Main; 1910, 119 S.

Schweitzer, A.
MLG. *Das Abendmahl. II. Heft: Das Messianitaets-
und Leidensgeheimnis.* Mohr, Tuebingen u. Leipzig; 1901,
109 S.

GdLJF. *Geschichte der Leben-Jesu-Forschung.* 2. Auflage des Werkes *Von Reimarus zu Wrede.* Mohr, Tuebingen; 1913, 659 S.

PBJ. *Die psychiatrische Beurteilung Jesu.* Mohr, Tuebingen; 1913, 46 S.

Siemerling, E.
*Paranoia. Verruecktheit* (Siehe Binswanger).

Smith, Stephen
*Who Is Insane?* MacMillan, New York; 1916, 285 p.

von Soden, H. F.
*Die wichtigsten Fragen im Leben Jesu.* Glaue, Berlin;
2. Auflage, 1909, 121 S.

Soury, Jules
*Jésus et les Évangiles.* Paris: 1878, 190 p.

Spitta, Friedrich
*Die synoptische Grundschrift in ihrer Ueberlieferung durch
das Lukas-Evangelium.* Hinrich, Leipzig; 1912, 512 S.

Strauss, D. F.
*Das Leben Jesu kritisch bearbeitet.* Osiander, Tuebingen;
2. Auflage, 1837, 2 Baende, 1559 S.

*Das Leben Jesu fuer das deutsche Volk bearbeitet.* Kroener,
Leipzig; 21. Auflage, 2 Theile, 326 S.

*Der alte und der neue Glaube. Ein Bekenntniss.* Emil
Strauss, Bonn; 12. bis 14. Stereotyp-Auflage; 1895,
278 S.

Venturini, K. H.
*Natuerliche Geschichte des grossen Propheten von Nazareth.*
Bethlehem; 2. Auflage, 1806, 4 Baende, 1809 S.

Voelter, D.
*Die evangelischen Erzaehlungen von der Geburt und Kind-
heit Jesu kritisch untersucht.* Heitz, Strassburg; 1911,
136 S.

Volkmar, Gustav
*Die Evangelien.* Fues, Leipzig; 1870, 660 S.

Washburn, L. K.
*Was Jesus Insane?* Truth Seeker, New York; 1889, 20 p.

Weber, William
Review of *Werner, Schaefer, Seeligmueller* in the *Theologische Literaturzeitung*, 1911, Nr. 8, Sp. 232-36.

Weidel, Karl
*Jesu Persoenlichkeit. Eine Charakterstudie.* Marhold,
Halle a. d. S.; 2. Auflage, 1913, 128 S.

Weinel, H.
IBN. *Ibsen. Bjoernson. Nietzsche. Individualismus und
Christentum.* Lebensfragen. Mohr, Tuebingen; 1908,
244 S.
*Jesus im 19. Jahrhundert.* Lebensfragen. Mohr, Tuebin-
gen; 3. Neubearbeitung, 1914, 331 S.
*Paulus—Der Mensch und sein Werk.* Mohr, Tuebingen;
2. Auflage, 1915, 294 S.

Weiss, B.
*The Life of Christ.* Translated by J. W. Hope. Clark,
Edinburgh; 1909, 3 volumes, 1224 p.

Weiss, J.
AeE *Das aelteste Evangelium.* Vandenhoeck and Ruprecht, Goettingen; 1903, 414 S.
PJvRG. *Die Predigt Jesu vom Reiche Gottes.* Vandenhoeck und Ruprecht; Goettingen, 1892, 67 S.

Weiss, J., u. a.
   SdNT.   *Die Schriften des Neuen Testaments neu ueber-
   setzt und fuer die Gegenwart erklaert.*   Vandenhoeck und
   Ruprecht, Goettingen; 3. Auflage, 21.-28. Tausend, Band
   I: *Die drei aelteren Evangelien,* 1917, 511 S.

Weisse, Ch. H.
   *Die evangelische Geschichte kritisch und philosophisch be-
   arbeitet.*   Breitkopf & Haertel; 1838, 2 Baende, 1157 S.

Weizsaecker, C.
   *Untersuchungen ueber die evangelische Geschichte: ihre
   Quellen und den Gang ihrer Entwicklung.*   Mohr, Tuebin-
   gen & Liepzig; 2. Auflage, 1901, 378 S.

Wellhausen, J.
   *Das Evangelium Lucae.*   Reimer, Berlin; 1904, 142 S.
   *Das Evangelium Marci.*   Reimer, Berlin; 2. Ausgabe, 1909,
   137 S.
   *Das Evangelium Mathaei.*   Reimer, Berlin; 2. Ausgabe,
   1914, 144 S.
   Einl.   *Einleitung in die drei ersten Evangelien.*   Reimer,
   Berlin; 2. Ausgabe, 1911, 176 S.

Wendland, P.
   *Die hellenistisch-roemische Kultur in ihren Beziehungen zu
   Judentum und Christentum.*   J. C. B. Mohr, Tuebingen;
   2. und 3. Auflage 1912, 448 S.

Wendling E.
   *Die Entstehung des Marcus-Evangeliums.*   Mohr, Tuebingen; 1908, 246 S.

Wendt, H. H.
   *The Teaching of Jesus.*   Scribner's, New York; 1892, 2
   volumes, 835 p.

Werner, Hermann
   PGJ.   *Die psychische Gesundheit Jesu.*   Biblische Zeit-
   und Streitfragen; herausgegeben von Kropatscheck,
   Verlag von E. Runge, Gr. Lichterfelde, Berlin; IV. Serie,
   12. Heft, 1909, 64 S.
   NKZ.   *Der historische Jesus der liberalen Theologie—Ein*

*Geisteskranker.* Neue Kirchliche Zeitschrift; herausgegeben von. W. Engelhardt; Deichert, Erlangen und Leipzig;
XXII. Jahrgang, 5. Heft, 1911, S. 347-390.

Wernle, Paul
SF. *Die synoptische Frage.* Mohr, Freiburg in B.; 1899,
256 S.
*Die Anfaenge unserer Religion.* Mohr, Leipzig und Tue-
bingen; 1901, 410 S.
*Die Quellen des Lebens Jesu.* Religionsgeschichtliche
Volksbuecher; Mohr, Tuebingen; I. Reihe, I. Heft, 3. Auf-
lage, 1913, 76 S. (*The Sources of Our Knowledge of the
Life of Jesus.* Beacon Press, Boston; 1907, 163 p).
*Jesus.* Mohr, Tuebingen; 1916, 368 S.

Westcott and Hort
*The New Testament in the Original Greek.* American
Book Company, New York.

Westphal, Alexandre
*Jésus de Nazareth.* Chez l'auteur, Lausanne; 1914, 2 volumes, 926 p.

Windisch, Hans
*Leben und Lehre Jesu. III.* Theologische Rundschau.
Mohr, Tuebingen; 16. Jahrgang, 12. Heft, Dezember,
1913, S. 439-443.

Wrede, W.
MGE. *Das Messiasgeheimnis in den Evangelien.* Vandenhoeck & Ruprecht, Goettingen; 1913, 291 S.
CuTdJE. *Charakter und Tendenz des Johannesevangel-
iums.* Tuebingen u. Leipzig; 1903, 71 S.
*Paulus.* Religionsgeschichtliche Volksbuecher; Mohr, Leipzig; 1. Reihe, 5/6 Heft, 2. Auflage, 1907, 112 S.

Ziegler, Theobald
*David Friedrich Strauss.* Truebner, Strassburg; 1908,
2. Teile, 777 S.

# INDEX OF SCRIPTURE PASSAGES

## Old Testament

## New Testament

283

# PERSONAL REGISTER

Hillel, 10.

Hirsch, xiiif, 30, 47f, 79ff, 110, 120, 122, 124, 128, 131, 143, 150, 153, 165f, 196, 200, 208f, 219, 224, 234, 257, 263, 267, 273.

Hoffmann, 160, 273.

Holbach, von, 168.

Holbek, 63.

Hollmann, 30, 40f, 124, 129, 228, 273.

Holtzmann, H. J., 2, 28, 40, 119, 157, 194, 200f, 205, 210, 216, 220, 222, 273.

Holtzmann, O., xiv, 7, 30, 40f, 48ff, 114, 116, 120, 123f, 149, 152f, 158, 161, 166, 169f, 173f, 181, 192, 194, 200, 207ff, 262f, 267, 273.

Horne, 145.

Hosea, 62.

Huck, vii, 139, 140, 142, 152, 154, 157, 167, 170, 178, 273.

Irenaeus, 151.

Isaac, 81.

Isaiah, 62, 81, 202.

Jackson, 128, 273.

Jacob, 81.

James, the brother of Jesus, 22, 70, 90, 95, 235f.

James, Wm., xiff, 30, 36, 263, 274.

Jeanne d'Arc, 8, 212.

Jeremiah, 48, 59f, 62f.

John the Baptist, 7, 9, 11, 13, 50f, 70ff, 81, 83, 95, 108, 117, 121, 130, 134, 149ff, 163, 170, 184, 207, 235, 236ff, 239.

Jonah, 105.

Jordan, 42, 123f, 274.

Joseph, the father of Jesus, 69, 84, 89ff, 235f, 238.

Josephus, 26, 236.

Judas, the brother of Jesus, 90.

Judas Iscariot, 77, 91, 102, 121, 187f.

Juelicher, 119, 142, 164, 226, 274.

Justin Martyr, 152.

Kaeferli, 4.

Kant, 36, 177, 263.

Keim, 2, 42, 69, 160, 169, 173, 233, 274.

Kent, 145.

Kepler, 37.

Kierkegaard, 60, 63, 67.

Klein, 197, 274.

Kneib, 29, 35, 42, 115f, 123f, 131, 274.

Knudson, viiif, 261, 274.

Koegel, 274.

Kraepelin, 175, 212, 234, 243, 247ff, 251, 253, 257f, 274.

Westphal, 169, 181, 281.
Windisch, 40, 124, 281.
Wrede, xii, 44, 91, 127, 131f, 135, 138, 162, 181, 205, 211, 214,
    228, 281.
Zelenka, 126.
Ziegler, 6, 119, 281.